Beautiful Mornin'

BEAUTIFUL MORNIN'

THE BROADWAY MUSICAL IN THE 1940S

ETHAN MORDDEN

New York   Oxford

Oxford University Press

1999

Oxford University Press

Oxford   New York

Athens   Auckland   Bangkok   Bogotá   Buenos Aires
Calcutta   Cape Town   Chennai   Dar es Salaam   Delhi
Florence   Hong Kong   Istanbul   Karachi   Kuala Lumpur
Madrid   Melbourne   Mexico City   Mumbai
Nairobi   Paris   São Paulo   Singapore
Taipei   Tokyo   Toronto   Warsaw

and associated companies in
Berlin   Ibadan

Copyright © 1999 by Ethan Mordden

Published by Oxford University Press, Inc.
198 Madison Avenue, New York, New York 10016

Oxford is a registered trademark of Oxford University Press

Library of Congress Cataloging-in-Publication Data
Mordden, Ethan
Beautiful mornin' : the Broadway musical in the 1940s
/ Ethan Mordden.
p.   cm.
Includes index.
ISBN 0-19-512851-6
1. Musicals—New York (State)—New York—History and criticism.
2. Broadway (New York)—History.   3. Popular music—New York
(State)—New York—1941–1950—History and criticism.   I. Title.
ML 1711.8.N3M768   1999
782.1'4'0973—dc21   99–10088

1 3 5 7 9 8 6 4 2

Printed in the United States of America
on acid-free paper

To my golden-age editor,
one of the last of his kind:
Sheldon Meyer

Acknowledgments

To my excellent copy editor, Rosemary Wellner; to the encompassingly presiding Joellyn Ausanka; to my excessively generous colleague Ken Mandelbaum; and to my wonder-working agent, Joe Spieler.

Contents

1. MUSICAL COMEDY I   3

2. STARS   24

3. THE ROAD TO *OKLAHOMA!*   43

4. RODGERS AND HAMMERSTEIN   70

5. AMERICANA   94

6. THE DANCE MUSICAL   120

7. OPERETTA   138

8. FANTASY   157

9. REVUE   176

10. MUSICAL COMEDY II   189

11. THE CONCEPT MUSICAL   212

12. THE CAST ALBUM   236

INDEX   271

Beautiful Mornin'

1

MUSICAL COMEDY I

The 1940s is in certain ways the unique decade in the musical's history, quite aside from the fact that almost half of it was played out during a war for the survival of Western Civilization. It was the first to leave substantial documentation in the form of cast recordings, giving us what the mere black-and-white of surviving scripts and music pages cannot: a powerful sense of Broadway performing style. This was also the first decade to produce an impressive amount of undisputed classics regularly performed today. And it was the decade in which the musical's artistry changed most decisively and even most suddenly, in what we might call "the Rodgers and Hammerstein revolution."

As we'll see, these three defining features are interrelated, for it was the impulsive nature of this revolution that inspired so many great shows in so little time; but it was also the invention of the "original-cast recording" that turned successes into classics, made them permanent.

Ironically, as the 1940s began, the musical was deeply vexed. Depression economics had all but banned the daring or even mildly unusual show, and the seasonal tally of new productions was down from an average of about forty-five in the 1920s to about fifteen. The revue, in its twenties heyday a showcase for special talents, had degenerated into a lumpy vaudeville. Hollywood had lured away many of the musical's most gifted performers, from Eddie Cantor and the Marx Brothers to Fred Astaire and Jeanette MacDonald. Another problem was the loss of writers who were especially influential when the musical's Golden Age started, at around 1920. Among composers, George Gershwin was dead, Vincent Youmans had retired, and Jerome Kern composed his final stage score in 1939. Lorenz Hart, though still active as Richard Rodgers' partner, had tired of his work and life and was soon to depart. Major new talents had arrived in the 1930s in composers Harold Arlen and Kurt Weill, lyricist E. Y. Harburg, and composer–lyricist Harold Rome; but in 1940 their distinguished work was, for the most part, still ahead of them.

Yet another problem was the paucity of good old-fashioned singing voices, a concomitant of the collapse of operetta in 1930 but another effect of Hollywood's buying up Broadway talent for the movie musical. And perhaps the worst problem of all was the Hoagy Carmichael–Johnny Mercer show *Walk With Music* (1940).

All right, not that show alone. But *Walk With Music* represents all that was wrong with the musical in general: lack of content. Musical comedy had been running on a formula most effectively set forth in the Alex Aarons–Vinton Freedley Gershwin piece for Fred and Adele Astaire, *Lady, Be Good* (1924): start with hot performers, add a hot score and hot choreography, and glue it all together with as much humor as possible. What this format didn't have was a story, characters, realism, irony, point. These were constructions without foundation, circles without centers. The genre depended entirely on the available talent. If the songwriters and performers came through, one had success—but even that success was fluff. It was tunes and charm, eccentric comedy, and a New Dance Sensation.

And that was all that the public wanted—in the 1920s. By 1940, this approach was so exhausted that only the most able performers and the most tuneful songs could draw an audience. *Walk With Music* might have done so, perhaps. It was no worse than many a twenties hit. Out of town, as *Three After Three*, it was bombing. Was it because theatregoers had had enough of the "three fortune hunters" plot popularized by Hollywood, as nightclub artistes Vivi (Simone Simon), Carrie (Mary Brian), and Rhoda (Mitzi Green) pose as, respectively, heiress, chaperone, and maid in Palm Beach to bag a millionaire? Was it because Vivi falls for a poor guy (Jack Whiting) while *Rhoda* loves the rich guy (Art Jarrett), just as we knew they would? (Carrie got her man, too—Lee Sullivan, who would introduce "I'll Go Home With Bonnie Jean" and "Come To Me, Bend To Me" in *Brigadoon* seven years hence.) Did the public regret the cliché figure of the man-hungry la-di-da (Frances Williams) and her wisecracking brother (Marty May)?:

WILLIAMS: Where's my bag?
MAY: My dear, you have one under each eye.
WILLIAMS: Look who's talking—Snow White! If you had a streak of decency in you, you'd go back and marry that five-year-old girl.
MAY: Why should I? I've had the best years of her life.

The Guy Bolton–Parke Levy–Alan Lipscott book, based on Stephen Powys' play *Three Blind Mice*,* was quick and dirty and the Hoagy Carmichael–Johnny Mercer score fast and loud, and *Three After Three* folded in Detroit, promising to hit New York after some revisions. They always say that; this time, they meant it. Three months later, as the title slithered from *Ooh! What You Said!* to *Walk With Music*, as Kitty Carlisle and Betty Lawford replaced Simone Simon and Mary Brian, as the girls became sisters (who left not a nightclub but a farm), and as the out-of-town song hit, "Darn Clever, These Chinee," was dropped because it turned on the "Confucius say" vogue that had suddenly become irritating, the show reached Broadway. To a man, the critics asked *Why?* Why labor to perfect a piece of junk?

Because, by the rules of the Aarons–Freedley formula, a poor show wasn't all that unlike a good show. They were separated by

---

* Filmed in 1938, *Three Blind Mice* spun off countless remakes and imitations, including the Betty Grable musical *Moon Over Miami, Three Little Girls in Blue,* and *How To Marry a Millionaire.*

differences of emphases, not of kind. For instance, the choreography of Anton Dolin and Herbert Harper was haphazard: someone would sing a number, and anyone else would dance it. Or now Dolin would direct a corps de ballet, and now Harper would set them tapping. Sloppy? Hit shows used dance in the same way.

Or: Mitzi Green, Paramount's former child star, now nineteen, found chances to slip in her impressions of Greta Garbo, Katharine Hepburn, and Fanny Brice's Baby Snooks. She did them well, and it must have been amusing to applaud a performer who had been around forever yet was still a teenager. But did celebrity imitations really help a show? In this age, they never hurt one.

Or: the two main ballads, "I Walk With Music" and "What'll They Think of Next (now that they've thought of you)," are simply less melodious than the popular Broadway ballads of 1940: "I Could Write a Book," "It's a Lovely Day Tomorrow," "Taking a Chance on Love." The score as a whole is not without invention. One number led to a mixed quartet singing bop scat on the names of New Jersey townships, with a lot of "doodle" and "chu de wa" in the delightfully tricky Hugh Martin manner—arranged, in fact, by Martin himself. Another number, "The Rhumba Jumps!," for Frances Williams, honored the craze for South American dances with a sharp lyric about a Harlem band's adventures south of the border (" 'Hep, hep,' they hollered, the moment they landed . . .") and a jagged tune bound to delight.

Or: the gaggy book ran from the pathetic to the workmanlike:

> PAMELA (*formerly* VIVI): You can go to prison for giving a bad check, can't you?
> RHODA: You get your choice—you can either go or they'll take you.

The book even ran—just once in the evening—to the stunning, though this *is* in bad taste:

> WING: (*hearing a crash offstage*) What's that?
> CARRIE: It's the new maid. She handles china like Japan.*

* This refers to Japan's brutal attack on Nanking and Shanghai in 1937, an operation that left some 370,000 Chinese dead.

"A blizzard of quips," Richard Lockridge of the New York *Sun* called *Walk With Music*, adding, "Somebody will have to do something about the musical comedy book someday"—really, I think, meaning Somebody will have to write shows with genuine content and integrity of elements rather than these assemblies of spare parts. This is why the good shows were more entertaining than but not much different from the poor ones. They were *all* concoctions, pranks, swindles.

Walk With Music gave up after six weeks, just as the only slightly more successful *Higher and Higher* (1940) folded. Here we find Richard Rodgers and Lorenz Hart screwing up almost as badly as *Walk With Music*'s authors, in a piece designed for Vera Zorina, the dancer who had proved a delight in the 1937 London production of Rodgers and Hart's *On Your Toes* (1936) and then on Broadway in their *I Married an Angel* (1938). Zorina turned out to be busy getting into Irving Berlin's *Louisiana Purchase*, so Marta Eggerth was substituted: a singer taking over for a dancer in a show that wasn't about anything in the first place. Well, okay: about servants passing off one of their number as a lady, to snag a millionaire. It's *Walk With Music* with Rodgers–Hart songs, mostly dull ones. The show did produce a semi-standard in Shirley Ross' solo "It Never Entered My Mind" and offered one forgotten but lovely ballad, "(You are) From Another World," when Eggerth has just fallen in love at sight of society scion Leif Erickson. This became a musical scene when the refrain leaped from the servants to soda jerkers and cops as news of the arrival of the fake debutante traveled the city, recalling the voyage of "Isn't It Romantic?" in Rodgers and Hart's Maurice Chevalier–Jeanette MacDonald film *Love Me Tonight*. Jack Haley, as another servant, was Eggerth's co-star, but both were upstaged by Sharkey the trained seal, who figured prominently in the show's poster and the largely favorable reviews.

These could not help a show that lacked the topline score, the irresistible performances, the opulent novelty background that filled in for the Broadway musical's typical insubstantiality. True, Rodgers and Hart had enjoyed a boom in the late 1930s with a string of insubstantial shows. But each of them had *something*— a dream ballet by Balanchine or Weidman, a star turn by George

M. Cohan, an endearingly youthful cast, a circus. Even *Too Many Girls* (1939), the Rodgers and Hart show that directly preceded *Higher and Higher*, had a secret ingredient: George Abbott. As producer and director, Abbott kept *Too Many Girls* taut and bouncy. He didn't need strong storylines or character development to make a hit show. On the contrary, he thought of such things as impediments to fun. What Abbott knew was editing wordy scripts, pointing a scene, a joke, an exit, and getting false but pleasantly functional performances from his actors.

A good idea for Abbott was *Beat the Band* (1942), which he not only produced and directed but co-authored, with *Too Many Girls'* librettist, George Marion Jr. *Beat the Band* typifies what could go wrong in an early forties musical comedy: everything. Not because the authors made crucial mistakes in delineating the material, but because there was no material. There was novelty color in a slight focus on the world of the swing musician. This made the leading man (Jack Whiting) a bandleader, brought noted instrumentalists (trumpeter Leonard Sues and drummer Johnny Mack) on stage with lines to read, and provided two big numbers, "The Steam Is on the Beam" (in a boiler room: because swing is *hot*) and the first-act finale, "America Loves a Band," a huge sequence in which the chorus' shouted "Sock!" is rhymed with "Rock!," the first instance I know of in which the latter word was used, on Broadway, in a musical context.

The score, by Johnny Green and Marion, is like that to most of the other forgotten forties musicals: melodic in the ballad "Let's Comb Beaches," with its rippling accompaniment; not funny in "I'm Physical, You're Cultured"; unnecessary in "I Like the Men"; and so on. But then, what do you sing when the plot is not only aimless but so convoluted that the theatre ushers couldn't have explained it by the final night of the show's nine-week run? The book was gags and song cues. A princess turns out to be from Oklahoma. How did she get to be a princess? "The hard way," she snaps back. "I married the prince." There was one bizarre moment, at least, when trumpeter Sues wanted to go bowling with drummer Mack, who said, "I can't—I got a date with your wife." Replied Sues, "Why don't you try and get away later?"

Any decade has its failures, but there is an awful emptiness about a forties failure. Complaining about *Beat the Band*, George Jean Nathan wrote, "The attitude of a portion of our theatrical producers seems to be that what people want in war time is not serious drama but entertainment, and then providing them with none of it." However, it wasn't wartime alone that produced these copiously vacant shows. Yes, the theatregoing public now included a great many servicemen and their dates who undiscerningly cheered cheap comedy and inadequate stagecraft. Still, the Broadway musical had been running on empty for years.

Even the hits could be . . . well, *Early To Bed* (1943), a one-joke farce in which a bordello in Martinique is mistaken for a finishing school by a surprising number of characters, including the California state track team. This leads to many doubles entendres, such as:

> COACH: I asked [the manager] if they had facilities here for
> a workout, and he said he guessed it could be arranged.

or, when club singer Lois tells newly arrived sex worker Eileen that Lois wants to rehearse her act:

> EILEEN: You have to rehearse it?
> LOIS: Of course. You can't go out and do your specialty before
> a lot of people without rehearsing.
> EILEEN: You have an audience? . . . I hope this place doesn't
> turn out to be too continental for me.

With the omnipresent George Marion and Robert Alton, *Early To Bed* counted one unusual credit: music by Fats Waller, in his second (and last) full-length Broadway score. It's a lively one, in "Hi-De-Ho-High" and "When Nylons Bloom Again," then torchy in "There's a Man in My Life," loving in "This Is So Nice." None of the tunes caught on, though the critics' favorite, "The Ladies Who Sing With a Band," was revived in the Waller anthology revue, *Ain't Misbehavin'*.

The reviews were raves, though, again, this title was hotter than, but not appreciably unlike, its brothers. Its cast—soprano Muriel Angelus as the madam, John Lund as her opposite (who frames the action as a flashback when he tells her story in a bar), Richard Kollmar as a vainglorious bullfighter, Jane Deering, Jane

Kean, and Bob Howard—was comparable to those of *Walk With Music, Higher and Higher*, and *Beat the Band*. So was its physical production, the quality of its choreography, and so on. It was state of the art when art is out of ideas, and this particular show was made notorious only because its no-no subject matter and grinning title suggested a bawdy night out. In fact, it was not unlike a college musical building up to a bullfight instead of a football game. "It's a show your sixteen-year-old daughter can take . . . the pastor and your maiden aunt to," said a doting Burton Rascoe of the *World-Telegram*. It even failed to be banned in Boston, though the script was temporarily tamed there, especially the lines of Yorba, a leftist mural painter (modeled on Diego Rivera) whose masterpiece is a large female nude holding *Das Kapital* over her genitals.

Today, we look back on the musical's history and decree that the key ingredient of a good show is its score: *Show Boat, Anything Goes, Carousel, My Fair Lady*. However, this overlooks the central importance of *Show Boat*'s epic narrative, *Anything Goes'* casting chemistry of Ethel Merman with the team of William Gaxton and Victor Moore, *Carousel*'s perfection of the new genre of American "folk" art, and *My Fair Lady*'s Shavian dialogues.

Furthermore, early forties thinking did not see the score as uniquely essential because scores were so often generic, with their go-everywhere ballads, dance setups, and comic novelties. Still, there were glimmers here and there, something unusual in the songs—even, something unusual to match the unusual nature of the show itself. If George Abbott's worst mistake in this era was *Beat the Band*—and he himself called it "the poorest job of producing and directing that I ever did"—it was very smart of him to hire Hugh Martin and Ralph Blane to write the score for *Best Foot Forward* (1941). The two youngsters, who collaborated simultaneously on both music and lyrics, raised the level of the piece to memorable, inciting a relatively faithful MGM film, a 1963 off-Broadway revival, and enough high-school drama-club stagings to threaten the supremacy of *Good News!* (1927).

Good News! is a college musical, but *Best Foot Forward* is even younger, with a prep school setting and a Big Dance instead of a Big Game. The plot hitch is that some smitten students have invited a Hollywood star whose career is suffering a slowdown. Her agent gets her to accept, for a PR coup, but her arrival on campus arouses the jealousy of the boys' dates. If *Beat the Band* is loaded with aimless action, *Best Foot Forward* is concentrated but short on action. In fact, virtually nothing happens till late in Act Two, when the girls attack the movie star on the dance floor, ripping her dress apart and causing a scandal.

To that point, *Best Foot Forward* is no more than who's dating whom, who's breaking up, and who's probably going to reconcile. But then, that's this show's peculiar charm: a long, loving look at what matters to carefree kids. Legend tells that producer–director Abbott was attracted to the script, by John Cecil Holm, because a cast of teenagers meant that the boys wouldn't be drafted; the United States was to enter World War II only nine weeks after the play opened. But in fact only the characters are teens: the players were more like twenty or so.

Abbott chose a jolly crew: Gil Stratton Jr. as the lead student and Maureen Cannon as his girl, Jack Jordan Jr. and big, dumb, and grinning Kenny Bowers as his buddies, June Allyson and Nancy Walker (the latter billed only as "Blind Date") as prominent girls at the prom, Rosemary Lane as the movie star, and, in the chorus, future Hollywood director Stanley Donen and Broadway choreographer Danny Daniels. Richard Rodgers, frustrated by Lorenz Hart's increasing torpor, signed on as Abbott's co-producer, though, ironically, he took no poster credit, to avoid antagonizing Hart. As their dance director, Abbott and Rodgers hired their pal Joey, Gene Kelly, in his sole Broadway production credit till he directed Rodgers and Hammerstein's *Flower Drum Song* seventeen years later.

As historian Stanley Green informs us, it was Rodgers who gave *Best Foot Forward*'s prep school its famous name, for the show had gone into rehearsal without anyone's being able to come up with a suitable sound for this place of youth in merry riot. The school's fight song had been written around a "working title," Wisconsin. This became "Tioga," but that felt like . . . well, the musical comedy version of a prep school. "What we need," said Abbott, "is a name that has has something to do with winning with a lot of sock in it." "That's it!" said Rodgers. " 'Winsocki.' "

Has any other musical boasted a major hit tune that serves the story as a football fight song? "Buckle Down, Winsocki" became so popular over the years that it made a merely pleasing show seem a giant by implication. But *Best Foot Forward*'s score is strong overall, its special quality being a youthful energy to match the youthful characters. It even has a couple of plot songs. "Three Men on a Date," for the central trio of students, affirms their unrepentant dumping of their girls for their Hollywood guest, Gale Joy. "Hollywood Story," a duet for Gale and her agent, gives us an intriguing portrait of a truly unhappy woman.

The other numbers are the usual ballads and up-tunes, turned out, however, with unusual skill. Hugh Martin had got his start charting vocal arrangements for Abbott–Rodgers–Hart and Cole Porter shows in the late 1930s; he was jazzy yet neat, lovingly aggressive, and one hears it in these songs. "That's How I Love the Blues," "The Guy Who Brought Me (can't send me)"—the lament of a girl stuck with the direst of dates, a non-dancer— "Just a Little Joint With a Juke Box," and a rousing tribute to the barrelhouse, boogie-woogie, and blues, "The Three 'B's'," are about music. "I Know You By Heart" and "My First Promise" are about dating. "Ev'ry Time," the daintiest of torch songs, is about getting stood up. It's all *youth*. "Shady Lady Bird" tells us "I've got an awful lot to learn" and "What Do You Think I Am?" goes on "Just a baby?" For once in this time, the score matched the subject: cute kids got cute kid songs.

The *Best Foot Forward* score continued to grow for MGM's 1943 Technicolor version, which, in wartime perforce, turned Winsocki into a military school. Lucille Ball played herself as the movie star, and on hand from Broadway were Walker, Allyson, Jordan, Bowers (the last two, for inexplicable reasons, exchanged roles), and Tommy Dix, graduated from a cameo, singing "Buckle Down, Winsocki," to playing lead. Ball (dubbed by Gloria Grafton) got "You're Lucky," Walker got "Alive and Kicking," and the kids in general got possibly the best song of all, the ultimate Hugh Martin choral spree, "Wish I May (Wish I Might)," ingenious in pinning down kids' interests—riding in a Cadillac with the top down, making out at the drive-in. All three numbers were retained in the 1963 revival, along with two unused titles that Martin and

Blane had written for MGM's *Meet Me in St. Louis*, "Raving Beauty" and, for Liza Minnelli's eleven o'clock spot, "You Are For Loving." It would be interesting to see, in these days when Broadway is stuffed with revivals, and with so many first- and second-rank titles already exploited, how a third-rank classic* would fare on The Street commercially.

In all, *Best Foot Forward* was an anomaly—a conventional piece particularized by an unambitious yet all the same *pointed* score. Broadway didn't have many pointed scores in the early 1940s; Broadway had "The Steam Is on the Beam" and "The Rhumba Jumps!."

Or: Broadway had Cole Porter, and that's where this imprisoning format for musical comedy had its release: in a brace of hot numbers. Add Porter's songs to a trashy Herbert and Dorothy Fields book about rich wives "entertaining" soldiers to avenge themselves on unfaithful husbands, create roles to make the most of an extremely fetching cast, and one has the smash-hit book show of 1941—in fact, at 547 performances, the longest-running pure-fun musical comedy since *Good News!*—*Let's Face It.*

Drawn from the 1925 play *The Cradle Snatchers*, by Russell Medcraft and Norma Mitchell, *Let's Face It* not only honored the Aarons–Freedley style but was a Vinton Freedley production. However, there was one major innovation in the style, a technical one that had a powerful effect on artistic matters. In the 1920s, when Aarons and Freedley formed their partnership, musicals were staged in one set per act, or in two sets per act separated by a minor scene played before the traveler curtain—what is called "in one." By the end of the 1920s, advances in the way shows were designed, in the way sets were hung, even in backstage discipline all enabled the creative team to count on four, five, or six sets per act.

This was invaluable, as writers no longer had to twist their sto-

---

* The first-rank shows are incontestable: *Show Boat, Carousel, West Side Story*. The second rank brings in popular yet not historically overwhelming titles: *Once Upon a Mattress, A Funny Thing Happened On the Way To the Forum*. In the third rank lie the once popular but now more or less neglected charm shows, like this one.

rytelling around the technical possibilities—such as where, physically, they were allowed to be at a given time, or how many characters they could bring onstage, or where people had to be while they were doing what. Narrative grew more fluid—really, more realistic. Finally, the story could dictate to the staging, rather than letting the staging limit the story.

One reason why was a new director's touch that found characters confidently moving downstage during a musical number to let the traveler close behind them (to give the stagehands the necessary privacy) even as the number continued. Once, this was thought threatening to the theatre's always perilous credibility. Changing the visuals *in front of the public* without a blackout? Worse, actors openly parading from one fake place to another, instead of making an official entrance from the wings? Wouldn't this only emphasize the very falseness of theatrical illusion? But, from the start in the late 1930s, when these changes were introduced, the public accommodated itself to the usage effortlessly.

So the traditional musical comedy could now toy with its own sense of artifice, move its folk around more easily, connect disparate places with a point of view. And, of course, as the storytelling improved, the songs had to keep up with the plot, work a little harder. Cole Porter's *Let's Face It* songs did include go-everywhere Cole Porter numbers: the ironic love songs ("You Irritate Me So" and the luxuriously coddling "I Hate You, Darling"), the Latin rhythm novelty ("A Little Rumba Numba," mainly an excuse for an appearance by ballroom dancers Mary Parker and Billy Daniel),* the list song ("Farming," on the bucolic amusements of the usual Porter celebrities, from "Kit Cornell" to the Duke of Verdura; and the wicked "Pets," dropped during rehearsals).

Yet "Jerry, My Soldier Boy" and "I've Got Some Unfinished Business With You" were locked into the storyline; and the

---

* The ballroom (i.e., "in evening dress") couple's adagio, tango, or choreographic medley, plopped into a book show with little or no motivation, dates back to the 1910s and was still a favorite makeweight in the early 1940s. As we'll see, by 1945 it was virtually extinct, though *Follies* (1971) looks back on it lovingly in the "Bolero d'Amour."

bouncy, brilliant "A Lady Needs a Rest," a cross section of the daily routine of the worldly socialite (who's "keeping her children in nights, and keeping her husband out") could only have been inspired by the show's central players: three bored, lonely, trendy, vital, satirically minded New York ladies:

Eve Arden, Vivian Vance, and Edith Meiser. Opposite them, as the soldiers they vainly attempt to seduce, were, respectively, Danny Kaye, Jack Williams, and Benny Baker;* and opposite *them*, as their ingenue sweethearts, were Mary Jane Walsh, Nanette Fabray, and Sunnie O'Dea. These were specialists, not just actors, and Let's Face It was organized around their gifts. Mary Jane Walsh, a suave singer in the belt range, was on hand to maintain a vocal standard. As Kaye's girl friend, she was strongly involved in the plot. But the Fieldses and Porter had above all to keep her positioned to put over the show's best melodies, perhaps especially "(Always have an) Ace in the Hole," with its ultra-Porter couplet in which "Bad times may bar you from Saks [Fifth Avenue]" abuts a warning about "a Satan in slacks." (Dancers Parker and Daniel made another appearance here, covering a set change and reminding us how easily the Aarons–Freedley format included miscellaneous talents without making the slightest excuse for their presence.)

Danny Kaye, fresh from his star's acclamation as an effeminate photographer in Lady in the Dark, was noted for retailing gibberish at a furious rate, and Porter gave him and Arden a dense patter number, "Let's Not Talk About Love," and also came up with "Baby Games," for the three ladies and their soldiers, similarly rooted in the frantically infantile mannerisms that Kaye specialized in. Then, too, Kaye's wife, Sylvia Fine, fashioned novelties for Kaye, "Melody in 4-F" and "Shootin' the Works." These interpolations into a Cole Porter score may strike us moderns as blasphemy. Yet this had long been common practice (though far more so in the early 1900s and less so now). Besides, why employ a zany such as Kaye and deny him material specifically provision-

---

* *The Cradle Snatchers'* founding sextet was even more impressive: Mary Boland, Edna May Oliver, and Margaret Dale facing off with Humphrey Bogart, Gene Raymond, and Raymond Hackett.

ing that zaniness? Fine could create it, and Porter probably didn't want to. The bulk of Kaye's script, too, gave the public full measures of his manic-depressive hysteria, not least in a scene aboard a canoe perched on a cardboard lake in which Arden tries to wring a little romance out of the soggy Kaye.

It was Arden, really, who got the most surely crafted tour de force, in a self-contained comic scene. Keep in mind that Arden, a sometime Hollywood player who by 1941 had appeared on Broadway in four revues and a book musical, commanded an established persona as elegant and ironic, with a clipped, deadpan* delivery and the ability to remain eternally bemused—or, rather, calmly staggered—by eccentrics. A decade after *Let's Face It*, Arden was to achieve ultimate completion with this identity in television's *Our Miss Brooks* as the schoolteacher surrounded by a daffy landlady, a befuddled though ceaselessly scheming principal, a libido-less boy friend, and so on. But here, in *Let's Face It*, is Arden at her peak, as she waits by a telephone on an army base. A soldier enters to place a call. As soon as he speaks, we hear a bizarre vocal impediment: he can't pronounce an "L." Worse, his girl friend, "Rirrian," apparently can't understand why he won't be able to see her that night. It seems that his leave has been canceled:

> SOLDIER: My reave! My reave! Can't you understand English?

As he goes on, Arden gives the audience her patented "how absurd does this world have to get?" look:

> SOLDIER: My reave got cancowed! My reave! (*He's frantic.*)
> My *reave*!

Arden can't take any more. As masterfully as a colonel, she holds out her hand, the soldier obediently gives her the phone, and in her very, very precise English, Arden speaks to the soldier's girl friend:

> ARDEN: Lillian—he says his leave got canceled.

---

* Literally "blank face": a now nearly lost art in which a comic performs his or her punch lines in a sardonic tone with expressionless features. Arden also specialized in "takes": reaction shots.

Arden hands the receiver back to the soldier, who now has another problem: Lillian accuses him of cheating on her with this other woman:

> SOLDIER: I am at camp! I ain't at Erinor's house! That wasn't Erinor!
> ARDEN: (*dryly flabbergasted*) Who?
> SOLDIER: (*To* ARDEN, *suddenly cowed*) Erinor.

And so on. In all, *Let's Face It* won its popularity on a plan that was by now nearly a generation old: start with a novel premise, develop farcically rather than realistically, and fill out with The Three Essentials: good score, good jokes, good players. (Sets and costumes were not regarded as crucial, and individualistic choreography was still being acculturated.)

The weakness in this format lay in the difficulty in rounding up all three Essentials at once. If even one of the three faltered, a show could dissolve, because it lacked foundation. *Let's Face It* could not have captivated Broadway without that Porter score, smart, loving, and constantly surprising with the customary Porter rhythmic sidesteps, pushbeats, and syncopations. Yet what would the songs have been worth without the pointed fun in the book and the expert comics socking that fun forth? The Essentials interlocked, cooperated, sustained each other.

A similar case can be made for *Louisiana Purchase* (1940), in which the Three Essentials were: one, Irving Berlin; two, a racy Morrie Ryskind–B. G. De Sylva book; and, three, the team of William Gaxton and Victor Moore with Vera Zorina, Irene Bordoni, and Carol Bruce. As well, this show boasted something special in its subject—political burlesque on Governor Huey Long's quasi-fascist rule in Louisiana.

Long was dangerous on the national level. At the time of his assassination, in 1935, he was poised to threaten Franklin Roosevelt's regime with a third-party candidacy that would have split the Democratic vote. However, producer and co-writer De Sylva was a retailer of the Aarons–Freedley shop, and he had no intention of tackling anything as serious as an Issue, even with the prickly former liberal Ryskind eager to observe ironies in Rooseveltian America. It was De Sylva who devised *Louisiana*

Purchase's storyline: straight-arrow but fuddled Republican senator (Moore) comes south to investigate shady yet likable politician (Gaxton). Politician falls for Hitler refugee (Zorina), who agrees to help compromise senator in an erotic scandal but then falls for *him* when he agrees to help her mother get out of Nazified Austria. That—along with the worldly commentary of restaurateuse Bordoni, the amiable company of songstress Bruce, the threats and sorties of Gaxton's corrupt cronies, and the "vocal stylings" (as they used to say) of the quartet billed as the [Hugh] Martins— is Act One.

The plot thins somewhat in Act Two. But by now we know that plot is not one of the Essentials. Expert makers of musicals were instead used to building their structures out of such other material as, say, the sheer discovery of the twenty-year-old Bruce, a real find for her strangely mature elegance, her plummy light mezzo. Or there was the reteaming of Zorina and choreographer George Balanchine, though this most snazzy and contemporary of musical comedies may seem an unlikely host for ballet. In fact, the ballet world had been moving from operetta into musical comedy for years. The brassiest, sauciest shows were on their toes nowadays. *Beat the Band* would be choreographed by ballet's David Lichine—yes, even "The Steam Is on the Beam."

Or take *Louisiana Purchase*'s curious opening number, no scene-setter but an "in real time" presentation of producer De Sylva's attorney, dictating a letter in which he frets over possible lawsuits unless the show pretends to take place in not the actual but a "mythical" Louisiana. The lawyer mentions Ryskind and Berlin by name, really worried at first and then avuncular, even gubernatorial, when he reveals the solution—and, of course, in a joke dating back to the early 1900s, he's one Sam Liebowitz, of the firm of O'Rafferty, Driscoll, and O'Brien.*

---

* The chuckling remark that all the lawyers of most common occurrence are Irish or Jewish presumably reflects the racial consciousness of early-twentieth-century show biz, heavily populated by minority groups who exploited stereotypical humor even as they tried to discredit it. I raise this point here because, under the influence of the racially sensitive Rodgers and Hammerstein and the culminating anti-stereotype sarcasm of *Finian's Rainbow*, the 1940s is

Given that every musical of the day began with a number of some kind but almost always a choral piece, it's arresting to find the tradition-loving Berlin tinkering with the protocols: bringing up his curtain on, first, the law firm's gum-chewing telephone operator and then the attorney, intoning in near-recitative. True, once the lawyer's solo is over, the ensemble takes stage for song and dance as in any show. Still, it's odd, even a wee bit Pirandellian, to spend a work's first five minutes on whether or not it's safe to stage the work in the first place. Today, we take such novelties in stride—indeed, we expect them. In 1940, when most musical comedies looked, acted, and sounded alike, a breakaway touch, however mild, was a stroke of lightning.

Berlin's score itself is otherwise conventional, even conservative in its retention of the hoary "finaletto" that habitually rounded off the first act in musicals of the early 1900s with one new tune, usually for the merrily entering chorus, then snatches of songs already heard in the act with new lyrics to advance the action in musical terms. It sounds like Gilbert and Sullivan; when George and Ira Gershwin used it in *Strike Up the Band* in 1927, it was already a wry pastiche. Now, in 1940, we wonder what Berlin was thinking when he included one in perfect earnest.

Perhaps he was defying the perception of his work as primitive hit-tuning without the craftsmanship of a Kern or Rodgers. A primitive Berlin certainly was, lacking even the rudiments of harmony and needing an assistant to notate his inspirations. Yet genius *can* be primitive. Berlin couldn't turn the music that he heard *inside* into notes on a staff, but he knew what he wanted, and held out until the chording that was offered him matched what he had conjured up in his mind.

In the end, Berlin's grasp of harmony equaled that of the best of Tin Pan Alley, though not on the level of Kern, Rodgers, or Harold Arlen. Anyway, primitive or not, Berlin was an innovator, for instance in the use of expansive song structures or in starting a melody on an unexpected tone of the scale. And, of course, his

---

the decade in which cheap racial humor was eradicated from the American musical.

effortlessly colloquial lyrics put everyday idioms into an earthy poetry. "It'll Come To You," one of *Louisiana Purchase*'s (cut) numbers, promises expertise in sex because that's simply nature's way; and "Latins Know How," sings Bordoni, about the same thing. (Note another stereotype, the endlessly amorous Mediterranean.)

It was Berlin's gift to absorb and then express what the nation was thinking at any given moment, from ragtime to swing and from Dressing Up Feels Powerful to Good Dancers Are Good Sex. The title number of *Louisiana Purchase* reconciles black music— in its "stride piano" left hand and jazzy chromaticism in the vocal line—to white, in the very concept of The Title Song of a Big Broadway Show. "You Can't Brush Me Off" borrows a slang catchphrase and returns a raucous love song, fond but aggressive. "It's a Lovely Day Tomorrow," very pure and diatonic in its melody and almost absurdly simple in its message, is the Berlin of the anthems, the idealistic and even epic Berlin. Remember, this is the man who wrote "White Christmas" and "God Bless America."

All this analyzing of Berlin's qualities obscures his greatest gift—sheer all-conquering tunefulness. Berlin's most character-oriented score is that for *Annie Get Your Gun* and his most elaborate score that for *Miss Liberty*, both later in this decade. But *Louisiana Purchase* is the most enjoyable Berlin score on the most basically sensual level, so rich in silly fun that the cut numbers— "Wild About You," "I'd Love To Be Shot From a Cannon With You," and the already mentioned "It'll Come To You"—are as good as everything that was actually performed.

Typically for the day, some of the score is more concerned with how Irving Berlin writes songs than with what his characters are actually up to in the story. So, when William Gaxton and Vera Zorina announce the love plot by getting on each other's nerves, they break into a Quarrel Duet. Fine: except Berlin's lyric finds them suddenly intimate with each other's smoking habits, jokes, and taste in clothing and poetry. What, after knowing each other for five minutes?

Comparably, a big gospel number called "The Lord Done Fixed Up My Soul" turns up in the action only because . . . well, why not? With almost all the principals facing exposure and prosecution, a minor character offers a non-solution. It's the south, and he's black, and while neither fact inexorably points to a soul rave-up, his logic seems persuasive to everyone on stage:

> BLACK MAN: I know what my mammy would do if she was in the trouble you all's in. She'd do some mighty deep praying.
> CAROL BRUCE: That's right, Abner.

And, after scarcely three seconds of orchestral introduction, Bruce sails into the verse: "I had a mammy for a nurse . . ." Note a third stereotype—*and* that suddenly it's *Bruce* claiming the background in the mammy arts.

But, once again, it was not realism that people wanted but entertainment. Jokes, songs, casting . . . and the dance, of course, peaking late in the second act in a dream ballet bearing a title, as all the best of the Big Ballets did. This one is "Old Man's Darling—Young Man's Slave," Zorina's vision of her future, married to either the pathetic Moore or the overbearing Gaxton. This sounds innovative, but the dream ballet was already a genre in the late 1930s, to be most famously realized in *Oklahoma!*'s "Laurey Makes Up Her Mind" (on a theme similar to that of "Old Man's Darling") three years after *Louisiana Purchase*. It is worth remarking, too, that while dance music in most shows had long consisted of repetitions of whatever song had just been sung, the Big Ballet's very grandeur called for something on a higher cultural level: *dramatic* dance music, descriptive, narrative, featuring developments and variations of themes from the show. "Laurey Makes Up Her Mind" calls on no fewer than seven of *Oklahoma!*'s songs, putting some of them through startling changes as the dream deepens into nightmare. "Old Man's Darling" focuses on a single number—grows out of it organically. After Gaxton sings "Fools Fall in Love," a solo violin echoes the main strain, then a fraught transition produces a waltz version, for trumpet and tripping woodwinds. Further transformations, now hushed, now wondering, lead into Zorina's vocal, and at last the violin returns as Zorina resolves her dilemma: it'll be Gaxton, warts and all.

What is important here is that the invention of the "symphonic" accompaniment to support the pretensions of the Big Ballet quickly influenced all dance music in musicals, lending atmosphere and point to shows whose books could not supply them. *Louisiana Purchase* has a good book for its day, functional and quick on its feet. But it's unreal without imagination and sturdy without substance. It's all frippery, field expedients, setups for the Essentials. Bordoni runs a restaurant because that makes it easy for characters to come and go in the restaurant scenes, and because that enables Ryskind to pile restaurant jokes upon the abstemious Moore. The Martins wander through the action as relentlessly as La Gioconda gets around Venice. Moore's hotel room is inundated by women because the era enjoyed sex farce. A supplementary couple with the most tenuous connection to the plot keeps snagging our attention for charm duets.

And then there's Ryskind's nagging Republicanism, a shock in Broadway's invariably liberal form, the musical. Ryskind has only just established Zorina as a victim of Nazi oppression when he paints her as yet another welfare-state freeloader: "In a few years, I get my second papers, and then I go on relief, eh? Heil Roosevelt!" Worse, the show's plot is rounded off when the quivering Moore, a presidential hopeful, cannot cross a picket line for any reason whatsoever because . . . well, in a freethinking republic, it just isn't being done.

Still, what are these cavils next to the pure *pleasure* of the piece? As with Porter's *Let's Face It*, it's absurd to complain about the parts that don't tally for us today. These two hit shows of 1940 and 1941 give us what Broadway then demanded of its top practitioners in the musical: a season's run, a solid tour of the major cities, a sale to Hollywood (Bob Hope starred in both movie versions, respectively in the Gaxton and Kaye roles), and some hit-parade action for the outstanding songs. Then the piece would fade, perhaps to be revived at the St. Louis Municipal Opera's summer season or, if innocent enough (and neither of these shows was), to be promoted for use by high-school and amateur dramatic clubs for a single generation. Then the show would vanish, but for echoes of its music on radio.

Nowadays we cultivate the classic: the *lasting* show. We await the next one each season—the new Sondheim? A sleeper from downtown, East Village Puccini? A spectacle drawn from an unadaptable novel with a killer score and a production of the Hal Prince school? Paul Simon on Broadway? A lynching?

To comprehend the 1940s, especially the Rodgers and Hammerstein influence that transformed the musical within the decade, we need to see how the concept of a successful musical changed. It had been a disposable money-spinner. Now it would be a cultural essential, something that would stay with us indefinitely in its complete truth as a Broadway show. Like the Mona Lisa and *Carmen*, it would be eternally on view, not just "recalled" in a radio medley by Gladys Swarthout and James Melton or summer-tented. It would not be given the crass "direct from Broadway" approach of a week on The Street leading to a national tour of cities that didn't know any better; that was mainly for *Naughty Marietta*, *Blossom Time*, *The Student Prince*, and other old operettas that no one cared about, anyway. Of course, there was always *Show Boat* and *Porgy and Bess*, whose scores were so very, very much alive that . . . but did one actually restage old shows? Ziegfeld had put *Show Boat* on in 1932, three years after the original had closed; but that was a remounting of the original: the whole thing as it had been, with some cast changes. To produce a *new* version of an old show, one would have to have . . . well, not just a hit show but a *great* show. And, by 1940, what would that even *be*?

2

ƒTARƒ

The star vehicle was the easiest musical to produce, because this extraordinarily central figure could walk onto the stage—even, into the first day of rehearsals—with an evening's worth of material all built-in. One had only to assemble the support group. The paying public was built-in, too, flocking to star shows as moviegoers patronized Clark Gable or Judy Garland. A star was the surest thing that a manager (today: "producer") could present, somebody famous whom a lot of people never tired of.

Of star shows, the easiest to produce was the revue. For instance, rent Jimmy Durante, Ray Bolger, singer Jane Froman, dry comic Ilka Chase, dancer José Limon, clown Emmet Kelly, wet comic Jack (later Jackie) Gleason, deadpan singer Virginia O'Brien, the indescribable "Peanuts" Bohn, the Morelli Singers, Dodson's Monkeys, and so on—from genuine headliners to available filler—and you have a showcase for talent called *Keep Off the Grass* (1940). The performers are self-starters, complete with their own time-tested (and -worn) material, and writers Mort Lewis, Parke Levy, Alan Lipscott, Norman Panama, Melvin Frank, and even others will run off a burlesque of *Life With Father* using

24

the Roosevelts as characters and of Laurence Olivier and Vivien Leigh's just-opened *Romeo and Juliet* in the style of zany *Hellzapoppin*. Or was it so easy? The Shuberts, *Keep Off the Grass'* producers, had been mounting such vaudevilles for decades, yet this one folded after five weeks.

Ed Wynn did better with *Boys and Girls Together* (1940) and *Laugh, Town, Laugh!* (1942), in both of which he served as absolute capocomico—star, producer, and author. As in Wynn's twenties shows, he filled the evening with his patented eccentricities—the crazy hats and demented inventions, the vocal delivery that loved to emphasize a minor phrase just *before* the punch line only to throw the punch line away, thus creating a double laugh as half the audience roared even while repeating the joke to the less alert half, who then roared in turn.

In *Boys and Girls Together*, Wynn extemporized, interfered in the acts (such as advising the woman in a Danse Apache how to get back at her manhandling partner), and revived his famous bicycle piano, riding around the stage as Jane Pickens sang "You Can't Put Catsup on the Moon" while perched upon it. *Laugh, Town, Laugh!* was less high-powered. An autumnal work, it brought back perhaps the most overviewed of the classic vaudeville sketches, Smith and Dale's "Dr. Kronkeit." (This was the inspiration for the pastiche sketch that Neil Simon created *en hommage* for *The Sunshine Boys*.) Wynn may have felt himself overviewed as well, for he was almost wanly deferential toward the acts he used to deconstruct. It was his last Broadway appearance, though he went on to major work on television in the 1950s and performs a cameo in the *Mary Poppins* movie.

Another performer of the Old School bade farewell to Broadway when Eddie Cantor fulfilled a long and constantly frustrated dream of playing Erwin, the greeting-card poet of the John Cecil Holm–George Abbott comedy *Three Men on a Horse*. Gentle Erwin, who falls into the clutches of gamblers because of his knack for picking winning horses, was the ideal Cantor role—as Cantor had realized when the play first appeared in 1935 (with William Lynn as Erwin, Sam Levene as the lead gambler, and Shirley Booth as his moll). Menaced by dangerous men and enchanted by a supernatural gift he himself has no interest in: this was the stuff of major Cantor shtick, as he cringes, wonders, hides, and whines.

With a book by Izzy Elinson and Joe Quillan, music by Vernon Duke, and lyrics by John Latouche and Harold Adamson, the show was presented as *Banjo Eyes* (1941), the title role belonging not to Cantor (as everyone was meant to assume) but to a horse. In fact, Banjo Eyes was a speaking part, played by the old vaudeville team of Mayo and Martin in an animal suit. Dream ballets showed how Banjo Eyes tips Erwin, always warning him that his gift will vanish if he tries to place money on a race. With the raspy-voiced (and strictly non-singing) Lionel Stander and the coldly tempestuous Audrey Christie as tout and moll, the ubiquitous De Marcos (though Tony had ditched wife Renee for Sally), a burlesque adagio trio billed as Lynn, Royce, and Vanya, and an interpolated wartime anthem by Cliff Friend and Charles Tobias called "We Did it Before (and we can do it again)," *Banjo Eyes* was very much of its day: an agglomeration of diversions loosely pursuing a storyline. The Three Essentials would have put it over; but it lacked two of them. It had the cast, but the fun was forced and predictable and the score ordinary but for one Cantor special, by Duke and Adamson, "We're Having a Baby (my baby and me)." As an appeal to auld lang syne, Cantor topped off the show with a medley of his old hits in his familiar blackface makeup—"Margie," "Ida," "If You Knew Susie." After four months of okay business, *Banjo Eyes* was forced to close when Cantor suffered a medical emergency.

This was an extremely disappointing showing for Cantor, whose twenties vehicles did turnaway business; but Cantor worked for Ziegfeld then. His rival in Jewish blackface singing comedy, Al Jolson, worked for the Shuberts, and Jolson, too, made a comeback, after a decade away, in *Hold On To Your Hats* (1940). All the town regarded it as a historic event, the *Herald-Tribune* entitling its review "First Minstrel." Cantor had maintained a more consistently successful career, especially with his radio show. But Jolson was perhaps more centrally, even primevally stellar: the man who popularized the "sell-it!" vocal style that eradicated nineteenth-century salon technique just as the first generation of all-American popular song was crystallizing (they called it "jazz"); who presided over the creation of the movie musical; whose very survival affirmed the vitality of the upstart, immigrant, earthy show biz that had entertained three generations of Americans. Where Cantor played the sissy, Jolson played the wise guy— though in *Hold On To Your Hats* Jolson tried on a Cantoresque role as a timid radio cowboy, the Lone Rider, who is inveigled on a trip westward to put down a bandit gang.

The production credits were typical B or B+: Jolson himself produced, with George Hale; the prominent (if by now written out) Guy Bolton wrote the book, with Matty Brooks and Eddie Davis; the promising Burton Lane and E. Y. Harburg wrote the score; Edgar McGregor and Catherine Littlefield, both uncelebrated experts, respectively directed the book scenes and choreographed; and the production as a whole—in the typical billing of the day—was "supervised" by Hale. Maybe a smarter or more original team of bookwriters might have significantly increased the show's chances; but there were no smart or original bookwriters in shows of this kind in 1940. Aarons–Freedley thinking, remember, required not good but *funny* writing. Good writers had better things to do.

The cast, at least, was hot: Martha Raye as Jolson's vis-à-vis, the dependable (if aging) Jack Whiting as the juvenile, and Bert Gordon, the "Mad Russian" on Eddie Cantor's radio show, as the Lone Rider's Jewish-accented cohort, Concho. The Lone Rider's horse was Goldie, which finally tells us how the evening's jokes skewed: the Lone Ranger Goes Yiddish.

As always, Jolson hogged the script and the best songs. He was at his most Jolsonesque even now, twenty-nine years after his Broadway debut, dancing as he sang, getting into drag as a señorita to attract the attention of the bandit leader and then sticking in an act as a Mexican street vendor, doing "love to hate you" courtship comedy with Raye, ad libbing with the frenzied Gordon, and assuming a wide range in the song formats, from the surprisingly downscaled "Walkin' Along, Mindin' My Own Business" to the imitation of a Vincent Youmans rouser, "There's a Great Day Coming Manana." Like Cantor, Jolson of course concluded his performance with a storm of old hits—"April Showers," "Swanee," "Sonny Boy"—just as he did in his Shubert shows so long before. First minstrel.

Hold On To Your Hats was a much, much better show than any of the ones that Jolson did in the 1910s and 1920s, when there was nothing but Jolson and his specialty numbers plus a bunch of goons singing swill. Raye faced off Jolson with the flirty "Would You Be So Kindly," detailed the horrors of modern life ("Were they ever scared by big squaw wife in Schiaparelli hat?") in "Life Was Pie for the Pioneer," and saluted Jolson's señorita disguise in "She Came, She Saw, She Can-Canned." Gordon's explosive Concho froze the real Lone Ranger's subservient Tonto like a deer in Nietzsche's headlights. A quartet of "dudettes" delightfully opened the show as hitchhikers, each with a red glove thumbing the air, singing "Way Out West (where the east begins)." And the entire cast serenaded Jolson at the finale with the touching "Old Timer."

Still, it was strictly performer art. The score no more than goes through pleasant motions. The humor, when the players weren't making it up, reads as simply stupid:

> DUDETTE: (*haughtily*) Remember, I'm one of the four hundred.
> MAMIE: Beat it, sister, before I cut you down to $3.98.

(This was also not the first musical—and not the last—to make a jest out of the mispronunciation of a New Mexico town as "Alber-cue-cue.") At that, *Hold On To Your Hats* might have made it on its strong cast. But Jolson tired of putting out eight times a week and, as co-producer, folded the piece after five months.

Incredibly, there was speculation that Eddie Cantor would take over for Jolson. The rules of stardom forbade any headliner of consequence to take a seat already warmed in public. But then, if one replaced a star with a journeyman, however adequate, would that not threaten the very reality of the work? The star not only defines but informs his show, provides its content. There is no show without him.

Those of my readers who are thinking of the many performers who successfully followed Ethel Merman in *Gypsy* revivals, or who took over Carol Channing's Dolly (Merman among them), are citing star shows of vastly denser story value than the star shows of the early 1940s. Right now, we're in a time dominated by Aarons–Freedley thinking, when the inspiration for an evening's entertainment is a mosaic of talents and not the delineation of character. There are no characters; or, rather, *stars* are the characters. So it's bad enough if the star leaves the show before it's ready to close. What if the star leaves before it opens?

Think of yourself as George Hale. You are producing a piece built around England's outstanding musical comedy talent, Jessie Matthews, in her first American appearance since three revues in the 1920s. Not only will this be Matthews' first American book musical but her American "debut" after having gained international fame as the queen of the English screen musical, so fetching that she could fill Radio City Music Hall (with *Evergreen*, in 1934).

Your show for Matthews is *The Lady Comes Across* (1942), in a punning salute to both Matthews' primly voluptuous je sais quoi and to her ocean voyage from London to Broadway. You envision a major production, although, penny-wise, you have bought the sets to a disaster called *She Had To Say Yes* that closed on the road the previous season. You will build your show's plot around those sets, but that's easy enough, as *The Lady Comes Across* will offer Matthews as an innocent caught up in wartime espionage . . . well, not really: it was all a dream. Still, such an adventure can occur pretty much anywhere.

Not being able to afford or interest anyone on the level of Rodgers and Hart or Cole Porter, you have turned to Vernon Duke and John Latouche, erratic but talented. In fact, Latouche will eventually write, for *The Golden Apple* (1954), arguably the most brilliant lyrics that Broadway will ever hear. And Duke has composed many a hit song—"April in Paris," "Autumn in New York," "I Can't Get Started," "Taking a Chance on Love"—just never a hit show.* Still, the songwriters are more promising than the book-

---

* In his entire career, from London in the 1920s, when he composed one success, the mystery thriller *The Yellow Mask*, to Broadway in the 1960s, when *Zenda* collapsed on its tryout, Duke was almost supernaturally dogged by

writers, Fred Thompson and Dawn Powell: the sharper talents tended to turn down assignments in which the script will be written around pre-existing sets.

And you at least have Jessie Matthews, perhaps the most bizarre heroine musical comedy had ever known: pretty, with a valentine-shaped face and enormous eyes; a wonderful singer and a stylish dancer; but a strangely plangent pixie, the kind who prefers to sing cheer-up ditties while her heart is caving in. Her romantic opposite will be Ronald Graham, as an FBI man who recruits Matthews and establishes her cover as a clerk in a bon ton dress shop, mainly because the shop was one of *She Had To Say Yes'* nicest sets. Nightclub comic Joe E. Lewis is the central wag, but Mischa Auer is also on hand, as a spy (in drag, disguised as "the Baroness Helstrom") who's hunting for the usual espionage macguffin, "the papers," hidden in the girdle of a dowager (Ruth Weston).

True, in terms of story value, this is no *My Fair Lady*. Nor, it turns out, have Duke and Latouche distinguished themselves. (One critic will term Duke's melodies "cold Porter.") But there is abundant extra fun—from the Martins, here cast as shoppers to sing the madrigal "Summer Is A-Comin' In," from Lewis' salute to one of radio's most constant voices, the "H. V. Kaltenborn Blues," from the dance team of Gower and Jeanne (actually Gower Champion and his pre-Marge partner, Jeanne Tyler), and from George Balanchine, who decided to stage *this* show's dream ballets as spoofs.

Hiring Balanchine was one of your smarter moves; and, in the aforementioned style of the day, you have balanced the choreographer with a director for the book scenes (Romney Brent) and then placed the pair of them under Morrie Ryskind's "supervision." However, from the first out-of-town performance, it is clear that something is very, very wrong with your show. It looks fine,

---

failure. No fewer than five of his scores were written for shows that closed out of town; and his one classic title, *Cabin in the Sky*—which we'll be hearing from presently—staggered through five months of half-empty houses and has never been successfully revived.

Joe E. Lewis is working out well, and Gower and Jeanne, barely
into their twenties, are entrancing, wowing the public with one
bit in which they pant spoken lines while dancing. One of Graham's numbers, the silky waltz "Lady (you're so deep in the dream
you can't hear me)," looks very winning. A solo for Lewis, "You
Can't Get the Merchandise," is amusing the public with digs at
wartime shortages. (Pearl Harbor was bombed just as you hit Boston.)

Unfortunately, the ludicrous spy story isn't holding up. Frantically, you change anything that can be changed, and the nagging
revisions are starting to tell on Matthews. In fact, something is
very, very wrong with your star. Like the character she's playing,
she feels menaced. People are opening her mail, murmuring pass-
words, kidnaping her.

No, really. Incredible to report, Matthews is actually suffering
a hysterical psychotic episode, and has got so deep in the dream
that she has to be hospitalized. She will be very honest about it
in her memoirs, thirty-two years later:

> I was in a dark room. Someone had dressed me in a rough
> shift that scrubbed against my skin. I was on a bed ... I
> couldn't move my hands, they felt manacled. Had the Ger-
> mans caught me? ... I heard someone screaming ... And
> then I knew that the woman who screamed was myself.

It ends well:

> A man stood at the foot of my bed. . . . He told me he was
> from the British Consul, and spoke gently to me. . . . In his
> hand he held the dog-eared script of *The Lady Comes Across*
> ... I could see the underscoring, the inserts, the deletions.
> "How did you ever manage to learn a part like this?" he asked.
> "It's enough to drive anyone crazy." I gave him a wry smile.
> "It did."

But that leaves you without the unifying personality that this
clumpy piece desperately needs. As you ready your troupe to open
in New York, one Evelyn Wyckoff, heretofore a soprano in Shubert Brothers operetta tours, steps in as leading lady. She's a
spunky kid with a sweet voice, and the critics give her high marks

for effort. Some of them almost like the show. But most of the notices are outright pans, and while no one calls it the worst musical since *Naughty Riquette* (1926), you have no chance to run. Exhausted, you fold after 3 performances, the shortest run of any book musical in the decade.

What went wrong? When the star departs a show with no substance in itself, there *is* no show. Louis Kronenberger underlined the importance, to a piece of this kind, of the Three Essentials: "Those arch saboteurs of musical comedy, the book and the gags . . . ruin what might have been a good show. . . . And [it also] lacks the two things that might have overcome such drawbacks: a brilliant score and a big personality."

Conversely, dancer Ray Bolger enjoyed a tremendous hit in *By Jupiter* (1942), though this piece was in its story material and character development no better than *The Lady Comes Across*. However, *By Jupiter* had a lot of bawdy gender humor, a wonderful Rodgers and Hart score, and a sharp cast supporting Bolger as a pantywaist married to the Queen of the Amazons. Like *The Lady Comes Across*, it was a stupid show: but a funny, melodic, and personable one, and it was still going strong at 427 performances—the longest opening run of any Rodgers and Hart title—when Bolger, his contract up, decided to Do His Bit and entertain the troops overseas, forcing *By Jupiter* to close. Had he stayed, it just might have lasted two years, the first story musical in history to do so.

Let's look at *By Jupiter* to see just how a hit star show of 1942 works when it has nothing but a headliner, a one-joke subject (women boss men around till Hercules, Achilles, Theseus, and other heroes show up), and whatever incidental charms it contrives to stick in. Most musicals of the time were originals, but *By Jupiter* was an adaptation, of Julian F. Thompson's 1932 play *The Warrior's Husband*, the work in which Katharine Hepburn first won the attention that eventually took her to Hollywood. Rodgers and Hart wrote the book themselves, despairing of getting anything valid from the hacks and duffers who wrote musical comedy books in 1942. Indeed, they had done so three times previously; and Rodgers co-produced, with Dwight Deere Wiman.

They chose a first-rate cast. None of the names besides Bolger's means anything today, but the leading Amazons counted a Mermanesque powerhouse in Benay Venuta, an amusingly icy Hollywood beauty in Constance Moore (in Hepburn's old part), and a delightful old bag in Bertha Belmore (an alumna of *The Warrior's Husband* in *her* old part, as a plutocrat who exploits a wartime emergency to ensure that her son, Bolger, is wedded to the Amazon queen, Venuta). Moore pursued the traditional "second couple" romance, with Richard Kollmar as the ice-melting Theseus; future leading man Mark Dawson helped fill out the Greek ranks; and future MGM cutie Vera-Ellen captivated the public in the dance numbers.

Immediately, we see a sharp difference between *The Lady Comes Across* and *By Jupiter*, for the critics groused about some of the casting in the former but enjoyed everyone in *By Jupiter*. Remember, this was a time when theatre held a powerful place in the structure of American show biz, smaller than movies but bigger than pop concerts and records. Theatre had prestige, too. Broadway was a magnet not only for audiences but for talent, which included more than those of a strictly thespian vocation, such as refugees from dead vaudeville, nightclub folk looking for something steady, and the determinedly Hollywood-bound.* A musical was supposed to be *stuffed* with ace performers. It wasn't George Hale's fault that he lost his star in Boston. But, except for Gower Champion's dance act, the rest of Hale's corps was dreary.

Then, too, *The Lady Comes Across* kept getting tangled in its clumsy plot, while book writers Rodgers and Hart made sure that *By Jupiter* emphasized not plot but personality. Oddly, *By Jupiter* treated the same absurd "quest" premise as *The Lady Comes Across*. Just as the latter found the good guys having to get to some fancy dame's girdle, so did *By Jupiter*'s Greeks have to steal

---

* The illustrative example of how crucial a Broadway success—even a mere Broadway appearance—could be is The Betty Grable Story: after ten years in the movies doing chorus, bit work, and featured parts in B films, Grable went to New York, got a supporting role in an Ethel Merman–Bert Lahr hit, *DuBarry Was a Lady* (1939), and was on her way back to California with a star's contract.

the Girdle of Diana from the Amazon queen. That, plus the two love plots—the pixilated Bolger finally stands up to his butch bride and instantly conquers, and Moore and Kollmar woo warrior-style—is virtually all that occurs the entire evening. The rest is nothing but fun: for instance, in the costuming of Hercules (the portly Ralph Dumke) to look exactly like Lauritz Melchior, the Met's main Wagner tenor. Or in the duet of Bolger and mother Belmore, "(I used to love my) Life With Father," a passable song made show-stopper when the sixty-year-old Belmore joined Bolger in a spot of dance.

True, some had a problem with the flamboyance of Bolger's mollycoddle act. As *The New Yorker*'s Wolcott Gibbs put it, "I am never quite sure . . . just how funny effeminacy really is on the stage." However, the public in general loved Bolger to the nth—and that public, by 1942, was very much another of those soldiers-on-leave-with-their-dates clientele. *By Jupiter* was brass and crass, and so they liked it. Indeed, it was nearly burlesque (in the Min-skyan sense), with the Amazons alluringly costumed in battle gear and short skirts, with the female Viking Jayne Manners on hand to recall burlesque's trope of six-foot-showgirl-playing-comedy-with-short-men, and many, many a double entendre, especially those examining the absurdity of a society in which men keep house and women kill.

Hart got off the wickedest such jest in the Amazons' chorus "The Boy I Left Behind Me," in which the infantry envys the navy "because a sailor has a boy in every port." This was perhaps Hart's wickedest show altogether: his best, then. For such a one-joke piece, he is wonderfully varied in tone. The ballads alone are an anthology of feelings, blissfully romantic in "Wait Till You See Her," despondent in "Nobody's Heart (belongs to me)," caressing in the hungrily syncopated "Careless Rhapsody," even brutally martial in "Here's a Hand," on the meeting of Moore and Kollmar. Hart's devilry reaches into everything, as when he concocts another ballad in the lovingly nostalgic "The Gateway of the Temple of Minerva" yet turns the number on its head with a punning turnaround in the final line—a kick gone on a tear when the chorus takes up the tune in boogie-woogie scat style. "Ev'rything I've Got (belongs to you)," a challenge duet for Bolger and Venuta,

provides a very center for this tale of sex war; and Hart even in-
dulges in a patriotic anthem, Hart-style, in "Jupiter Forbid," the
Amazons' big scene-setter, but really a jazzy hymn to democracy.
Irving Berlin did it in anthem. Cole Porter did it in saucy list
songs. But Hart—greatest of all?—did it lightly, sweetly, and most
truly.

Rodgers matched Hart with some of *his* best work. None of the
songs has endured importantly,* but they are all enjoyable and
three or four really sing. There's another difference between this
show and *The Lady Comes Across*, which tried to skid by on the
kind of mediocrity that Rodgers and Hart at their weakest invariably surpassed.

One last difference between our two star vehicles: Jessie Matthews was a lot bigger than her show was, so it couldn't have done
her much good. However, Ray Bolger was no more than prominent before *By Jupiter*; the show anointed him. He did far better
than Jolson and Cantor, for they were playing their long-
established personae. Bolger made himself a novelty, playing a
character far removed from the goofy sidekicks and hoofers he
was known for (not to mention his Scarecrow in the film *The
Wizard of Oz*).

Still, there was nothing as solid as a talent absolutely guaranteed to be big and do big and stay big, and that, in the Broadway
musical circa 1940, was Ethel Merman. Since her discovery in
Girl Crazy (1930), Merman had spent the years sharing top bill-

---

* "Wait Till You See Her" did become a standard, but it was actually dropped
from the show just before the New York opening. The fourth love song in the
Moore–Kollmar subplot, it was situated so late in the story that it slowed the
whole show to a stop. In Boston, where *By Jupiter* was called *All's Fair*, the work
seemed a sure hit but for a saggy second act, so Rodgers and Wiman decided to
drop the scene. In his memoirs, Rodgers mentioned omitting the song during
the New York run. That was in fact the theory of his ghostwriter, Stanley Green.
"Wait Till You See Her" was cut in Boston but shows up in the first New York
playbills because the printer wasn't warned in time. My proof: critics in those
days made a big deal out of singling out the three or four songs they most
enjoyed. Almost all mentioned "Nobody's Heart" and "Life With Father," and
many cited "Ev'rything I've Got" and "Careless Rhapsody." *Literally none* named
"Wait Till You See Her," so none, surely, can have heard this outstanding example of the famous "Rodgers waltz." The 1967 off-Broadway revival found a
solution to the number's odd placement, redepositing it early in Act Two.

ing, mainly with comics. The 1940s reinstalled her as protagonist, to carry shows single-handed and play romances that really mattered. Her type had been set for some time: as a city girl, gutsy and funny, easily offended, fierce when crossed, but very loyal and so guilelessly unpretentious that she was constantly going up against, and ultimately either charming or defeating, various haughty aristocrats. But now her love plots would gave her a vulnerable side to display, a tender note to sound amid the brassy clamor.

Why had it taken so long for this most essential of stars to find her identity? Oddly, while her no-nonsense side-street dame seems perfect for wartime, she was an odd item when she first arrived. Remember, in 1930 the musical's version of America's Sweetheart, Marilyn Miller, was still in her prime and the very opposite of Merman: blond, ethereally demure, a country girl who mainly danced but also sang, in front-parlor, Saturday-night-musicale soprano. Merman, of course, was dark and lowdown, never danced, and sang red-hot trumpet.

It was the singing that made Merman so necessary to the musical that it had at length to reinvent the very concept of the heroine in order to let her run her own show. Hers was the kind of voice that can sing the heck out of a rave-up like *Girl Crazy*'s "I Got Rhythm." But Merman could also dip into a ballad with delicacy. She had a pianissimo to fill the Alvin and Imperial Theatres, yet her grace notes (as in "There's *no-oh* business like *sho-oh* business . . .") went off like bombs. She had a comic touch, too—but I mean in her singing. She would sharp or flat a note for verbal effect, yet intone the most ribald pun in apparent innocence. These contradictions within the fortress-mentality consistency made Merman dependable yet surprising. True, she was— at least, at this time—no actor. Was Jolson? Cantor? Bolger? Rather, she put her lines over with tremendous verve, was indefatigable to the point of never missing a performance no matter how long the run, and spit out her lyrics with faultless articulation in the days before electrical amplification. She was huge, wondrous, and long-lived, the musical's ultimate star from her first show—her first phrase, even—to her last. She was Ethel Merman rolled into one.

We can catch Merman at her early zenith in *Panama Hattie* (1940) and *Something For the Boys* (1943). Both, typically, were Cole Porter shows. Merman had sung Gershwin, Youmans, and Arthur Schwartz in one work each and would get to Irving Berlin twice. Porter and Merman, however, collaborated five times, because no one but he could taste so surely of her dirty grandeur, her effortless uniting of class, place, era, gender—that is, proletarian Golden-Age show-biz Big Lady glamor—just by being who she was. It's outrageously apropos: Porter the Yale man and Merman the upstart as a matched set.

But they were, as he designed her entrance "I prevail" number, her loony friendship duet, her torch song, and so on; and as she worked into it so ingenuously that one wonders if she got all the double meanings. Porter's most sympathetic librettist was Herbert Fields, who wrote or co-wrote seven Porter scripts and who, in the 1920s, first edged musical-comedy librettos into the racy. Fields collaborated with B. G. De Sylva on *Panama Hattie* and with sister Dorothy Fields on *Something For the Boys*, but they are basically the same piece: Ethel defies the snobs to win over the hero in exotic locations with a strong wartime atmosphere in which she pulls off a stunt advantageous to the war effort. *Panama Hattie* gave Merman her second title role (after *DuBarry Was a Lady*) as Hattie Maloney, a Canal Zone nightclub owner courted by a naval officer, a divorced blueblood with an eight-year-old daughter, Geraldine. The girl at first laughs at Hattie's grammar, dress, and overall style, but becomes her warm ally by the first-act curtain. A shadowy spy plot designed to fill up an empty second act finds the kid unwittingly carrying a bomb to her father's office, but Hattie saves him, at great personal risk.

Even in a show re-envisioning Merman with a sweetheart side, *Panama Hattie* observed the Merman conventions. The Grand Entrance:

> MAC: (*calling up to an unseen Merman*) Hey, Hattie!
> HATTIE: (*still unseen*) What do you want?
> MAC: There's four guys down here to see you.
> HATTIE: Only four? I must be slipping!

Thus anticipated, Merman finally enters, dolled up in an apotheosis of streetwalker chic and leading a titanic poodle named Serutan.*

Another Merman convention was the Heavy Retort:

> HATTIE: One more wisecrack out of *you* and you'll be wearing
> this *cuspidor* as a *snood*!

and another was the Demotion of the Socially Arrogant, when a certain Leila Tree resents the insolence of the Hattie–Gerry alliance:

> LEILA: How dare you two? I'll have you know that I'm a Tree!
> HATTIE: (*with the chatty brightness of a Mermanesque "innocent" reply*) I must tell Serutan about you!

Something For the Boys presented Merman as Blossom Hart, one of three long-lost cousins inheriting a rundown ranch near San Antonio, which they rehabilitate as a hotel for wives visiting soldier husbands. Blossom herself has an eye on Sgt. Rocky Fulton, already engaged to a creepy socialite who misrepresents the hotel as a bordello and has it declared off-limits. But Blossom, who can receive radio transmissions through fillings in her teeth, helps guide an ailing warplane and its crew to safety, thus winning vindication for her ranch and Sgt. Fulton's love.

Again, there was all that Merman stuff. Here, her best Heavy Retort was aimed at Rocky, who goes all wolf at the sight of Blossom's legs:

> ROCKY: Boy, look at those drumsticks!
> BLOSSOM: How'd you like a kick in the teeth from one of
> those drumsticks?
>
> . . .
>
> ROCKY: (*mock-ruefully*) And *this* is the womanhood I'm fighting to protect?
> BLOSSOM: And this is the womanhood *I'm* fighting to protect!

What mainly differentiated *Panama Hattie* from *Something For the Boys* was the subsidiary casting. As the boy friend, *Panama*

---

*A now forgotten but once ubiquitous health tonic. Note that Serutan is "Nature's" spelled backwards—as the commercial promotions always emphasized.

Hattie's James Dunn was one of those dim talents common in American show biz back then—a man, one imagines, who got work more out of Irish charm than capability. Over at *Something For the Boys*, Bill Johnson gave Merman someone to look up to, big, cute, and young (twenty-five to Merman's thirty-four), with a formidable high baritone that sailed up to a resounding G to cap the devilish "When My Baby Goes To Town."

The comics, too, separated the shows. *Panama Hattie* featured three sailors (Rags Ragland, Pat Harrington, and Frank Hyers), Hattie's pals and apparently former burlesque clowns—appropriately enough in a work heralded with the boast "50—Dazzling Panamamas—50." For example, Woozy (Ragland) is annoying two women:

> FIRST GIRL: (*irritated*) What do you want?
> WOOZY: I want to make some new acquaintances.
> SECOND GIRL: Oh, you do?
> WOOZY: Yeah. I'm tired of making all the old ones.

Panama Hattie also offered Betty Hutton and Arthur Treacher as the second couple, the raucous Hutton chasing the primly English Treacher for the entire evening.

Something For the Boys' jesters were Blossom's two cousins, played by Allen Jenkins and Paula Laurence, the one a sidewalk con man and the other a stripper. This helped center the story. Hattie's sailors, so busy in the action, had nothing whatever to do with the plot. *Something's* cousins were the center of that show's plot, their ranch no macguffin but the reason why everything happens, literally from the opening curtain to the finale. Another difference from *Hattie* was *Something's* gentling of the ingenue role from the spirited Hutton to the low-key Betty Garrett, who got a major solo in the lazy boogie "I'm in Love With a Soldier Boy."

One thing one must praise in Cole Porter is his ultra-contemporary sound, astonishing in a songwriter whose Broadway debut occurred in 1916, when Victor Herbert and George M. Cohan ruled. As in *Let's Face It*, little of the two scores really digs into the stories. *Hattie* includes a characterful duet for Hattie and Gerry (Joan Carroll), "Let's Be Buddies," that captures in a patter section their class distinctions even while harmonizing them.

"They Ain't Done Right By Our Nell," for Hutton and Treacher, similarly compares Yankee bluntness with British ceremony, at that in another of Porter's delighted spoofs of country music.

In *Something For the Boys*, the opening number is pure action, as a lawyer (Jed Prouty) contacts the cousins one by one to tell them of their inheritance, the scene bound by a single line—"But I haven't any cousins!"—repeated by each cousin in turn as the audience starts to catch on. A droll and unexpected beginning, the number contains an insider's joke in that, following Paula Laurence and Allen Jenkins, Merman will have to "pop up" in the show rather than make one of her Big Entrances. (Of course, the impromptu materializing of the headliner is in itself a kind of Extra-Big Entrance, as the startled public gasps and applauds.)

Still, these are not site-specific scores but rather Merman-specific scores. Hattie's "My Mother Would Love You" (the ballad) and "I've Still Got My Health" (the novelty spot); or Blossom's "Something For the Boys" (the rouser) and "He's a Right Guy" (the torch number, in Porter's favorite Latin shuffling beat) were the usual great Merman songs by the great Merman composer. The two were most surely in cahoots in Hattie's "Make it Another Old-Fashioned, Please," a torch spot with a beseeching coda ("Leave out the cherry, leave out the orange . . .") that Merman exalts by flatting the "Leave" into a drunken whine.

What mattered, then, was not how carefully Porter discovered music in the scripts, but how well Porter wrote songs. Keep in mind that not only much of American life but a significant fraction of American business was plugged into the music of Broadway—on radio and anywhere bands played for singers, in the making of movie musicals, in sheet music and record sales, and, by *Something For the Boys'* 1943, wherever servicemen were. Broadway did not constitute American pop music exclusively, but Broadway led it, and Porter was one reason why. It was craftsmanship, precision, genius. Just one example: in *Something For the Boys*, when Rocky is recounting the meeting that sparked love with his fiancée, the scene moves into song as the chorus of soldiers responds to Rocky's tale. "The place?" they sing, and Rocky answers, "A big shindig in Baltimore." "The time?" they ask. Rocky replies; "The girl?" they insist. And so it continues, no mere intro to a ballad but a parody of an intro in the form of a burlesque of a discussion, shaped and goaded till it finally gives way to the serene jazz of "Could It Be You?" Because the sheer deadly *routine* of the musical as a whole was infecting the vitality of its songs, the best composers and lyricists were fooling with their forms— in effect, trying to create novelty within the routine. No way: the routine itself, the very subject matter of the musical, would have to be re-created first of all.

Neither *Panama Hattie* nor *Something For the Boys* is major Porter. In the first show, all of Betty Hutton's numbers are terrible. (Perhaps her bombs-away energy defeated him.) The later show includes, along with the brilliantly racy "The Leader of a Big-Time Band" (Porter's salute to the sex appeal of swing and, by synecdoche, its archons), some of the most futile comedy songs ever written.* But Porter was so big at this point that his contract gave him billing as large as Merman's; indeed, the two names were as imposing in their era as a rock or movie star's would be now, when few Americans care who is starring on Broadway and even fewer know who the songwriters are. Two days before *Panama Hattie* opened, Merman graced the cover of *Time* magazine; the *New York Times* review of *Something For the Boys* called her "truly immense." Both shows were huge hits (at, respectively, 501 and 422 performances); were bowdlerized in Hollywood, with shredded scores; and were then retired. But for Merman's television version of *Hattie* in the early 1950s, the two were gone almost as soon as they had closed.

It was an ephemeral art. That did not suit a tradition of greatness compounded in the 1920s, when the established Irving Berlin and Jerome Kern were joined by the Gershwins, Rodgers and Hart, Cole Porter, Vincent Youmans, De Sylva, Brown, and Henderson, and, above all, Oscar Hammerstein. These men invented the very sound of American pop. *Invented* it. Some of their songs had become standards; but their shows were always vanishing.

---

*One of them, "By the Mississinewah," a duet for Merman and Laurence, costumed as squaws, is so witless that one wonders what staging tricks director Hassard Short dreamed up for it, as it was hailed as the funniest musical number in Broadway history.

Isn't the *play* the thing? Maybe the plays weren't good enough to last. But how could such gifted writers not be making good plays—a generation after *Show Boat*? Surely, something more . . . well, not more amusing or captivating than *Panama Hattie* but more . . . *intelligent* . . . could be the work of these outstanding authors.

And now it happens.

3

THE ROAD TO OKLAHOMA!

It is a historian's privilege to point out how many shows, whether they hit or failed, seemed impossible propositions when new. *Cabin in the Sky* (1940) falls into this category: a black show some ten years after black shows had lost their vogue; written by a librettist (Lynn Root) unacquainted with the musical as a form and a songwriting team (Vernon Duke and John Latouche) who, we already know from *The Lady Comes Across*, never really had a hit separately or together; and a fantasy in a time when the musical obsessively favored realism. Nor did *Cabin in the Sky* boast audience-baiting stars, though Ethel Waters did get above-the-title billing.

Few shows, however unique, have no antecedent. *Cabin's* is *The Green Pastures*, Marc Connelly's 1930 "folk play," in which Bible stories were retold in Dixie dialect by an all-black cast. *Cabin* observes Connelly's focus on warring strains in black village life—prayer versus the crap game, the wife versus the available "high-yaller" bombshell, the sweepstakes ticket that redeems the penniless life, the thuggish versus the peaceable. Root added something that Connelly hadn't thought of: opposing armies from heaven (led by Todd Duncan, George Gershwin's original Porgy) and hell (led by Rex Ingram), fighting over the soul of Little Joe (Dooley Wilson), the ever-sliding but well-intentioned husband of Petunia (Ethel Waters). With the addition of the temptress, Georgia Brown (Katherine Dunham), we have the show in a nutshell: Duncan and Ingram, with their respective cohorts, constantly materializing or perching on bits of scenery as Waters chides and loves and Dunham flirts and Wilson doesn't know which way to turn.

It's a parable, and thus, despite a powerfully felt black ethnicity, a universal tale. What man doesn't want to slide, what wife doesn't fight to hold him? Interestingly, Harlem's intellectuals, offended by *The Green Pastures* and *Porgy and Bess*, were largely sympathetic to *Cabin in the Sky*—though this, too, was the work of whites, and lavish in the folklore and lingo that made black commentators uncomfortable when adopted by whites, however sincere their intent. One scene, set in hell itself, finds the devil's man referring to Georgia Brown as "the best gong-kicker I got"—gong-kicking being Harlem argot for sex, popularized in many a song lyric (most notably in Cab Calloway's "Kicking the Gong Around").

Perhaps it was this very ease of idiom that helped put over the fantasy, for *Cabin in the Sky* really exploits it. At the show's opening, Little Joe is actually dead and Petunia already mourning. (In an old trick, a barely seen double, supine on the deathbed, impersonates the corpse; a bit later, Dooley Wilson, as Little Joe's ghost, simply rises from behind the bed.) The moment cannily combines comedy and sorrow, as the devil's man tries to put his grip on Little Joe even as Petunia prays—but so powerfully that the dead man is granted a six-month reprieve in which to whitewash his soul. Later, after an apocalyptic tornado blows all the town's fancy folk away, we find Petunia and Little Joe on a great stairway in white sackcloth. They're *dead*. Petunia, of course, is admitted to heaven. But Little Joe is denied entry, till Petunia finds a loophole in the rules. It seems that Little Joe spent all his money on Georgia Brown, and Miss Brown, having gone and found religion, has given all her money to the church. So Little Joe is a donor to holy work—and, lo, heaven buys it. Little Joe is Saved.

What sets *Cabin in the Sky* apart from early forties musicals, besides its fantasy and blackness, are strong characters. For once, a musical isn't a novelty act filled with generic songs, go-everywhere jokes, and the De Marcos, but a deeply felt story unfolded in a special atmosphere that of itself inspires unique songs, dances, and jokes—even unique sets, designed by Boris Aronson to capture the fantastical realism that Root, Duke, and Latouche were striving for. Ghosts walk a fish fry. Love and death shoot craps for souls. The cabin where Petunia and Little Joe dwelled looked real enough, but so did Lucifer Jr., ensconced on a bit of debris and dressed in red and black, and The Lawd's General, all in white (complete with wings), sitting on a telephone pole, as if God Himself had the show under His survey.

This *precision* of delivery is evident in every aspect of *Cabin*'s production—but it could not have been so well staged if it had not been so well written. Here's a story! Here's characters!: the almost forbiddingly strict yet loving Petunia, resourceful enough to beat dice cheaters at their own game, but vindictive and even bitchy when she shows up in a dance hall, turned out in unaccustomed sweepstakes-winner finery, for the climactic confrontation with Georgia Brown. Little Joe is quite charming, no sinner but a nice, dim guy in a tough spot. Georgia Brown, interestingly, doesn't function as a stereotypical temptress but rather as a sweet kid whose narrow culture doesn't give her a lot of maneuvering room. And the two representatives of the hereafter are caricatures mocking caricature, The Lawd's General so dogmatic that he can lose his professional cool. Lucifer Jr. is a real cutup, as in this exchange when Georgia Brown steps in to complicate Little Joe's afternoon:

> LUCIFER JR.: (*beaming*) Well, is *dis* a break! And Petunia gone, too!
> LAWD'S GENERAL: (*hotly*) Some mo' of yo' debbiltry, huh?
> LUCIFER JR.: (*chuckling*) No, Ah didn't figure on dis. But it sho' works in nice!

The score, like the book, abjures anything typical of Broadway, any "Steam Is on the Beam" or "Rhumba Jumps!" But then, what could typify this black parable but songs of a new like? True, we expect, and get, the spiritual ("Wade in de Water," the curtain-raiser); the revivalist rave-up ("Dem Bones"); perhaps even Petunia's comic take on the turn-of-the-century "coon song" ("In My Old Virginia Home [on the River Nile]"). But the rest of the score is as characterful as the script—The Lawd's General's weighty paean to "The Man Upstairs"; Lucifer Jr.'s correspondingly sybaritic "Do What You Wanna Do"; Little Joe's "please don't" duet with Georgia Brown, "Love Me Tomorrow (But Leave Me Alone Today)"; Georgia's wanton theme song, "Honey in the Honeycomb"; Petunia's response to the news that Little Joe might take Georgia to Havana, "Savannah," a rhythm number hymning delights closer to home; and the rhapsodic title song, for Petunia and Little Joe, in happier times.

Because producers Albert Lewis and, of all people, Vinton Freedley had so much trouble capitalizing the production—because, in fact, Depression economics had made feasible only the mindless musical comedy that Freedley had helped create—*Cabin* couldn't afford an out-of-town tryout. It previewed entirely in New York, most unusually for the era. With but three performances left before the opening, everyone decided that something was missing—a charm song for Ethel Waters, something to lift Petunia from her bossy piety, yet wistful, with a touch of irony. Vernon Duke uncorked an old measure of the bubbly, a number he had written with lyricist Ted Fetter, "Fooling Around With Love." Waters herself suggested reblending it as "Taking a Chance on Love," and Latouche reworked Fetter's lyrics. It proved to be Waters' great moment, especially at the refrain's opening "Here I go again," sung with a sunniness that only emphasized the character's misgivings. As so often happens, the insertion of this one number utterly rebalanced the show, married its contemporaneity with its timelessness, its spirituality with its earthiness. Put simply, *Cabin in the Sky* took the critics' breath away.

However, the show's warm reception raises a vexing aspect of the reexamination, reconstruction, and revival of old shows that is so much a part of the musical's profile today. All the reviewers heavily promoted Waters and the Duke–Latouche score, but something else indefinably arrested them. Brooks Atkinson, for instance, called *Cabin* "a labor of love . . . bursting with life. Mr

[Martin] Beck will need plenty of fire insurance as long as 'Cabin in the Sky' remains at his theatre." Other reviewers said the same thing in other words—"exuberant" and "exciting" over and over.

What they were referring to was the staging itself, by George Balanchine. Heretofore only a choreographer, Balanchine now got one of those "entire production staged by" credits, with the direction of the book scenes credited to co-producer Albert Lewis. Clearly, Balanchine didn't just toss in the indicated dances here and there. He styled the entire show, in its pungent attitudes and restless motion: and nearly lost his job when Lewis and Freedley kept wanting the hoofing routines popularized in the black shows of the 1920s (such as *Shuffle Along* and *Blackbirds of 1928*) while Balanchine kept finding new ways to beat out the tempo of the story.

What vexes is that all of this is lost. *Cabin in the Sky* survives as a composition but not as a theatre experience, so it's difficult to know exactly what happened at the Martin Beck. We know what happened at MGM, where *Cabin* was given a misleadingly faithful film version in 1943. Actually, the movie sale put the show into the black, for its 156 performances saw a lot of empty nights. So far, so good, and along with Waters and Rex Ingram in their Broadway roles, MGM set forth Eddie "Rochester" Anderson as Little Joe, Lena Horne as Georgia Brown, and John Bubbles, Butterfly McQueen, and Louis Armstrong, all topmost talents. The score was savaged, though traditional interpolations and three new numbers by Harold Arlen and E. Y. Harburg honored the sound style heard on Broadway.*

Yet this cinema *Cabin in the Sky* really *looks* representative and *isn't*. Georgia Brown was planned primarily as a dancing role, to counter Petunia, primarily a singer, but the movie gives the dancing to Waters. All Balanchine's slithery, curvy ensemble move-

---

* The main Arlen–Harburg addition, "Happiness Is (Just) a Thing Called Joe," sounds so authentic that many believe it's Duke–Latouche. But Arlen and Harburg were more imposing in two unused numbers. "I Got a Song" made its way into *Bloomer Girl* a year later. "Ain't It the Truth," filmed as Horne's solo in a bubble bath, was deemed too risqué for a "family picture," and was released only as a short. It, too, got into an Arlen–Harburg show (and for Lena Horne, at that), *Jamaica* (1957).

ment is gone, all the saucy posturing, the high stepping. The movie *Cabin* is a play with songs; it doesn't even credit its choreographer, Busby Berkeley. And Broadway's fantasy has now become another Hollywood "dream," which robs the tale of its all-or-nothing, spared-or-damned intensity. There should have been a City Center revival in the 1950s, when Balanchine, Dunham, and some of the original dancers might have collaborated on a resuscitation. There should certainly not have been the dreadful 1963 off-Broadway revival, short on dance and bankrupt of vocal tone. *Cabin in the Sky* remains a lost classic: a beautiful language that no one living can speak.

With *Pal Joey* (1940), which opened exactly two months after *Cabin in the Sky*, we find something even more unlikely than fantasy: real life. "An uninhibited musical comedy" the posters called it, alluding to its demimondain setting of back-alley Chicago, where everyone, rich or poor, is a user or a hustler and adultery is a rich wife's hobby. There had long been a bawdy strain in the American musical; Cole Porter's shows in particular were anything but family fare. Still, Porter's shows were froth. *Pal Joey* has the bite of a mean reality, an extraordinary lack of warmth, and bitterness for fun.

We see this most of all in the two leads—very long parts, by the way, in a show that was not a star vehicle of the Ray Bolger or Ethel Merman kind. Most musicals offer as leading characters fortune-hunting ingenues or prep-school prom dates or an FBI man and his wannabe spy. *Pal Joey* gives us smart-alec Joey, an extremely smalltime club performer of impudent charm who is screwing his way to the bottom; and Vera, the older sophisticate who picks him up, fondles him, and drops him. There had simply never been anything like these two in a musical, speaking and even singing in their own hard-and-tight vernacular.

Pal Joey began as a series of short stories by John O'Hara that had run in *The New Yorker* and then appeared in book form. The pieces are all letters written by "pal Joey" to "pal Ted," a bandleader. Joey is only half-lettered and amorally unreliable, yet his tales of life on the margins of show biz have the sting of an almost Balzacian honesty, where the detail of observation never obscures the comprehension of survey. O'Hara's anti-hero is all too knowable, not very talented but funny and dumb-shrewd, as when he charms a "mouse" and takes her home:

> She was staying with her grandma and grandpa, two respectible old married people that lived there all their life. They were too damn respectible for me . . . nine oclock was the latest she could be out. That to me is the dumbest way to treat that kind of a mouse. If its going to happen it can happen before nine oclock and if it isnt going to happen it isnt going to no matter if you stay out till nine oclock the next morning. But whats the use of being old if you cant be dumb?

Joey has a mean side, too:

> As for you my ex-pal you know what you can do and also you can sing for the $20 I owe you. I am making a little trip to N. Y. in the near future and we will have a little talk and you can explain your positon, altho the way I feel now if I saw you now your positon would be horizontle . . . because I could always slap you around when ever I wanted to.

Why O'Hara thought that these stories would suit the by then strait format of musical comedy is a question that no one has answered. Maybe O'Hara had never seen a musical and had no idea how limited its humanistic purview really was. In any case, he invited Richard Rodgers and Lorenz Hart to collaborate with him on the project, and the team, just then struggling (and failing) to discover life in that dying swan of a seal opera, *Higher and Higher*, agreed. George Abbott signed on to produce and direct and Robert Alton declared himself happy to choreograph—so at least four experienced musical comedy men thought the material workable. True, the nightclub setting was a natural for "floor" numbers and dance routines outside the action proper, and the theatregoing public, then as now, dotes upon novelty. Nevertheless: what did the credit "book by John O'Hara" really promise, especially as the stories were made of separate incidents whose only throughline was Joey's self-absorbed journey to nowhere?

Years later, Abbott claimed that O'Hara's book was "a disorganized set of scenes without a good story line and required work before we would be ready for rehearsal." But it would appear that O'Hara did indeed conjure up a plot. He saved little from the *New*

Yorker pieces—the scene in which Joey enchants the mouse in front of a pet store, his interview by newswoman Melba Snyder, and the address of his hangout on Cottage Grove Avenue. Vera was entirely invented for the musical. Her sponsoring of Joey in a bon-ton nightclub, the mouse's development as the nice girl used as a foil to the rich bitch Vera, and a subplot involving the attempted blackmailing of Vera by a club dancer and her con artist boy friend were all new.

In short, O'Hara finally wrote a real *Pal Joey* story: a linear narrative not only saturated with the very sound of the kind of people he told of, but disclosing for us the world they inhabit, with its unique customs, totems, and laws. Best of all, O'Hara's ignorance of musical comedy tradition led him to supersede it, and to give Rodgers and Hart a number of "first time" opportunities in the planning of the numbers. The love-at-first-sight duet early in the first act—a spot so honorably filled in the past by such titles as "Deep in My Heart, Dear," "The Best Things in Life Are Free," "Make Believe," and "Outside Of That I Love You"— is "I Could Write a Book," no more than a guy making a pass. The real love duet, "In Our Little Den of Iniquity," is a gavotte for hedonists who do it to Ravel's *Bolero* under a mirrored ceiling. Instead of the nearly de rigueur opening ensemble number, *Pal Joey* raises its curtain on a razzmatazz *intro* for an ensemble number—but only shows us Joey and his might-be employer, dully taking in Joey's audition.* In his stage directions, O'Hara envisions the club manager starting to respond to the audition: "He likes Joey in spite of himself—and in spite of Joey."

That's a key line, for Joey is partly a charmer but mainly a loser, self-destructive in the long run. He's hip. He's fast. He knows the answers. In the awkward silence that follows his singing of "Chicago" for an as yet unimpressed club owner, Joey says, "Where *is* that Alice Faye?," a line we no longer hear because a show this

---

* The obliging O'Hara thought this would be a great spot to feature Rodgers and Hart's "Blue Moon," a tune they had failed to place throughout the 1930s in a variety of guises. Far too placid a noise with which to launch a musical comedy, "Blue Moon" gave way to the snappy "Chicago," one of those insipidly rousing geographical salutes (c.f., "San Francisco," "New York, New York"), perfect for the brainlessly phoney Joey.

realistic has to update itself at each generation. Who now recalls, as *Pal Joey's* original audiences would have done, that Alice Faye (with Tyrone Power and Don Ameche) starred in a Twentieth Century-Fox disaster spectacular (imitating MGM's *San Francisco*) called *In Old Chicago* in 1938?

Better than hip, Joey's hot. Women fall like October's red leaves. Here's the Meeting:

> VERA: Oh, you're going to be difficult. Secretive.
> JOEY: Sure. If I gave it to you all at once, you wouldn't come back.
> VERA: You're about the freshest person I think I've ever met. What makes you think I care enough to come back?
> JOEY: Lady, you can level with me. You'll be back.

and the Skirmish:

> VERA: So I can go to hell?
> JOEY: You can double go to hell. You know what else you can do?
> VERA: Something about a galloping rooster, I imagine?

and the Score:

> VERA: (*rising from the nightclub table*) I'm a very smart and ruthless woman, so don't try any fast ones. Come on.
> JOEY: Where to?
> VERA: Oh, you know where to.

What Abbott did to O'Hara, mainly, was edit. He dropped the unnecessary scenes—Joey picking out a new car on Vera's money; Joey begging Vera not to have the lead dancer, Gladys, fired from his new club, Chez Joey, because Vera suspects that Joey has a thing for Gladys; Vera and the mouse's heart-to-heart in the mouse's bare room in the Florence Kling [Mrs. Warren G.] Harding Club for Girls.* Abbott shaved off the ends of garrulous scenes, tucked in useful gags, and completely rewrote the all-

---

* An inside joke, like the Alice Faye reference, lost to moderns. Harding, our twenty-seventh president, was popularly supposed to have sired an illegitimate daughter. The mother, Nan Britton, even published a book about it, *The President's Daughter*, an under-the-counter best-seller in 1927. O'Hara's point is that adultery, among the rich and powerful, is pervasive.

important blackmail confrontation. O'Hara's version ran far too long, and centered on Vera's eventual recognition of the blackmailer's partner, Gladys, as one of her husband's castoff doxies. Abbott replaced that with a deus ex machina, Deputy Police Commissioner O'Brien, who runs the blackmailers out of town.

Oddly, O'Hara saw Joey as ending up with the mouse in a conventional happy ending. Maybe he thought musicals had to close soft, no matter how hard their nature. Cast out and penniless, Joey still has the mouse, who invites him to dinner at her sister's:

> JOEY: I feel like walking. Is it far?
> LINDA: Oh, I don't really mind. Do you?
> (*He takes her arm as the music swells, and the curtain falls.*)

Abbott heard that music as out of tune, and added a coda: after the dinner, Joey and Linda part in front of the pet store where they met. Linda goes, Joey calls out, "And thanks, thanks a million"—a rich little line, which Joeys can tenderize, throw off in a shrug, or spit out with sudden scorn—and a new mouse crosses the stage. Joey pauses, looks after Linda for a moment, then abruptly follows the new girl, an unreconstructed little rat.

Now Abbott had a tight show: a two-character piece with a colorful song-and-dance background and, in place of the traditional second couple, two vastly different ingenues to interact with Joey, the innocent Linda and the scheming Gladys. Moreover, the only genuine piece of plot action after Vera and Joey hook up—the blackmail setup—claimed an amusing character in the greasily dapper Ludlow Lowell, who speaks in an odd combination of salesman's hustle and emcee's patter. He is a charmless version of Joey: to remind us that Joey does have, if nothing else, charm. And Joey has nothing else.

Commentators ceaselessly praise this piece for giving the musical its first cad hero—not a weak, prideful dress suit like *Show Boat*'s family-deserting Ravenal nor a corrupt politician like *Of Thee I Sing*'s presidential candidate John P. Wintergreen, but a sociopath. However, what is more chilling about Joey is that, for all his manipulating and using—and charm—he is a loser. Ravenal at least has his times of success, and Wintergreen is elected to the presidency. But Joey is a failure even as a phoney. True, he does get a shot at headlining at a club of his own. But, by show's end, he is out on his ear with nothing saved from his days of glory, literally broke and homeless.

This reveals one of the libretto's major errors. The finale of Act One and the first half of Act Two treat the creation of Chez Joey, but we never actually see how the inescapably smalltime Joey goes over when playing to his first real test, a smart crowd. O'Hara provides a scene in which Joey reads the opening night's reviews, but these are inconclusive, reports on who attended. How does Vera's set respond to her boy friend professionally? Is the club a hit? A flop? Does Joey truly have career potential? We never learn.

Worse yet is the moment in which Ludlow Lowell passes himself off to Joey as a talent agent and Joey—on Gladys's say-so—signs with him. Would a born con man like Joey be so easily taken in by the sleazy Lowell? Would he trust anything that Gladys says, after the two have spent most of the show sparring (and, in O'Hara's first script, dating for purely sexual reasons)?

And what are we to make of the second-act interview with Melba, an amusing interlude in which we see Joey's charm fail to work? Still, it's something of a set piece, bringing nothing to the show but a song spot for Melba, "Zip," in which this frosty damsel takes stage with a striptease that is a takeoff on stripteases.

Pal Joey is not, after all, a breakthrough in storytelling per se. It is a breakthrough in character writing. The two leads and Linda are extremely well drawn, and everyone else works in that flavorsome nightclub lingo. Before *Pal Joey*, musical comedies often talked tough only to reveal a sugared-cherry center. *Pal Joey* is tough, period, its script true to its characters even as its characters hold true to its script: a tiny civilization is exposed in the very way its people express themselves.

Then, too, the show finds Rodgers and Hart at their best. The jazzy club numbers brought out the racy, "Thou Swell" Rodgers who virtually took over Broadway in the 1920s, and Hart fell neatly into the O'Hara idiom, even unto splicing grammatical errors into the lyrics of "That Terrific Rainbow" and "The Flower Garden of My Heart" (a miniature Ziegfeldian spoof, with the girls costumed in floral motif), as if the songs sung by club trash some-how must be written by trash as well.*

Rodgers differentiated the character songs from the hip, syn-copated sound of the club numbers, as if creating two worlds, one devoted to "You Mustn't Kick It Around" and "That Terrific Rain-bow," all brass and blue notes, and "Bewitched" and "Take Him," given to legato and strings: an Esau-and-Jacob score, part-hairy, part-smooth. What unites them is Joey, the sole character who appears in both halves of the music and who also ties the cho-reography to the book with his heavy involvement in both. He has three major dance routines, all in Act One—"You Mustn't Kick It Around," "Happy Hunting Horn," and the dream ballet, "Joey Looks Into the Future"—while Vera makes less telling appear-ances, in the dream and in the dance section of "In Our Little Den of Iniquity." But all this makes Joey a difficult part to cast: a star dancer may fail to act his way through the role, or simply seem too gifted for the bottom-feeder that O'Hara created (just as star singers can throw the part of *Cabaret*'s Sally Bowles off its pins, with vocals too impressive for this other great loser–charmer).

Vera, too, was someone new to the musical, though the original Vera was not. Vivienne Segal had been on Broadway since taking over the heroine's part at the last minute in *The Blue Paradise* (1915!), and had reigned in operetta in the 1920s. Yet offstage she had the sardonic humor and healthy social perspective that made her the ideal rich bitch who only calls herself one. Actually, Vera is fair, generous, intelligent, and funny. She isn't even cheat-ing on her husband with her various Joeys, for—as O'Hara re-vealed in that overlong first draft of the blackmail scene—Vera and Mr. Simpson have a *mariage blanc* in which the two amicably "go our separate ways."

Vivienne Segal must have been in everyone's mind from the first; but there was a very available Joey as well. Gene Kelly's timing was perfect: chorus in *Leave It To Me!* (1938)—he is to

---

* On the other hand, orchestrator Hans Spialek gave *Pal Joey* a boost of class with a quotation of Siegfried's Horn Call from Richard Wagner's *Der Ring des Nibelungen* in the dance section of "Happy Hunting Horn."

be seen in the ubiquitous still of Mary Martin's "My Heart Belongs to Daddy" scene, grinning skyward to Martin's right—then a dancer's spot in the revue *One For the Money* (1939), followed by a straight role, albeit as an entertainer, in William Saroyan's *The Time Of Your Life* (1939). Robert Alton had choreographed *Leave It To Me!*, and Rodgers, a tireless theatregoer, had seen *The Time Of Your Life*. Kelly had the looks and the moves for Joey; and it is worth recalling that when he made Hollywood, in MGM'S *For Me and My Gal*, he was first cast as a good guy, to George Murphy's heel, but was quickly ordered to switch parts with Murphy: as if Joey's self-absorption was built into Gene Kelly's charisma.

Both Kelly and Segal were listed below the title, along with Jack Durant (Lowell), June Havoc (Gladys), and Leila Ernst (Linda). (Kelly's future MGM cohorts Van Johnson and Stanley Donen were in the chorus.) *Pal Joey* was in excellent shape when it came into New York, though everyone remained anxious about how it would strike the public. Sure, the evening played well; but Philadelphia's audiences had been openly hostile to Kelly's Joey. Even Abbott was unnerved. Still, he realized that *Pal Joey* had the integrity that most musicals lacked, however appalling its characters, and that it could not be modified, only ruined. There was no attempt to sweeten it up—and, bear in mind, this is a piece that puts it out there from the first scene, right after Joey's rendition of "Chicago":

> MIKE: Well, I don't know. What do you drink?
> JOEY: Drink? Me—drink?
>
>   . . .
>
> MIKE: How about nose-candy?
> JOEY: Nor that, either. Oh, I have my vices.
> MIKE: I know that. Well, we have a band here. The drummer
>   is just a boy.
> JOEY: Hey, wait a minute.

Cocaine and homosexuality within a few minutes of the overture: yet the critics mostly loved the show. Even Brooks Atkinson, troubled by the material, had to admire *Joey*'s one-of-a-kind brilliance.

Legend loves a failure that eventually makes good: what the Germans might call *Candidefreude*. In fact, *Pal Joey* ran 374 performances, to a nice profit. There could be no immediate movie version, of course, but O'Hara, Abbott, and Rodgers and Hart knew that from the start. What may have surprised them was the score's failure to catch on. "I Could Write a Book" was popular, losing its context of a pants putting the make on a believe-anything skirt to become just another Broadway ballad. But there were few recordings—no runthrough of, say, four sides by the cabaret chanteuse Hildegarde (as Rodgers and Hart's *By Jupiter* was to have), not even a single of Vivienne Segal (or anyone) singing "Bewitched" and "Love Is My Friend," the reflective solo that underwent a lyric change, during the show's run, to "What Is a Man."

Then something very odd occurred. In the late 1940s, every major record label released at least one cut of "Bewitched," and some half-dozen of them hit the charts. Why had this song, featured in the overture, given full play within the action (including a reprise), and also plugged in a sweeping waltz version to climax the dream ballet, not struck the public's ear in the first place? Was it because Hart's lyrics so intimately penetrated Vera's soul that the audience processed only the words and "lost" the music, even in the ballet? Was it simply too sexy for 1940? Hart was especially keen on the couplet in which Vera identifies Joey as a "laugh" then admits that she loves having the laugh "on me."

Whatever the reason for the belated popularity of "Bewitched," its phenomenal resurgence renewed interest in *Pal Joey*'s score generally, prompting Columbia Records' Goddard Lieberson to record the show as a whole. Lieberson, whose firm had developed and then put the unbreakable, long-playing 33-RPM disc on the market, in mid-1948, was about to embark on an archeological dig through some of Broadway's outstanding old scores. Largely avoiding operetta, Lieberson especially favored Rodgers and Hart, and *Pal Joey* was thus very appropriate: and an instant hit. It became one of those products that—like Caruso 78s, *The New Yorker*, and volumes of Degas reproductions—gave middle-class households a sense of cultural identification.

But how to cast this epochal album? As Vivienne Segal was still active on Broadway, she was the obvious choice as Vera; and in

Kelly's role Lieberson chose a Broadway dancer with a better singing voice than Kelly's, Harold Lang—as if casting a revival rather
than a recording. True, Lieberson's Gladys and Lowell were vo-
calists rather than the "personalities" that had occupied these
roles in 1940; Lieberson bowdlerized a bit, omitted "Chicago" and
"The Flower Garden of My Heart," and tacked on a risible plugola
finale; and he refused his listener even a snatch of the lead-in and
between-the-verses dialogue that had already proved so effective
in 78-RPM Broadway cast albums. Nevertheless, this was *Pal Joey*
reinstated, even including the original overture and the ballet. Indeed, while crediting the orchestrations to Ted Royal, Lieberson
actually had Royal only dust off Hans Spialek's 1940 parts, leaving
in such quiddities as the violins' keening harmonics during the
release of "Bewitched," though the sound was strangely pointed
for the smoothed-out tones that would colonize early-fifties pop
music.

So Columbia's *Pal Joey* was a "virtual" cast album: how *Joey*
would have sounded had they been making cast albums in 1940.
Composer Jule Styne got so excited that he wanted to produce a
Pal Joey revival. What, just ten years after the original had closed?
Revivals were *old* shows—*Blossom Time*, *The Student Prince*,
Show Boat. But Styne was serious, even purist: he wanted to star
Segal and Lang. So it *was* a cast album! Styne was also trying to
promote Helen Gallagher to stardom and saw Gladys as an ideal
stepping-off place, and he figured that Robert Alton could simply
rework his original dances. No wonder Styne had trouble financ-
ing his revival. It was too soon for even a newfangled reinterpre-
tation of the piece, much less a replica staging. Styne's folly very,
very painstakingly got its backing, and finally opened (1952) to a
feast of raves, including a repentant Brooks Atkinson.

Again, there were lyric changes, for in the twelve years since
Pal Joey had appeared, some of Hart's references had simply evap-
orated—and remember that, in those days, audiences delighted in
songs like "Zip" that perused a Blue Book of Names.* (Will we

---

* Over the years, "Bewitched" lost one of its most endearing triplets, when
"dumb again" and "numb again" lead to "like Fanny Brice singing 'Mon Homme'

of today ever hear such a song in a musical?—something with saucy allusions to, for example, Rosie O'Donnell, Liam Neeson, and the latest scandal?)

Also again, a new orchestrator was credited, though Don Walker, named with Hans Spialek, so updated the sound that Spialek all but vanished. Because Styne cast raspy-voiced Lionel Stander as Ludlow Lowell, the character's two numbers had to be reassigned, one to Gladys as a floor number and the other to Joey. The latter, "Do It the Hard Way," might have been dropped, as it's somewhat incoherent, and musically no more than schlocky fun. Perhaps Styne and his two directors, David Alexander and Alton, were wary of failing to duplicate the contents of Lieberson's album. Remember, for most Americans who cared about musicals, *Pal Joey* was one of the first shows whose music they could play over and over without having to turn a side and fix a needle every three or four minutes. By 1952, it was a classic.

The revival ran 542 performances, spun off a (debut) London showing in 1954 with Lang and Carol Bruce, and finally inspired a prim movie in 1957, with Frank Sinatra, Rita Hayworth, and Kim Novak. (Sinatra ended up with Novak, in a return to O'Hara's first thoughts.) Since then, *Pal Joey* has been one of the most insistently revived musicals: a favorite in regional theatres; always tempting to prima donnas of a certain age because so is Vera; a hot item, twice, at the City Center with Bob Fosse (Lang's understudy in 1952); in a disastrous both-the-leads-quit-yet-we're-opening-anyway viewing at the Circle-in-the-Square; back at the City Center for an Encores! concert with Patti LuPone and Peter Gallagher; in London in a cheap but tangy staging for Sian Phillips and Denis Lawson; with Julie Wilson here and even non-dancers Johnny Desmond and Steve Lawrence there; and counting a thrilling rota of Melbas, from 1952's Elaine Stritch through Renee Taylor and the City Center's Eileen Heckart and Kay Medford and then Josephine Premice in a 1978 Civic Light Opera (of California) mounting starring Lena Horne and Clifton Davis up to Bebe Neuwirth at Encores!

---

again." Of all lyricists, only Cole Porter was as clever as Hart, and only Stephen Sondheim is as intelligent.

I go into this copious detail to emphasize how vulnerable major forties titles could be to certain rules for survival: there had to be a recording; the recording had to permeate the culture; and the lead and even supporting characters had to be strong enough to entice gifted performers in each new generation. Thus, even if *Something For the Boys* had been recorded, it wouldn't have helped, for the score wasn't wonderful enough to have put the show over as a national treasure. Or: if *Louisiana Purchase* had been recorded, it might well have done very, very well commercially, for the score is wonderful—but the characters aren't. Yes, Victor Moore and (some say) William Gaxton and certainly Irene Bordoni and Vera Zorina were wonderful: but how does an actor play these parts if he or she isn't Moore, Gaxton, Bordoni, Zorina? And Carol Bruce didn't even have a character to play: she sang the up-tunes.

This outlines the difference between *Pal Joey* and *Cabin in the Sky*, and tells why they went to such different positions in the canon, despite being equally innovative in the musical's search for real stories to tell. *Pal Joey* was a popular recording leading to a popular revival and does not need a staging genius to set it forth. *Cabin in the Sky* got neither recording nor revival in any real sense, and as a staging it was an alchemy—three Russians (Vernon Duke, George Balanchine, and designer Boris Aronson) and two white Americans (Lynn Root and John Latouche) leading an all-black cast through a fantastic fable that employs stereotypical black tropes dating back to the nineteenth-century minstrel show in order to liberate them from stereotype. It's a stunt of its time. It's unrepeatable, while the story of *Pal Joey* is being enacted in real life in every city in the country as we speak.

But it was a forties discovery that a great musical was a unique one. Even: it was a forties discovery that there could *be* great musicals, not just more *Panama Hatties* but more *Show Boats*. So, as the notion of a permanent repertory of great shows began to take hold, some of the greatest works made such special demands on the staging team that they could not properly be revived at all.

Lady in the Dark (1941) can't. It has been done here and there, but never with anything remotely like the success that the original enjoyed. It may be the most famous American musical that doesn't get performed a lot (unless one counts *Rose-Marie*), combining as it does *Cabin in the Sky*'s vulnerability with *Pal Joey*'s survivalist strength. That is, the show itself is always available, orchestrations and all, yet we will never again see the like of Gertrude Lawrence, the first Lady, and perhaps the most enchanting of all the American musical's heroines. She was not a singing star, like Ethel Merman; nor a dancing star, like Gwen Verdon; nor a devastating blond beauty, like Marilyn Miller. Lawrence was an erratic singer, a just-barely dancer, and no beauty. Worse, she read lines in a wistfully unrealistic delivery of her own invention, in an accent absurdly advertising her English origin. But Lawrence was magic; one might call her "talent in spite of itself." She dominated the English-speaking stage in both musicals and straight plays for at twenty-five years, a reign ended only by her death, and at the time that Moss Hart conceived *Lady in the Dark*, Lawrence was at the utmost of her majesty.

Like a number of Broadwayites, Hart had undergone psychoanalysis with Dr. Gregory Zilboorg, apparently because of his sexual ambivalence, well-known to everyone in the business. It is not known what Dr. Zilboorg prescribed for Hart's quandary, but he did recommend that Hart end his longtime collaboration with George S. Kaufman and work on his own: in other words, grow up and leave Daddy. Hart had in fact written the odd title as a single, but his first produced play and all of his major successes were composed with Kaufman, including *You Can't Take It With You* and *The Man Who Came To Dinner*. Now Zilboorg was freeing Hart to abandon the overwhelming authority figure and write about the man Hart had always wanted to be: a gay one.

Of course, they worked in codes then, and Hart made his protagonist a woman, a business executive, desperately out of touch with her true feelings, who keeps finding excuses not to marry till she falls under the spell of a Hollywood hunk. Finding herself desirable for the first time, she turns into a New Woman, less wedded to her work, almost carefree. But the hunk turns out to be a weak little piece of a thing emotionally, and the heroine at last finds her match in one of her employees, an aggressive man who has always challenged her. Admitting her love for him, the woman learns to share authority rather than fear or isolate it.

If that isn't a gay coming-out parable, Cole Porter wrote *Show Boat* with Herbert Fields. The "lady executive" is clearly a likeness of a gay man, capable and creative but alternate, not like most of us—even lacking something, as 1940 saw it. The Hollywood beauty as icon, the unnervingly masculine challenger who is at the same time an erotic figure . . . this is more gay imagery. And note that Hart intended his play for Katharine Cornell, a real-life lesbian wedded to a gay man, Guthrie McClintic.

However, Dr. Zilboorg was a conservative Freudian, very interested in his patient's dreams, and at some point Hart realized that not only must dreams form part of the show but that song and dance was their natural element. So Hart's great post-Kaufman graduate project would be a musical—all the better, to distinguish it from his Kaufman comedies. But could Cornell sing? Of course not. Who would then play Liza Elliott, the editor of a fashion magazine who tells American women how to dress and think and love while her own romantic life is falling apart?

Gertrude Lawrence said yes. With composer Kurt Weill and lyricist Ira Gershwin, first-call director Hassard Short, and producer Sam H. Harris, Hart had his show. The "psychiatry musical," they called it. But was it a musical? There was no overture, no reprises of big tunes, no comical second couple, no fiddly dancing after the vocal, no scenes "in one" in front of the traveler while the stagehands readied the next big set, no opera soprano ringed in for a Big Sing, no radio jokers. No *genre*.

Because it wasn't a musical. It was, as Hart had planned it, a play—but one with musical sequences, the dreams, built out of recitative, arioso, outright song, and underscored dialogue. There were four: the Glamour Dream, the Wedding Dream, the Circus Dream, and the Hollywood Dream: symphonically speaking, the argument, the slow movement, the scherzo, and the argument's resolution.

The fourth dream was ultimately axed: too much music. Actually, Hart's heroine enjoys too much immediately successful therapy. People generally spend many years at it before learning anything about themselves. In Hart's scenario, Liza's doctor reveals to her—in the span of a few weeks—a crippled sense of self-esteem thanks to a beautiful, jeering mother and a few early humiliations in the romantic sphere. Instantly, Liza wises up, ditches the fatherly protector who started her magazine (Hart's "protector," Kaufman, who started Hart's career?) to renegotiate her relationship with her very masculine managing editor, the man who wants to run Liza's magazine—that is, in gay sexual terms, to "top" her.

Whether or not all this reflects the conflicted Hart's personal feelings or is simply a story that he concocted doesn't matter. What interests us is how Hart stumbled on the unique musical play between *Show Boat* and *Oklahoma!*. The very *motion* of *Cabin in the Sky*'s folk-ballet staging will have impact in the development of choreography as an indispensable element in the elaboration of atmosphere, spirit, attitude. The naturalism of *Pal Joey* will have impact in the gradual disappearance of stock characters and formula dialogue. But the very structure of *Lady in the Dark* will have impact: in a renegotiation of the relationship between the script and the score, of how much dramatic weight the song-and-dance portion of a show will be asked to carry, of how the performers relate to the score separately and together, of how song relates to dance. Within a few years of *Lady in the Dark*, we'll meet up with: shows as much danced as sung (*Song of Norway, On the Town*); yet more plays "with" music (*Lute Song, Around the World*); shows cast with more non-singing principals than vocal leads (*Brigadoon*); shows virtually made of bits and pieces of score (*Allegro*); shows staged without a choreographer (*South Pacific*); shows almost entirely sung (*Regina*); and shows *entirely* sung (*Ballet Ballads*).

Here is a two-act play containing three little operas (the dreams), along with one song, "My Ship."* So this isn't in any real sense a musical. It's a show that, like its heroine, is *haunted* by music.

Consider the show's geography. Musicals typically moved from, say, a hotel lobby to a rehearsal hall to a bar to the stage of the

---

* *Lady in the Dark*'s romantic plot climaxes when the managing editor coincidentally recognizes Liza's "dream motif"—a vaguely threatening melody, this same "My Ship," that seems connected to her emotional problems—and finishes it for her. This is exactly how Victor Herbert's *Naughty Marietta* (1910) climaxes, as Captain Dick completes Marietta's Dream Melody. Hart's inside joke?

Something Theatre to an army camp, and so on. *Lady in the Dark* moves strictly between two offices—that of Liza's magazine and of her psychiatrist—except when it slips into those operatic dreams, which, in the Glamour and Wedding sequences, are very fluid and, in the Circus sequence, very fixed: because Liza is nearing a resolution of her problem. *Lady in the Dark* stands out because it doesn't behave like a musical even while using a musical's means to reach a musical's ends. The work combines dialogue, song, and dance, only not as normally—even not as *ever*—combined. What Hart, Weill, and Gershwin eventually came up with is a kind of vivid haze broken by a spotlight that dogs the protagonist of the greatest star show ever devised. What's bigger than Gertrude Lawrence in *Lady in the Dark*? The conclusively self-renewing Ethel Merman in *Gypsy* (1959)? The emphatically emerging Barbra Streisand in *Funny Girl* (1963)? These are comparable. *Nothing* is bigger.

Yet Lawrence made no Star Entrance. In fact, given the thinking of the times, her first appearance was perversely downbeat; perhaps that was the point. I have said that *Lady in the Dark* began without any orchestral instigation, without music of any kind, an act of genre-bending simply undreamed of at the time. Musicals begin with music, evocatively; *Lady in the Dark* just begins. Curtain up, dull establishing dialogue in psychiatrist's office, Star is announced, but then . . . well, let Hart tell us:

> Liza Elliott is a woman in her late thirties, plain to the point of austerity. She wears a severely tailored business suit, with her hat pulled low over her eyes. No single piece of jewelry graces her person and her face is free of make-up. There is an air of the executive about her, yet at the moment she seems to be fighting hard for a moment of calm before she can speak.

It was in the dreams, of course, that this almost pugnaciously crestfallen Lawrence cut loose as the musical-comedy heroine the audience doted on, for *Lady in the Dark* was in one sense an epitome of Lawrence's career: half in musicals and half in straight plays. What a rich part, then, showing so much of her at once—businesslike over the clinical depression, bewitched and dazzling and terrified in the dreams, so naturalistically fantastical, confronting while fleeing. Her portrait will grace the new postage stamp—but the managing editor shows up as the painter, and when Liza views his version of her she screams in horror and society renounces her. Or now she marries, and must choose the ring: but the managing editor, playing the jeweller, draws a knife on her. Or she is put on trial for vacillation in not a courtroom but a circus, with the managing editor as prosecuting attorney. Liza's defense is one of the great show-stoppers of all time, "The Saga of Jenny," and she seems sure to win vindication when that dreaded dream tune reappears and the circus dissolves around her as she is left alone in the, yes, dark.

Given its unheard-of structure, *Lady in the Dark* had to *sound* different from other musicals, for it lacked the spots every show left for the typical numbers. It even lacked characters who "typically" sing. As the show took shape, it was felt that only Lawrence should solo in any meaningful way; everyone else would have bits or ensemble work. Two magazine staffers, Miss Foster (Evelyn Wyckoff) and Russell Paxton (Danny Kaye) enjoyed a scene leading up to a Lawrence–Wyckoff duet, "Huxley (wants to dedicate his book to you)," and Kaye took stage as the judge in the circus trial. The managing editor, Charley Johnson (Macdonald Carey), sang a bit. The Hollywood heartthrob, Randy Curtis (Victor Mature), was to sing a ballad with Liza, "This Is New," but Mature couldn't hack it, and his musical chores were limited to a bit of *Sprechstimme* during the trial. Liza's wealthy protégeur—another mollycoddle whose love she cannot use—is Kendall Nesbitt (Bert Lytell), whose lines in the Circus Dream, as witness for the prosecution, are pure speech. Still, all these people were at least connected to the music, if only by being in sight while it was heard. Only one principal was absolutely cut off from the music—the psychiatrist, Dr. Brooks,* because he is the sole person in Liza's life who does not appear in the dreams.

Actually, Kaye did claim a solo. Rather late in the day, it was

---

* Has anyone noticed how smartly Hart named his characters? They bear the descriptive precision of the nomenclature in Restoration comedy without the punning overkill. What's more purely supplementary than "Miss Foster," mintier than "Russell Paxton," virile than "Charley Johnson"—exactly the qualities these people respectively represent?

decided to take advantage of his penchant for rapid-fire diction in "Tschaikowsky," the ultimate list-song in that it is little more than the names of fifty-three composers of Tsarist and Soviet Russia.* The number is excrescent, having nothing to do with the action. Worse, it's terrible music, though Weill humorously set it in *Allegro barbaro*, launched by a quotation of the famous march theme from Tchaikofsky's Sixth Symphony. Worst of all, it comes *just before* "The Saga of Jenny," thus flirting impudently with the grandeur of the protagonist and star. It should have been cut in Boston.

And, indeed, a famous story tells how warmly the audience cheered Kaye's "Tschaikowsky" in, yes, Boston, and how, at the back of the theatre, one of the production team cried, "Now we've lost our star!"

What nonsense; who makes up these apocrypha, anyway? *If* it happened, what the man would have said was, "Well, there goes that number," meaning "Lawrence won't stand for some juvenile's crabbing her act."

But, remember, "The Saga of Jenny" is a *great* number, "Tschaikowsky" an idiot's piffle. "Jenny" catches Liza at the high point of her wonder and worry in its biography of her opposite: a woman without fear. It's her go-for-it moment, throwing off the harness of this densely difficult *character*, Liza Elliott, for a taste of that densely delightful *performer*, Gertrude Lawrence. Keep in mind that the notoriously improvisational Lawrence would vary her rendering from night to night, providing an electric atmosphere on stage as her co-workers strained to stay with her. What, in the end, was "Tschaikowsky" but a tension to play off of, an illusion of challenge that Lawrence could humiliate? A *warm-up*? As Ethel Waters put it to this same Moss Hart, out of town with the revue *As Thousands Cheer* (1933), when faced with following a high-powered act, "I like working on a *hot* stage!"

It was so hot that *Lady in the Dark* sold out the Alvin Theatre on weekdays for months at a time, an unprecedented success when Broadway maintained thirty-nine houses that knew few dark

---

* The citations include one Dukelsky: *Cabin in the Sky*'s Vernon Duke, who was indeed an émigré, né Dukelsky and named Vladimir.

weeks between productions. In those days before air-conditioning, shows closed for the summer, and, anyway, Lawrence needed a vacation badly enough to take ten weeks off before reopening in the fall of 1941, leading the show on tour, then playing a final limited run back on The Street at the Broadway Theatre.

In all, the piece racked up 550 performances in New York alone, making it the eighth-longest-running book musical since 1900. At that, it closed only because Lawrence had had enough and must not be replaced. Her personal triumph may have clouded the show somewhat, kept it off the list of eternally renewable classics. Plenty of forties shows with roles for stars have lasted without them—*Pal Joey, Annie Get Your Gun,* and *South Pacific,* for instance, though obviously they nourish headline talent where available. *Lady in the Dark,* however, eked out its survival. "My Ship" is a standard, and the show did get a major filming at Paramount with Ginger Rogers in 1944 and a prominent television airing with Ann Sothern in 1955.* The show occasionally turned up in summer stock in the 1950s and 1960s; I saw Jane Morgan do it at Westbury Music Fair. Risë Stevens recorded it, lamely. Neither City Center's Encores! concert nor England's National Theatre staging, both in the 1990s, has conclusively reproposed it. It remains a ghost: there yet not there. But then what actress can comprehend, as extensively as Lawrence did, the eerily compromised glamor of the dream Lady, the shallow power of the real Lady, the pair of them so wound-up, so top, so soigné, so tight? Rosalind Russell and Alexis Smith are generally right, but would have been overextended by the music; rumor doted for

---

* Paramount saw a correspondence between the non-musical portions of Hart's conception and the kind of romantic comedy that, say, Mitchell Leisen directed for Claudette Colbert and Ray Milland. With Leisen in fact directing the film *Lady* and Milland opposite Rogers as Charley Johnson—right, a constipated English pin-stripe in for a coarsely dynamic American—the studio saw just another Paramount sex play, in need of no music. Though it had paid $283,000 for the show, the highest amount yet spent for the film rights to a Broadway musical, Paramount eviscerated the score. The TV version was much more faithful; and while Hollywood's Ginger is amusing in a prestigiously artificial way, Sothern is quite persuasive. She feels the woman's fear; Rogers feels her salary.

years upon a Julie Andrews revival for her gala Broadway comeback, till she indeed came back in a dud revival of a movie. I think
only Julia McKenzie could have pulled it off, in about 1980—and
she would not only have sung it better than Lawrence but brought
a frightening intensity to the nervous breakdown that underscores
the entire show.

But this emphasis on the star part obscures *Lady in the Dark*'s
lasting impact on the way drama and music interact in the dreams.
Yes, they're opera, but *musical comedy* opera. Weill, a refugee
from the Nazis, was so enthusiastically naturalized an American
that he changed the pronunciation of his name from *Vial* to *While*
and threw himself into his new country's music. His previous musicals, *Johnny Johnson* (1936) and *Knickerbocker Holiday* (1938),
were on one hand an American version of the political parables
he had written in Germany and on the other a satire set in old
Nieuw Amsterdam. Their music could come from anywhere. But
in *Lady in the Dark* Weill was determined to, so to say, teach
Broadway its own music: employ the usual noises in unusual ways.

The result—though it's difficult to single out "songs" in such a
restless score—was "(You've only) One Life To Live," Liza's gently
swinging "what I want" number, urging everyone to follow her
lead in making the most of one's days. Naturally, she is serenaded
as the "Girl of the Moment" in a chorus, Allegro Giocoso, that
goes into a Larghetto Religioso (during the painting of the as-
saulting portrait) and then a manic rhumba, all on the same melody, as Liza staggers around and the crowd denounces her as a
fraud. Or consider the "Mapleton High School Song," a parody
of the alma mater so fairly observed—by a foreigner, remember—
that it is no parody.

"The Princess of Pure Delight" is a real novelty, a strophic narrative with a twist ending and spoken jests appended to each of
the verses. Its lesson tells that the most obvious solutions are right
before us, hidden in plain sight—like the Dream Tune, which Liza
thinks is her curse but is in fact the clue to the resolution of all
her grief. And, amid a number of leitmotifs, there is that tune
itself, "My Ship," the musical center of the entire show as it se-
renely pulses in phrases that rise then immediately fall, at peace

with itself. For, of course, when Liza at last faces up to this music and all that it represents psychologically, she conquers fear and becomes whole.

In short, Weill *created* a style that the Broadway musical *should have had* all along. Ironically, early in *Lady in the Dark*'s run, another European emigré tried American musical theatre in a style less assimilative than commentative. Benjamin Britten's *Paul Bunyan* (1941), given at Columbia University, so stylized the American folk sound that Americans couldn't recognize it—not even the bluesy Act One quartet "You Don't Know All, Sir," almost a dead ringer for the kind of thing Weill was doing just then. Despite the genius of librettist W. H. Auden, the critics definitively scoffed, hurling *Paul Bunyan* into the oubliette for two generations.

Speaking of masters, we should note the influence also of Gershwin's *Porgy and Bess*, revived in 1942, seven years after its unsuccessful premiere. Producer Cheryl Crawford unveiled an extremely spare version: minimal decor, small cast, many cuts in the score, and the orchestration gypped down to not much more than half the forty-four players heard in the 1935 pit. Worse yet, Crawford banned all the music between the set pieces—the recitative, arioso, and character bits—to turn an opera into a musical play. At least Crawford troubled to rehire the original Porgy, Bess, Crown, Serena (the one who sings "My Man's Gone Now"), Robbins (her man), Maria, a few minor characters, and the original conductor, Alexander Smallens, who apparently encouraged Crawford's emasculation of Gershwin's operatic conception, out of what evil or stupid motivation we shall surely never know. Gershwin's career—no, life—can be read as a single arc rising inexorably and combatively toward this one feat, the writing of the Great American Opera about racial and cultural outcasts by a racial and cultural upstart. To bargain it down to its hit tunes is to deny not only Gershwin's genius but the greatness of his subject matter.

As if Crawford cared about the arc of Gershwin's life. She had two hunches. The first was that recordings and radio performances of such passages as "Summertime," "A Woman Is a Sometime Thing," and "Bess, You Is My Woman Now" had created for the show an audience that had not been ready in 1935. She was right. Her second hunch—that the original *Porgy and Bess* had failed because Broadway couldn't use an opera—was incorrect. For, once Crawford's production had affirmed the power and beauty of this masterpiece, it sprang right back into its original form with no loss of appeal, and has remained the fully sung piece that Gershwin composed. Revivals have not only reinstated the recits but opened the cuts imposed on the work in 1935; this rich piece must be taken whole.

Rich pieces are what led to *Oklahoma!*: *Cabin in the Sky*'s Gesamtkunstwerk staging of a folk parable in 1940, *Pal Joey*'s earthy honesty later that year, *Lady in the Dark*'s psychological examination of character wedded to an experimental musical structure in 1941, and *Porgy*'s passionate outpouring of song the following year all contributed to the creation of an audience conditioned to and thus eager for more unusual fare.

After two decades, the Aarons–Freedley musical was about to be replaced. Not revised. Not developed.

Replaced.

4

RODGERS AND HAMMERSTEIN

We know how unsuitable *Oklahoma!* was for the Broadway of
1943; that is what centers its legend. First, it was based on a flop
play, Lynn Riggs' *Green Grow the Lilacs* (1931), that was more a
study of a community than a story. A dark play, at that, in which
a degenerate farmhand menaces a young couple till the boy has
to kill the creep. Then think of the decor—flannel, jeans, and
gingham against a background of cornfields and barns. A musical
wants color, flamboyance, the exotic. And where would the choreography fit in, as square dances? Would wartime audiences, so
eager for escapist entertainment, be remotely interested in a piece
of history on life in the last territory within the national borders
to be granted statehood?

How often legend misleads. In fact, *Green Grow the Lilacs*—
the musical's working title, altered to *Away We Go!* by the start
of rehearsals and again to *Oklahoma!* just before the New York
opening—was a fine idea for a musical in 1943. The story is actually quite strong—not busy, no, but rich in character development. As for decor and choreography, don't think literally; think
of panorama, evocation, poetry. Cornfields? How about a *vista* of

them, stretching as far as imagination can reach? Consider the costume designer's many options, playing around with the men's great hats, the women's frontier finery, with stripes and colors all zigzagging against each other. And *history*? When better to consider the national pageant than in wartime?

No, the idea itself was a sharp one, however much the usual swamis predicted disaster. What was wrong with *Oklahoma!* right from the start was the writing team, Rodgers and Hammerstein.

What team? Composer Rodgers had spent an entire generation working strictly in musical comedy with the ultra-witty *flâneur* Lorenz Hart. Librettist and lyricist Hammerstein had spent the same years mainly in operetta and its derivations, where waltz mattered more than wit and the *poète* roamed, not the *flâneur*.

All Broadway gaped as these two partnered up, and not only because they were so ill matched. Of Hammerstein's most constant collaborators, Sigmund Romberg was still very much on the scene, and Jerome Kern, though living and working in Hollywood, remained available for stage work—he in fact was to have composed *Annie Get Your Gun* before his sudden death in 1945. Rodgers' Hart, however dejected in his personal life, had just produced the lyrics *and* (with Rodgers) the book for *By Jupiter*, and would work with Rodgers on a revision of *A Connecticut Yankee* (1927) after *Oklahoma!* had opened.

So what did this mating of such opposites mean? SMART WEDS HEART (as *Variety* might have put it)?

But if the Rodgers and Hammerstein coupling hadn't existed, Broadway would have had to invent it. There were simply too many *Walk With Music*s and *Beat the Band*s, too much decrepit genre, junk about nothing. Theatregoing, so reduced during the Depression, had been expanding since the late 1930s. Money was more available, hit shows were running longer, and a huge audience was awaiting a long overdue revolution in the writing and staging of musicals. The form, cautious throughout the 1930s (with a few exceptions), was stale by the early 1940s, so 1943 was about as late as the revolution could happen if the musical was to survive. In essence, the Rodgers and Hammerstein show turned out to be the converse of the Aarons–Freedley show: start with a solid story, then let all the showman's arts follow that story.

True, many operettas, the odd musical comedy such as *No, No, Nanette* or *Dearest Enemy*, and the always exceptional *Show Boat* had followed this line back in the 1920s. But the lesson had not taught in any real sense till *Oklahoma!* restated it, on March 31, 1943, in the St. James Theatre, to an opening night audience that had been hearing two very conflicting reports from the New Haven and Boston tryouts. One was that the show was too . . . well, too cowboy to go over. It was corny and . . . okay, not *corny* but . . . different. The other report called it the greatest musical that Broadway would ever see.

This is the part that gets left out of the legend. We hear of the Theatre Guild's financial dismay, of countless backer's auditions to deaf ears. We hear of Mike Todd's "no gags, no gals, no chance" after the New Haven opening.* We don't hear from spectators who rushed back to New York virtually trumpeting, or how Boston audiences screamed and leaped to their feet in a day when standing ovations were unheard of.

Are we really to believe that, before the New York critics wrote their reviews, *Oklahoma!*'s audiences didn't know a good thing? In fact, the reviews varied picturesquely, from comparisons to *Show Boat* and *Porgy and Bess* to Stark Young's being reminded of a "good college show"—that cheap production, again, no doubt. *Oklahoma!* has always been an audience show, whatever the critics think.

Let me point out something special about the piece: the songs pop out of the script so naturally that the singing is like dialogue, only more so. Of course, you reply: that's what musicals do. Not in early 1943. Songs tended to block the action, stop it dead. *Oklahoma!*'s songs convey it. The conversational nature of such first lines as "I Got to Kansas City on a Frid'y," "Sposin' 'at I say 'at yer lips're like cherries," or "You'll have to be a little more standoffish" is something that only Hammerstein of all lyricists

---

* Another of Todd's comments, this one seldom quoted, was "I spent more on *Something For the Boys*' curtain calls." Remember, part of what made *Oklahoma!* so unusual was its cheap staging, inevitable given the Guild's economic problems and beautifully papered over by the ingenious designs, but all the same disconcerting in an era that liked its musicals *big*.

ever employed before, and sparingly; in *Oklahoma!* he exploited it. The times loved genre numbers; Hammerstein wrote none. On the contrary, *Oklahoma!*'s opening number is a tiny tone poem on dawn in God's country followed by a cowboy's waltzy hymn to life and love on a lavishly sunny summer day. *Oklahoma!*'s major courtship duet is contentious, couched almost entirely in the imperative voice. Don't do this. Don't do that. It's a bossy love song. Two of the show's major comedy numbers, "I Cain't Say No" and "Many a New Day," not only make no allusion to current events or town topics but trouble to oppose two types of woman, the roughhewn sensualist, with plenty of basic rhymes, and the idealist, with the poet's devious alliteration, internal rhyme, and metaphor. And *Oklahoma!*'s most dramatic number, "Lonely Room," goes to the villain, in an anguish of sexual appetite and psychopathic rage.

It is especially odd that Rodgers fell right in with Hammerstein's program—odd because, with Hart, Rodgers wrote the melody first, sometimes on a lyrical hook ("This can't be love," Hart suggests, and Rodgers is already composing) and sometimes out of thin air. This had long been the practice throughout American songwriting. But Hammerstein wanted a chance to initiate an entire lyric for each musical number, and perhaps the inverted procedure is what called up an entirely new sound in Rodgers. Perhaps the material itself did. Certainly, Rodgers had never written anything with Hart that anticipated the stylistic world in which "It's a Scandal! It's a Outrage!," "Out Of My Dreams," or "All Er Nothin'" operates in.

Maybe the two authors worked so distinctively here because their characters gave them so much to investigate. Curly (Alfred Drake) and Laurey (Joan Roberts) are bickering lovers, mainly because Laurey is too headstrong and wishful for her narrow frontier culture and Curly is too typical of it. She's a landowner, a free woman—and a hungry one, though she doesn't know what she wants. It *should* be Curly: he's got charm and smarts, and he really loves her. Still, something about him gets on her nerves. His abundant self-confidence? His teasing need to control? She's restless and he's bewildered; so the bad guy, Jud Fry (Howard da Silva), tries to push in and take Laurey to the big social that forms virtually the entire second act. Why would she even consider going with this monster? Is she too terrified of Jud to refuse? Protecting Curly from Jud's rage? Lost in *nostalgie de la boue*? Eventually, Jud attacks Curly with a knife and, in the ensuing fight, gets stuck on his own piece, canceled out.

Thin plot or no, that's already more "there" than most musicals had. But this heavy triangle is lightened by the secondary couple, Will Parker (Lee Dixon) and Ado Annie Carnes (Celeste Holm), he so direct and she so flirty that it takes the ultimate Traveling Salesman, Ali Hakim (Joseph Buloff), and Annie's suspicious, gun-toting father (Ralph Riggs) to firm up the happy romance. Laurey's Aunt Eller (Betty Garde) supervises, as a figure Rodgers and Hammerstein would make generic, the Earth Mother (in Nettie Fowler, *Allegro*'s Grandma, Bloody Mary, *Pipe Dream*'s Fauna, a diaphanous version in *Cinderella*'s Fairy Godmother, and the Mother Abbess), who understands and guides, sometimes in an operatic contralto.

So there's not much in the way of actual events here. It's mostly courtships of various kinds, even imaginary, as Curly proposes to take Laurey to the social in a deluxe hired rig that doesn't exist (the famous Surrey with the Fringe on Top), though it somehow makes an appearance during the finale. The "Surrey" number is another very special thing about *Oklahoma!*: a musical scene rather than a song, using underscored dialogue to maintain the personal interplay between choruses and even changing the nature of the music itself, from braggadocio to lullaby.

The musical scene was not new to the musical. Hammerstein and Rodgers both had employed it throughout their careers. Yet neither had tried anything like "Pore Jud Is Daid," a funereal comedy number in which the hero tries to get the villain to kill himself even while goading him into a fight as the insults helplessly pour out. Like "Surrey," it mingles song with speech and even includes recitative, as Curly pictures the preacher's eulogy. The scene nudges the story along, develops character, and reveals how a primitive culture looks at death. That's a lot to do in four minutes, yet there's nothing apparently artful here, no demonstrations. It's natural.

Better, it's unique, like all the rest of *Oklahoma!*—and that explains this show's overwhelming role in the musical's evolution. One might say that *Cabin in the Sky*'s folkloric tone, *Pal Joey*'s naturalistic character development, and *Lady in the Dark*'s imaginative music-making all saw climax in *Oklahoma!*; but that's no more than a historian's irrelevant symmetry. What really matters here is how, at exactly the historical moment when Broadway needed it to, *Oklahoma!* applied unconventional storytelling arts to unconventional content in a way that seemed, if not imitable, inspirational.

That last statement may seem odd considering how many professional know-it-alls thought the piece would fail. But then, know-it-alls are always perplexed by novelty. Of course *Oklahoma!* could be copied, at least in part. Indeed, its use of choreography was almost immediately influential—specifically in the way the dancing fit into emotional grooves cut by the score. For once, in "Many a New Day," the dance following the vocal was not decoration but extrapolation, the women styling in movement the feminist independence that Laurey had been singing about. At the same time, the scoring of the song's verse ("Why should a woman . . .") in the dance music uses the rich major seventh and 9/6 chords that we associate with the "heartland" sound pioneered by classical composers in the 1930s. It's folk ballet.

So is the second-act curtain-raiser, "The Farmer and the Cowman," which might easily have been any banjo-friendly ditty quickly followed by its true *raison d'être*, a lively western dance. Not in this show: Rodgers and Hammerstein carefully twisted the song to highlight the social background, with a touch of range war implied. In fact, a scuffle does break out, ended only when Aunt Eller shoots off a pistol and forces the formidable Carnes to restart the number, a cappella, at gunpoint. When everyone else joins in—and only then—a dance of social harmony can proceed.

Clearly, director Rouben Mamoulian and choreographer Agnes de Mille found a way to mesh their work, to hold all of *Oklahoma!*'s staging in balance the way its authors had matched the score to the book. True, one piece did stand out: the dream ballet, "Laurey Makes Up Her Mind," because of its unusual length, its lyricism corrupted by brutal violence, and because the first act builds up to it so intensely that it makes a tremendously—and unpleasantly—decisive curtain before the intermission.*

This ballet typifies the way Hammerstein used Lynn Riggs' play—cutting down dialogue while remaining faithful to the central triangle, wholly inventing Ado Annie and Will Parker out of a bit part and a mere name, and always looking for ways to expand a chance line into music. In Riggs, the peddler tries to sell Laurey something, and she's a willing but difficult customer. Here's the *Oklahoma!* version:

> LAUREY: Want a buckle made outa shiny silver to fasten onto my shoes! Want a dress with lace. Want perfume, wanta be purty, wanta smell like a honeysuckle vine!
> AUNT ELLER: Give her a cake of soap.
> LAUREY: Want things I've heard of and never had before—a rubber-t'ard buggy, a cut-glass sugar bowl. Want things I cain't tell you about . . . Things so nice, if they ever did happen to you, yer heart ud quit beatin'. You'd fall down dead!

That's a wonderful moment, underlining Laurey's impulsive, confused personality; it's very close to what Riggs wrote. But in Riggs, the peddler offers Laurey only perfume. "Smells like the Queen of Egyp'!," he explains.

Hammerstein pounced on that, turning the perfume into the "Elixir of Egypt," a potion to clear muddled minds. "Smellin' salts!" Aunt Eller remarks. "Throwin' away yer money!"

But Laurey believes in it: because she needs to. Later, the elixir cues in a fifteen-minute musical segment, moving from underscored dialogue to "Out of My Dreams," which starts as an en-

---

* Actually, though *Oklahoma!* revivals do sometimes close Act One with the end of the dream—Jud's murder of Curly and abduction of Laurey—the original production topped off the dream with about thirty seconds of real time, as Jud awoke the drowsing Laurey and led her off to the dance while Curly looked on, "dejected and defeated." This may seem anti-climactic, but to end a dream sequence without ushering the public back into daylight violates one of the theatre's most useful rules. *Lady in the Dark* made no such error. It would be not unlike ending *Follies* after "Live, Laugh, Love." Dreams don't tell *what* happened; dreams tell *why.*

semble number, as the girls advise Laurey to consult her own feelings and not the potion, and ends as Laurey's solo. Or does it end? For Curly enters during the chorus, and at the song's final phrase the dancing counterparts of Laurey and Curly come on, in effect taking over for the actors, who drift off. Nothing has ended: something is about to begin.

This is, of course, the dream ballet, designed to explore Laurey's worldview: her love for Curly, her doting friends, the vain, horse-proud cowboys (who dance on bowlegged, as if riding, to a clopping rendition of "The Surrey With the Fringe on Top"), the threatening Jud (also played by a dancer), Jud's "bad" women (three can-can girls, who strut and kick to "I Cain't Say No"), and Jud's solution to Laurey's emotional chaos: a date with Jud, which is murder and rape.

No wonder *Oklahoma!*'s dance plot impressed Broadway so quickly. Here at last was the reason all those ballet people had been choreographing musicals: to do in dance what the script and score could not do in words and music. To consult a character's feelings. Surely, one of the attractions of the forties classics was their choreography, exposing to an uninitiated public the excitement of high-maestro dance.

The designs, as I've said, were limited by the Guild's desperation budget, though costumer Miles White managed to exploit the fantastic possibilities in frontier chic, if such there be. Lemuel Ayers' sets were functional, though he did capture those vistas. At least both men held true to their subject, never sending everyone on-stage for, say, a Latin number in rhumba ruffles and capes. Don't laugh—costuming the ensemble in irrelevantly coordinated outfits to dress the stage for a number was routine in the early 1940s, as if shows had not characters but dolls. No, everything in *Oklahoma!* kept faith with everything else. "The orchestrations sounded the way the costumes look" is how Richard Rodgers explained it: integrity.

Didn't earlier shows have it? Yes, at times; but even *Show Boat* contained moments given over to performer's specialties, not to mention a parade of Ziegfeldian beauties in the World's Fair scene. Even *The Cat and the Fiddle* let Odette Myrtil play her fiddle: because she could. Even *Lady in the Dark* gave Danny Kaye

"Tschaikowsky." And even *Oklahoma!* had one conventional and even ancient excrescence, the Jewish comic.

This early-twentieth-century stereotype, preserved in many an early talkie, had almost vanished from the musical when Rodgers and Hammerstein revived him for the role of the peddler. In Riggs, played by Lee Strasberg, he was simply exotic—"a little, wiry, swarthy Syrian," Riggs tells us. "His speech is some blurred European tongue with middle western variations." But *Oklahoma!*'s Joseph Buloff, a veteran of New York's Yiddish theatre, made Ali Hakim into a throwback to *Rose-Marie*'s Hard-Boiled Herman, a dialect comic, with the gestures and the inflections. It's worth noting that, when Rodgers and Hammerstein superintended the *Oklahoma!* film in 1955, they deracinated the peddler, giving him to the gently all-American Eddie Albert: as if admitting that Buloff's performance was the one piece in the original show that wasn't quite correct.

Oklahoma!'s success was instantaneous, and eventually worldwide. It played New York for 2,212 performances, five years; the national tour (with, at first, Harry Stockwell, Evelyn Wyckoff, Pamela Britton, and David Burns as the peddler) lasted so long that it got back to New York in 1953, after ten years on the road, as *Oklahoma!*'s first revival. The film, though it dropped two numbers, is immensely faithful and brilliantly cast (including a splendid piece of genuine acting from the usually dizzy Charlotte Greenwood, the authors' original choice for Aunt Eller in 1943). Revivals are perennial. The very title of the show has become a summoning term meaning "The work that changed the form."

Well, it did. Its immediate and all-encompassing influence takes in: a cycle of shows with historical American subjects; a fascination with characterful rather than plot-filled stories and with conversational lyrics, leading to a concomitant decline of the genre number; a proliferation of musical scenes, especially in the addition of a few spoken lines between the vocal choruses, thus to keep story tension vital; a layout of long first act and short second act (because the stronger stories need more exposition time and the act break must now arrive at a genuine dramatic climax and not because the candy counter is ready for business);

and in a sudden emergence of atmospheric, personalized, narrative dance, not for prestige but to bridge the gap between the
script and the score, that place where neither speech nor song
quite expresses what we need to know. True, not every choreographer tilling de Mille's field added all that much to his shows,
and some of the imitations were embarrassingly slavish. For instance, the once occasional dream ballet would become de rigueur: there were at least four others in the eighteen months after
Oklahoma!'s premiere. But there were some wonderful side effects
as well, not least in a new sophistication in the composition of
dance music. Indeed, *Oklahoma!* made dancing so integral to the
. . . well, the integrated musical that high-maestro choreography
became the fourth Essential.

Oddly, Rodgers and Hammerstein temporarily parted company
for separate projects after *Oklahoma!*, Rodgers with Hart on that
revised-for-wartime *Connecticut Yankee* revival (the poster presented an armoured knight and damozel speeding along in a jeep),
and Hammerstein on a kind of life's-dream undertaking, a translation and resetting of Georges Bizet's *Carmen* with an all-black
cast as *Carmen Jones* (1943). Hammerstein had actually conceived it for Hollywood, in 1934. What an idealist! The movies
had treated black subjects early in the talkie era and returned to
them in the 1940s: because the first sound films were nervously
trying anything, anything, and because the 1940s saw a partial
melting of the business-as-usual racial chill typical of Hollywood.
But the mid-1930s were hopelessly unfriendly to black stories.
And an *opera* at that!

"When I was a small boy," Hammerstein later wrote, " 'opera'
was a bad word in our home. Opera was a way people lost money,
especially Grandpa." This was Oscar Hammerstein I, one of those
amazing folk of the early twentieth century that Europe produced
but America developed. A manufacturer and inventor, Hammerstein senior was officially in two businesses, cigar-making and
vaudeville. He was a genius at both. He wasn't too bad as an opera
impresario, either: his Manhattan Opera Company, founded in
1906, counted some of the greatest singers alive, saw the American premieres of *Pelléas et Mélisande*, *Thaïs*, *Louise*, and *Elektra*
(and took over *Salome* after the Metropolitan Opera's board

enjoined manager Heinrich Conried from running the piece after a scandalous first night), and so challenged the Met that the latter paid him over a million dollars to take his music someplace else.

With such a background, it's easy to see why Oscar II was aware of opera. Maybe not as much as Lorenz Hart, who routinely alluded to it in his lyrics. But Hammerstein may have been wondering why opera as a rule had the cultural authority that the musical could never challenge, any opera at all. So, at some point in the early 1940s, he took on a hobby: writing *Carmen Jones.* And, at some point in 1943, after *Oklahoma!* had been launched, he sent the script out to producers. Maybe he was goaded by *Once Over Lightly* (1942), an "Americanization" of Rossini's *Il Barbiere di Siviglia* and a six-performance flop. Americanization? The adaptors retained the Spanish setting and larded the dialogue with slang and catchphrases. No. You move the action to the contemporary United States, and you don't goof the libretto. You translate it.

A number of producers turned down *Carmen Jones* till Hammerstein ran into Billy Rose, fastest and flashiest of all producers. "What's next?" caws Rose: What are you working on lately? Hammerstein tells. Says Rose, "Why didn't you show it to me?"

"You're the last person I'd show it to," Hammerstein politely doesn't say. You produce events, not shows. Nightclubs, Aquacades, *Jumbo.**

"Send it to me," Rose urges; Hammerstein does, and Rose takes it on.

Well, why shouldn't he? *Carmen* is a masterpiece, and Hammerstein no more than, yes, Americanized it: his changes are of tone, not content. Bizet's heroine works in a cigarette factory; Carmen Jones works in a parachute factory. Her next boy friend, Don José, soldier, becomes Joe, soldier. Torero Escamillo—her next one after José—is now Husky Miller, prizefighter. José's

---

* The Aquacade was water sports, and *Jumbo* (1935) was a circus staged in the world's biggest theatre and containing, by the bye, a bit of story and a Rodgers–Hart score. A former lyricist, Rose had at this point never produced a genuine book musical and was not highly regarded culturally.

hometown sweetheart, Micaëla, is Cindy Lou, and Carmen's smuggler friends turn into all-purpose lowlives. These are 1943 America's counterparts to what Bizet's characters represent.

Otherwise, the original material stands virtually unchanged. Hammerstein added in a very minor principal, Poncho, as Husky Miller's boxing challenger, dropped a snatch of music here and there, and reassigned Carmen's Gypsy Song to one of her side-kicks, meanwhile allowing for a copious drum solo (originally by Cozy Cole) that serves Hammerstein's 1943 and not Bizet's 1875. Yet otherwise Bizet's original orchestrations were honored, cut down (by Robert Russell Bennett) for a Broadway pit—and, most arrestingly, the work's spoken dialogue, ballooned into recitative by another's hands after Bizet's death, was brought back to earth, making *Carmen Jones* a more virtuous version of Bizet than those heard in most opera houses.

If *Carmen Jones* is so great, why did so many turn it down before Rose? Because it was uncastable. Where would one find black opera singers in a nation with a whites-only opera policy? (The so-called "color bar" was not broken till the original Porgy, Todd Duncan, sang Tonio in *Pagliacci* at the New York City Center in 1945, though an American Indian, Chief Caupolican, sang a lead in Karel Weis' *The Polish Jew* at the Met in 1921.) However, Rose knew something that no one else did—or, rather, someone: John Hammond Jr., who had made a career out of discovering and developing black musical talent. Some of Hammond's people were very Up There, such as Count Basie and Billie Holiday; but the main thing is how many black artists Hammond knew of or could seek out. Not overestimating Hammond's diligence, George Jean Nathan wrote:

> Using trains, airplanes, buses, bobsleds, bicycles, street-cars, taxis and in some desperate instances roller-skates and coaster wagons to get places, he penetrated into the lairs of bellhops, chauffeurs, chicken-kitchen cooks, policemen, photograph developers, crap game professors, stevedores, steerbusters, and countless other such bizarre haunts . . . and he came away with such a new, fresh and exciting lot of musical play competences as has not been seen on a single stage in years.

I'd like to know how the Carmen, Muriel Smith, felt when she was told that Billy Rose wanted her on Broadway. A former voice student at the Curtis Institute in Philadelphia, Smith was the photograph developer cited by Nathan when Hammond found her. The Joe, Luther Saxon, was also oddjobbing, though six-foot-five Glenn Bryant, the Husky Miller, was a New York City cop and had to go on leave of absence to perform. Only Smith had a world-class voice, and some of the others had to strain in those pre-microphone days. Still, given Bennett's reduction of the scoring, they held up nicely—and, not surprisingly, outdid the average opera singer in their delivery of the spoken lines.

Rose hired a huge cast, big as that of a twenties operetta. This was *spectacle*. Charles Friedman staged the book scenes, ballet man Eugene Loring did the choreography, and all-around wizard Hassard Short "directed the production." It was Short's idea to give the show a color code: Bizet's first act (and the Séguedille, staged in one as "Dere's a Cafe on de Corner") was set in yellow; his second act was purple. Here Hammerstein laid his intermission. Bizet's third act, moved from a smuggler's hideout to a country club, was blue, and the last scene rioted in black and white. Throughout, costumes either complemented or, dramatically, clashed with the pervading motif. Carmen, for example, always had something red on her.

A big show plays big theatres—first that old barn the Erlanger in Philadelphia for three weeks, then the Boston Opera House for two-and-a-half weeks, and at last New York's Broadway Theatre, for fourteen months. Except for the *New York Post*'s idiot Wilella Waldorf (who also didn't like *Show Boat*, *Lady in the Dark*, and *Carousel*), the reviewers raved as, truly, never before or since. Resurrection Itself won't get these notices: "Brilliant." "Incandescent." "Superb." "Enchantingly beautiful." "A terrific job." "Magnificent." "Thrilling, human, and altogether three-dimensional." "Terrific b. o. [box office] appeal"—that's *Variety*, which went on to view Hammerstein as "now at the peak of his career."

They might say that now and then of a composer: because the music always overwhelms the words. When they say it of a lyricist, you *know* he's good.

Rodgers certainly did; he and Hammerstein pursued their

Oklahoma! partnership by doing what must have appeared to be exactly the same thing as before: the Theatre Guild producing a staging by Rouben Mamoulian and Agnes de Mille that would faithfully adapt and expand an old play that surely wouldn't make a satisfying musical: *Carousel* (1945).

Here's a truly bizarre item, even if it's too familiar now to startle. But where *Green Grow the Lilacs* seemed a risky point of origin for song and dance, we can with hindsight discern possibilities in the bumptiously lyrical downhome dialect, the dream ballet, the "Surrey" scene, and the title song. Ferenc Molnár's *Liliom*, however, is no folk play. Its hero dies; and he's no hero, but a lowlife. Worse, the story blithely turns from mean-streets realism into fantasy for its last two scenes, and it ends in utter despair. *Liliom* makes *Green Grow the Lilacs* look like a natural, an *Ah, Wilderness!* or *The Matchmaker*, easy to do.

Still, Rodgers and Hammerstein had learned the central lesson in the making of musicals: the hard ones bring out the best in you. They challenge, incite, make one invent. Nothing about *Liliom* deterred them except its setting. The Hungarian Molnár had not unnaturally placed *Liliom*'s action in Budapest, a locale that, in the American musical, signaled an operetta. Rodgers and Hammerstein didn't write operettas. They were archons of the "musical play," as the posters put it: something using operetta's musical intensity and musical comedy's vitality, yet avoiding operetta's starchy grandeur and musical comedy's lack of consistency and rationality.*

The Theatre Guild wondered if *Liliom* could be transported to the United States. New Orleans, perhaps? New England in the 1870s? Now, *that* sounded right—and while the "Soliloquy" was the first number written, surely the composition of the sea chantey "Blow High, Blow Low," "June Is Bustin' Out All Over," and "This Was a Real Nice Clambake" told the authors that they had another folk rhapsody on their hands: another *Oklahoma!*.

---

* The term "musical play" was not coined at this time. Twenties operettas sometimes billed themselves thus. But in an era dominated by musical comedy as the 1940s was, the distinctive old phrase came off as a revelation, as the unveiling of a new kind of show.

Liliom had been staged three times on Broadway when Rodgers and Hammerstein began writing *Carousel*. Joseph Schildkraut and Eva Le Gallienne played Liliom ("Lily," a tough guy's ironic nickname) and Julie in 1921, Le Gallienne revived it at her Civic Repertory Theatre in 1932, and Burgess Meredith and Ingrid Bergman played it for producer Vinton Freedley in 1940. It was never a draw; the 1940 version folded inside of two months. Still, the piece does offer what all the Rodgers and Hammerstein classics exploit: extremely rich roles for the male and female lead.* Liliom (in *Carousel*, Billy Bigelow, his last name scanning with "Lil-i-om") is a charmer, a jerk, and trouble: you can't live with him and you can't live without him. Julie is steady, moody, independent, especially in Hammerstein's rendition. They destroy each other, he through neglect and a pointless death and she by trying to give him the thing that most terrifies him: responsibility.

No wonder the "Soliloquy" came first. It's Billy's apologia and epiphany all at once, a moment in which a man without self-esteem begins to like himself (because he is loved and is thus freed to give love) but who at the same time maps his doom (because he will have to steal to provide for his expected baby). The equivalent moment for Julie is "What's the Use of Wond'rin'?," an act of self-acceptance by a woman who loves a man who harms her self-esteem, and who will stay with him anyway.

The man–woman thing is what makes *Carousel* go: the sacrifices women make that men never even notice; the first-night pickup (Julie and Billy's) as opposed to the delicate courtship (Carrie and Enoch Snow's); the thug (Jigger Craigin) who puts the moves on Carrie, to Snow's gravely whining dismay; the apparently spiteful and jealous yet in the end well-meaning Older Woman (Mrs. Mullin); the one unusual woman who does not rate her self-image by whether or not men desire her (Nettie Fowler); the rowdy lyrics of "June Is Bustin' Out All Over," in which all na-

---

* *Oklahoma!*, *South Pacific*, and *The King and I* all have them, while the neglected *Allegro*, *Me and Juliet*, and *Flower Drum Song* are ensemble shows. True, the also neglected *Pipe Dream* has the strong couple, but they are overshadowed by the Earth Mother figure; and *The Sound of Music*, though a classic, suffers a male lead deliberately underwritten (by Howard Lindsay and Russel Crouse, not Hammerstein) to focus attention on star Mary Martin.

ture is likened to a bacchanal; the "June" dance, a sensitive feminist celebration in de Mille's spring-rite ballet, promptly countered
by the testosterone-oozing "Blow High, Blow Low," with *its* horny
courtship ballet; the daughter of Billy and Julie (Louise), who
bears his anger and her tenderness, and who dominates the second act's Big Ballet as the tomboy in love—at first sight, like her
mother—with an alluring vagabond described in the program as
"A Young Man Like Billy." If *Oklahoma!*'s subject was the folkways of incipient citizens, *Carousel* dealt with the more universal
issue of gender conflict—why men and women don't understand
each other, or even why women understand and men don't.

How does one cast such a show? Were there singing actors in
1945 who could live up to these roles? Although the Theatre
Guild was the nominal producer, *Carousel* was *in cura di* Rodgers
and Hammerstein, who liked to cast young, with some experience
(especially in *Oklahoma!* as replacements or on tour), and better
a solid singer who can act than an actor who "gets through" a
song.

Those solid singers are one reason why *Carousel* is sometimes
thought of as an operetta, despite the intensely naturalistic feeling
of its central romance and an overall earthiness amid the lyricism.
Indeed, the two romantic couples (John Raitt and Jan Clayton;
Eric Mattson and Jean Darling) could have soared through Romberg, the comic villain (Murvyn Vye) was a genuine bass, and the
Earth Mother figure (Christine Johnson) had just sung the ultimate Earth Mother, Wagner's Erda, at the Met.

To be fair, *Carousel* casts almost immediately began getting
even stronger vocally. Jean Darling's "Mister Snow" was surpassed
by many a Carrie; Vye's delivery rasped here and there. It is notable that *Carousel* was the first musical to get the "crossover"
treatment in a recording by opera singers (on Victor in 1955), and
notable too that, when England's National Theatre staged *Carousel* in 1992, all the imagination and nuance of director Nicholas
Hytner and designer Bob Crowley could not soothe a minority's
complaint that the Billy, Michael Hayden, was Short on Voice.

Carousel is a Big Sing, the piece that truly tells us what a Rodgers and Hammerstein show was: operetta by other means, those
gala voices put to serious use. That was another of the many

reasons why their shows stood out when new, as if constituting a movement of some kind. Yet one of *Carousel*'s major numbers—the *most* major in terms of how much plot it covers—isn't sung at all.

So much is made of *Oklahoma!*'s beginning with a bit of sunrise music and an unaccompanied voice that one is liable to forget how uniquely *Carousel* launches its narrative: in an eight-minute pantomime to music. Then, too, *Oklahoma!* began with a conventional overture; to the uninitiated in 1945, *Carousel*'s first minutes must have been astonishing. Hurdy-gurdy "tuning up" noises eventually congealed into a waltz tune. Was this an overture? It wasn't acting like one, for just when the orchestra should have been moving into the second number of the medley, the music became dramatically invocational, the house lights dimmed to black, and the curtain unexpectedly shot up on an amusement park: families, sailors, mill girls, an ice-cream wagon, a juggler, the "Three Beauties of Europe," and of course the playful little carousel. In the course of the scene, five of the show's seven principals appeared, and the exposition was laid out as instantly as *Oklahoma!*'s had meandered: all women are drawn to Billy, while Billy is drawn to one new woman (Julie) to the helpless fury of his current woman (Mrs. Mullin), the shock of another woman (Julie's confidante, Carrie), and the uninflected witness of a third woman (Julie's cousin, Nettie), who will remain oddly neutral to the Billy–Julie romance for the next fifteen years.

"The Carousel Waltz" might easily have been a dance number; Big Ballet was virtually as elemental in the evolving musical play as a brilliant story score was. But in fact this waltz prologue is simply an expansion of a prologue in *Liliom* itself. A spectacle out of style with the rest of the dour little story, it is usually cut in performance. "The Carousel Waltz" could be cut, too, without harming *Carousel*'s continuity, as the following scene—a fight among Julie, Carrie, and Mrs. Mullin, succeeded by Billy's intrusion—restarts the exposition all over, this time verbally. But then an essential piece of the musical play would be missing: the surprise.

Rodgers and Hammerstein did their work with a most wonderful unpredictability. They hook you, not with novelties, but discoveries. Such as raising the curtain before you're ready, to music of such irresistible sweep that it seems criminal not to dance to it—and the stage keeps *threatening* to, only adding to the suspense of the action unfolded before us. Or such as giving silly Carrie the deeply romantic "Mister Snow," or letting the pompous Snow start "When the Children Are Asleep" obsessed with his commercial aspirations and end it in a pre-nuptial reverie, a capitalist's serenade. Such as the "Soliloquy," so daring—another eight-minute number, this time for one person—that it's almost too daring for today, fifty years on. Rodgers and Hammerstein's unpredictability works in small but also very large ways—in *Allegro*'s naked stage, the racism that haunts *South Pacific*, or simply the fact that every character in *Flower Drum Song* is Chinese. In *Carousel*, it tells most importantly in the score, the team's richest, densest, most detailed. And that brings us to the Bench Scene.

Stephen Sondheim has called it "probably the singular most important moment in the revolution of contemporary musicals," and he ought to know. But I think that moment actually comes one number earlier, in the Julie–Carrie duet that runs into "Mister Snow." It's the first time a *Carousel* character actually sings—or, rather, talks to music. "Julie," says Carrie, and "*Julie!*," to the outline of an insistent violin figure. "Do you like him?"

"I dunno," Julie replies, and as they converse they begin to sing. But this is no "People Will Say We're in Love" construction, not a *song*. It's a scene, a characterological transaction, like "The Surrey With the Fringe on Top." It swiftly moves into "Mister Snow," a song. Still, opera is now in the air, not through-sung music drama but something more than a musical, because at times the music seems to be invading the script, even feasting on it.*

The Bench Scene certainly typifies the way *Carousel*'s score impatiently injects itself into the action. The number gets its nickname because, after "Mister Snow," a long book scene involving

---

* "Through-sung" denotes a theatre piece depicted entirely through a vocal text: *L'Incoronazione di Poppea*, *Il Trovatore*, *Miss Saigon*. The widely misunderstood "through-composed" denotes something else entirely—any musical work without movements, structured scenes, numbers. Few operas are through-composed, and virtually no musicals. Arguable exceptions include Marc Blitzstein's *Reuben Reuben* (1955) and Michael John LaChiusa's *Hello Again* (1994).

three different characters' warning Julie that Billy is bad news does not discourage her interest in him, leaving the two sitting on a park bench. They talk of any old thing—love and death, actually—in pointedly underscored dialogue, arioso, and the vocal centerpiece of the sequence, "If I Loved You." It's the same procedure as in the preceding scene, two people talking. But if the authors hadn't first introduced this method in the Julie–Carrie duet, smaller and tighter, the Bench Scene might have overwhelmed the audience. The first duet is two chums confiding in each other. The second is two incipient lovers trading worldviews, from a look heavenward at the stars to a glance at leaves falling from trees in the natural order of things. It is, in fact, the show in miniature: the Starkeeper gazing down upon men and women. "Two little people" is how Billy sees him and Julie, compared with those stars. "We don't count at all." Wrong, says Hammerstein; and he sends the dead Billy back to earth to prove it.

We take musical scenes in stride now. But in the 1940s, when many theatregoers hadn't seen an operetta since the 1920s—or had never seen one—the genre was alien. True, there were *Lady in the Dark*'s dreams, but they were surrealist cartoons. *Carousel*'s musical scenes—and this show has rather a number of them—are naturalistic. An important difference between musical comedy and the musical play is that, in the former, characters aren't really "singing." The musical itself is singing. In the musical play, the characters are singing. They have to—or the audience won't know how they feel.

Each of *Carousel*'s musical scenes expresses different feelings. The choral scene leading up to "June Is Bustin' Out All Over" portrays gender war comically ("Get away, you no-account nothin's . . ."), a corresponding scene in Act Two, uniting Snow's plaintive "Geraniums in the Winder" with Jigger's sardonic "Stonecutters Cut it on Stone," treats the subject with irony, only to be trumped by what is in effect the show's motto song, "What's the Use of Wond'rin'?." Yet it's all commentary on the man–woman thing, or at least on the destiny of Julie and Billy. Their stormy love all the same proves so powerful that the Starkeeper must visit mortal earth to preside, in the guise of a small-town doctor, at the high school graduation of Billy and Julie's daughter, where the ghostly Billy passes essential messages to his survivors to strengthen them for life without him. Surveying the youngsters before him, the good doctor comments, "Brought most of you into the world." No, all of you. And, after Billy has executed his amazing penance and is leaving the stage with the Heavenly Friend as the chorus swells in the climax of "You'll Never Walk Alone," the doctor and the Heavenly Friend lock eyes, God nods Yes, and the curtain falls.

Carousel opened at the Majestic Theatre, directly across from *Oklahoma!*'s St. James Theatre, on April 19, 1945, and among the many raves was Louis Kronenberger's very prescient notice in *PM*:

> I suppose a comparison between [*Carousel* and *Oklahoma!*] is inevitable. . . . The high spirits of *Oklahoma!*, the meadow freshness of it at its best, its fetching qualities as a "show" have no counterpart in *Carousel*. . . . But *Carousel*. . . . may yet seem more of a milestone in the years to come.

True, the show did not at first enjoy *Oklahoma!*'s success. At 890 performances, it was the fifth-longest-running musical of the decade (promptly surpassed by *South Pacific, Annie Get Your Gun,* and *Kiss Me, Kate*), but it never rivaled the first Rodgers and Hammerstein title as The One. *Carousel* didn't attract supplementary PR events (cutting anniversary cakes, receiving citations); didn't catch on as a show for servicemen to take their dates to or revisit with their families; and was, of course, far more about class and gender than about American life. *Oklahoma!* tells of a community striving to perfect democracy. *Carousel* tells of: one, the destructive stupidity that men bring to marriage; two, the ruin of a friendship between two proletarian women because of the social ambitions of a husband; or, three, how some men commit crime out of necessity and others out of sheer selfish evil.

Musical plays are stuffed with content; that's, really, how they differ from musical comedy. No wonder the form permeated Broadway. It even began to rewrite history, in 1946, when Jerome Kern and Oscar Hammerstein produced a revival of *Show Boat* in a revision that changed it from a musical comedy with serious parts into a Very Respectable Musical Play. Of course, by the mid-1940s, this show of 1927 was the champ classic, with perhaps the best known score of all time. Other famous shows of the 1920s were revived in the 1940s, but the stagings were generally makeshift. The new *Show Boat* was produced so handsomely that even after a year's run on Broadway it didn't pay off till the eighteen-month national tour got underway.

We now know that each generation revises this national property to suit trend. It becomes racially delicate in the 1960s, a gala Harold Prince pageant in the 1990s. Preparing their revival in mid-1945, after Hammerstein had seen *Carousel* to its opening and six years after Kern had been on Broadway at all, the authors had no particular agenda. They took advantage of improved technology to drop the inessential "in one" scenes that covered set changes. (In 1927, before a drop representing the facade of the Palmer House Hotel, Parthy Ann warned Captain Andy to return in one hour and went inside, whereupon Andy picked up three tarts and went off carousing. In 1946, he simply showed up at a nightclub with a reduced company of two tarts and a few lines covering this unimportant plot action.) This tightening of the scene plot made one song "redundant," as the English put it, and the authors also dropped a charm number and wrote a new eleven o'clock song, "Nobody Else But Me." They as well pruned the specialty material that, in 1927, served not the story but the quarreling talents of the original cast—Sammy White's hoofing solo, Tess Gardella's vocal tour de force, "Hey, Fella!," and Norma Terris' celebrity imitations.

More: they abolished the incidental dances that, in the 1920s, followed a song without anyone's wondering why, in favor of the Big Ballet. Helen Tamiris was the choreographer, a new talent, having debuted the previous season with *Up in Central Park*. All this was state of the art, circa 1946. There was no intention to rob the original of its robust gaiety, of the eccentric old-show-biz tricks that rode right along, in 1927, with the ecstatically outpouring melody.

Yet this is exactly what Kern and Hammerstein ended up doing. Much of the 1927 *Show Boat*'s fun lay in how producer Florenz Ziegfeld and (unbilled) director Hammerstein allowed the gifted cast to show its individual strengths. That's Aarons–Freedley

thinking, though, isn't it? Ironically, the show that virtually created the musical play had as much rococo drollery as any musical
comedy. The 1946 *Show Boat* got serious and cut much of that
out, partly because American show biz had so changed in twenty
years that the drolls had largely vanished, and partly because a
musical play of the 1940s exploits the fun thought up by the authors, not the fun thought up by the performers. It has no space
for hoofing solos and vocal specialties. Celebrity imitations?
Right—and Curly's going to wow the crowd at the Farmer and
Cowman Dance with his impressions of Jimmy Stewart, Humphrey Bogart, and Sonja Henie.

We see how vastly *Show Boat* changed—had to change—when
comparing the 1946 cast with the original lineup. The 1927 crew
had one weakness, the boring (probably more truly the stage-
frightened) Jules Bledsoe as Joe, the character who does very little
more than sing "Ol' Man River" and its several reprises, though
some revisions give him more to do. Everyone else was top of the
line, but of a special line, schooled in arts that had come to seem
quaint and irrelevant a generation later. The Magnolia, Norma
Terris, had a cute comic edge that was typical of a twenties operetta heroine but would simply be erroneous in a character who
must now be a sister to high-strung Laurey and the wanly doomed
Julie. The 1927 Ravenal, Howard Marsh, was, unlike the baritone
heroes of *Oklahoma!* and *Carousel*, a tenor. It's skirty, too lavish,
a student prince in a part meant for a man. Even Charles Winninger, a wonderful blend of comic and actor whose Captain Andy
centered the piece in 1927, was not useful to Broadway by 1945,
not in the musical play. Winninger was too much the improviser;
he left his mark on the show in the four-minute Comedian's Specialty Spot in the Cotton Blossom's auditorium after the hillbillies
have broken up the performance of *The Parson's Bride*. Taking
stage to explain to his public how the melodrama was supposed
to conclude, Captain Andy plays all the parts, fakes a titanic fist-
fight, and more or less reviews a century of theatre shtick in a set
piece that has less to do with *Show Boat* than with the expertise
of the Captain Andy. Or simply consider that Tess Gardella, the
1927 Queenie, was an Italian woman who worked in blackface,

billed as "Aunt Jemima." (Try to imagine a blackface performer in *Oklahoma!* or *Carousel*—not to mention *Carmen Jones*.) The 1946 Queenie, Helen Dowdy, was not only genetically black but genetically musical play, having appeared in that key forerunner *Porgy and Bess*, in both its premiere and the 1942 revival (and going on to even later stagings in the 1950s, including the famous international tour with Leontyne Price). *Carousel*'s Jan Clayton played Magnolia, baritone Charles Fredericks was her Ravenal, and Julie—so silky and pathetic in 1927, so tragic, so soprano, so Helen Morgan—was now Carol Bruce, *Louisiana Purchase*'s belting sophisticate. The Captain Andy and Parthy Ann, Ralph Dumke and Ethel Owen, were the very first players to vanish utterly in these parts, to fail to play. It was a shock, after Winninger and Edna May Oliver. But then, Buddy Ebsen and Colette Lyons, as Frank and Ellie, were no better. *Show Boat*'s cast, once so vital and self-willing, had become functional. Clayton and Bruce, at least, were very appealing singer–actors, and Fredericks worked hard to substantiate the flighty Ravenal. But in all, this was a *Show Boat* entirely dependent upon the powers of its story, score, and choreography: a musical play. And that deletes much of the fun from *Show Boat*, which is, after all, a backstager about the delight of performing.*

To be fair, the 1946 *Show Boat* was only trying to meet its public in the style that it had come to expect from an Important Show. Still, this wasn't *Show Boat*, but rather a musical play based on it. With "Rodgers and Hammerstein" now Broadway's designated revolution, a tension set in between the debased successors to the Aarons–Freedley format and the musical play or derivations thereof. "Music and girls are the soul of musical comedy," wrote one critic around this time, though he was in fact speaking of the musical in general. No: they *were*.

Because musical comedy as it was has run out of steam. The musical play now holds the power, and it will draw many—not

---

* Oddly, one twenties-style performer got into this *Show Boat*, not in New York but on the tour, replacing Buddy Ebsen: Sammy White, the 1927 Frank, closing down a long career in the only part that had brought him glory.

all—writers into its aura. The 1950s can be seen as the decade in which the oldtime musical was subsumed into the musical play.

But the 1940s is when the oldtime musical made its last stand. As we'll see, not everything that matters is *Oklahoma!*, *Carousel*, or their children.

5

AMERICANA

After *Oklahoma!*, the musical went into a wartime cycle of shows similarly devoted to American culture and folklore. These were not the first in the musical's history, however. If musical comedy is urban and up-to-the-minute, operetta loves exotic settings, the faraway and long ago; twenties operetta sometimes ventured into the American past in search of novelty, as in three Hammerstein titles, *The New Moon* (1928), *Rainbow* (1928), and *Sweet Adeline* (1929): old New Orleans, the west, and turn-of-the-century New York.

Thirties operetta concentrated almost exclusively on foreign climes, but this was a decade rediscovering American culture after the twenties debunking of it, in films and the concert hall especially. And we note Hammerstein, with Romberg, back in old New Orleans for *Sunny River* (1941). The story itself could have been set anywhere: a cafe chanteuse (Muriel Angelus) and a society woman (Helen Claire) both love an aristocrat (Bob Lawrence). The rich one gets him by cheat, he dies, they weep. The performers' names mean nothing even to aficionados (though Angelus introduced "Falling in Love With Love" in *The Boys From Syra-*

cuse), yet the critics thought the show a wonderful sing. They also enjoyed the return, after a fifteen-year stay in England, of veteran Ethel Levey (George M. Cohan's first wife), on hand to put over the title song. Tom Ewell, the show's comedian opposite the future Laurey, Joan Roberts, also won praise, never easy to do with what passed for humor in operetta. These were regarded as the best parts of a dull show, and it died in a month. Still, it must have had something, for impresario Emile Littler presented it two years later in London, with dueling divas Evelyn Laye (as the chanteuse) and Edith Day (in Levey's role). This time it died in three months.

Whatever *Sunny River*'s quality as entertainment, it was not at all the kind of show that *Oklahoma!* and *Carousel* represented, at once social, commentative, populist, and political. *Oklahoma!*'s farmers versus cowmen background is meant to show how democrats must learn to work out their differences peacefully—a lesson taught at a time when democrats were fighting fascists, because those differences cannot be solved except by the eradication of fascism. *Carousel*'s "Stonecutters Cut It on Stone" is social rather than political, a kind of invented folk song that reflects on the dramatic situation with a fatalistic worldview: men are an eternal problem, and women must suffer. It seems the center of the story—but only until the final scene. Hammerstein had followed Molnár's tale right up to the moment when the hero tries to give his daughter a star, slaps her when she refuses it, and is led away to the hereafter, a loser in death as in life: and there *Liliom* ends. Hammerstein added one last bit, the high-school graduation. And then, of course, the story's center seems to lie in "You'll Never Walk Alone." The tension between what the first song tells us and how the later song corrects it gives the whole a moral ambiguity. Compound the fantasy with the ascetically religious nature of the finale, whose sense of sorrow and ecstasy has the air of a church service, and *Carousel* takes on the format of a parable.

We expect such intelligence of the musical play; it is deceptive, complex. *Oklahoma!* and *Carousel* both use their American settings ontologically, whereas *Sunny River* was just another operetta.

So there was an important breakaway at this time in the musical's history. There will be more *Sunny Rivers*, and they, too, will fail. But interspersed among them will be other musicals seeking some meaning in the very idea of "America."

One other show preceded *Oklahoma!*'s wartime sensibility, the all-soldier revue *This Is the Army* (1942). With an Irving Berlin score and a script by James McColl devoted to military life, this was the ultimate patriotic piece. Rodgers and Hammstein *styled* their perceptions of America. *This Is the Army* simply *was* America—at least, male America in 1942, arising in darkness to a bugle call, undergoing basic training, nursing a crush on a Stage Door Canteen doughnut girl, dreaming of one's stateside sweetheart. All this was on display in song and sketch: goofy recruit chirping "The Army's Made a Man Out of Me" even as his voice is breaking; a nighttime barracks scene leading up to "I'm Getting Tired So I Can Sleep," for sleep brings dreams "of you"; Berlin himself, a sergeant in World War I, leading a line of doughboys in front of a risible tent to revive "Oh, How I Hate To Get Up in the Morning." Never able to resist what was then termed a "race" number, Berlin gave a group of black soldiers "What the Well Dressed Man in Harlem Will Wear," an excuse for some expert dancing around and under gigantic cardboard figures sporting the striped suits and broad-brimmed hats that had only just given way to GI khaki. Other services got a look-in in "American Eagles" and "How About a Cheer for the Navy," but the three-hundred-strong cast was strictly army personnel, as was the staging team—the orchestra was led by one of Broadway's former conductors, Corporal Milton Rosenstock. Even the few women's roles were filled by men in drag, reducing the dream visions of "I'm Getting Tired So I Can Sleep" to galoots in mop-top wigs and satiric ball gowns, their décolletage trimmed by chest hair.

This Is the Army was essentially an amateur night. Besides Burl Ives and Gary Merrill, none of the performers went on to a notable thespian career, the decor was merely functional, and the costumes mainly uniforms. Still, the show made a powerful impression on all who saw it, and could probably have run for years. Instead, the army booked a national tour of limited runs (three months in New York, with three showings a day) till it closed in

San Francisco, having raised two million dollars for the Army Emergency Relief Fund.

Oddly, for such a patriotic show, there was little jingoism in the material. In fact, though the war was implicitly omnipresent, it was treated almost in passing, except in the jazzy "That Russian Winter," on Hitler's eastern campaign, in which the title phrase is sung to the familiar melody of "The Volga Boatman."

Still, the very appearance of such a show at such a time is a jingoistic event, and many a heart thrilled to the finale, in which Berlin stood at front and center of some one hundred fifty soldiers in battle gear, row after row standing on risers, carolling out "This Time Is the Last Time." The sight became so identified with *This Is the Army* that Warner Brothers retained it in the film version, wherein the backdrop was made of giant statues of the eagle and Uncle Sam and the risers bore something like four hundred men. The rest of the movie was less faithful to the show, using a back-stager plot and a coed cast, though some of the drag material was honored. A surprising amount of the score got into the adaptation, as did Berlin and his reveille number. But what typified the stage version was the sheer informality of what amounted to an army talent show celebrating the men who were fighting for democracy's life. What typified the Hollywood version was Kate Smith singing "God Bless America."

There is no question that *This Is the Army* filled a need, an important one. At its opening, on July 4, 1942, the United States had been at war for seven months and getting the worst of it. The show, with a score by one of the most enthusiastic immigrants in the nation's history, was nothing less than an ode to democracy as the political form preferred by good guys everywhere. Good guys have a sense of humor, dance well, try not to be racist, and sing Irving Berlin songs.

Alternatively, good guys ride horses, try to get along with their neighbors, and sing Rodgers and Hammerstein. But they don't jail or sue the bad guy: they kill him. You have to, or he'll keep coming at you.

So, in many different ways, the wartime musical took a look at why we *were* the good guys. According to Harold Arlen and E. Y. Harburg's *Bloomer Girl* (1944), it was because of feminism.

Set at the very start of the women's movement, when they were still battling for the vote, *Bloomer Girl* also dealt with white racism and the dangerous unity of government and the money bosses, and even found time to fit in the Civil War. It owed a lot to *Oklahoma!*: its star, Celeste Holm; its supporting comic, Joan McCracken; its choreographer, Agnes de Mille; its designers, Lemuel Ayers and Miles White; and its orchestrator, Robert Russell Bennett (though the busy Bennett would have been there anyway). Most of all it owed to Rodgers and Hammerstein a new way of conceiving musicals that was very relevant to the wartime 1940s. The art of *Bloomer Girl*—how it looked, moved, sang— was very strongly derived from *Oklahoma!*. But the aim of *Bloomer Girl* was to hearten and improve democrats. Like a nineteenth-century Chautauqua, it was lecture–entertainment.

Book writers Sig Herzig and Fred Saidy set their tale in 1861, in "a small Eastern manufacturing town" that they called Cicero Falls—clearly the real-life Seneca Falls, New York, where a feminist congress was held in 1848. They wrote a real-life feminist into their piece, too—"Dolly" Bloomer, an advocate of trousers for women. Her imagined niece Evalina (Celeste Holm) is the show's protagonist, the rebellious daughter of the "enemy," a hoop-skirt maker. Aunt Dolly of course encourages Evalina in all the feminist isms of the time, especially abolitionism.* But Evalina's father has engaged her to a slaveholding southerner, Jefferson Calhoun (David Brooks). In fact, Aunt Dolly is hiding one of Calhoun's runaway slaves, Pompey (Dooley Wilson). Calhoun, however, charms us by mixing his misgivings about Pompey's defection with sympathy for Pompey's position. That makes it tough on Evalina. She was all set to loathe the slaveowner: how does she relate to a slavefreer?

It's a good story, because it has a ton of conflict but no genuine bad guy, even if Evalina's father exemplifies as many traits of the intolerant capitalist patriarch as the authors can work into a three-

---

* Tactfully deleted was any mention of another early feminist cause, in fact an obsession: prohibition. Remember, *Bloomer Girl* opened a mere twelve years after Franklin Roosevelt's administration finally repealed the loony national ban on liquor.

hour musical. There's a lot of historical color, too: when the spinet exercise of one of Evalina's five sisters becomes the accompaniment to the first number, "When the Boys Come Home"; in a ten-minute second-act opener called "Sunday in Cicero Falls," in which Arlen, Harburg, and de Mille take a cross section of the local social structures; in a replica of the oldtime "Tom show" (any of the countless adaptations of Harriet Beecher Stowe's *Uncle Tom's Cabin*), complete with placards at the side of the tiny stage ("Topsy and Eva," "Eliza Crossing the Ice"), and a number of ditties, creating a mini-musical in itself; and a Big Ballet centered on the Waiting Women who guard the homefront while the men are at (the Civil) War.

Yet all this would be little without the throughline of Evalina's *Bildung* as a freethinking woman in a world ruled for the betterment of men's projects, whether industrial or martial. Her sisters are devotees of marriage and duty, but Evalina, under Aunt Dolly's tutelage, is a confronter. The first-act curtain can fall only after Evalina, taking part in a fashion parade of hoop-skirts, drops her outer layer to reveal a set of bloomers, inciting a riot.

As always with Harburg, the political is not an aspect of the show, but its endowment. It's in the jokes:

> EVALINA: What ever happened to that young man of yours, Aunt Dolly?
> DOLLY: He came to a bad end—got to be governor.

It's in the characters:

> GOVERNOR: (*to* DOLLY) And I still haven't given up hope of making Miss Bloomer the Governor's Lady.
> DOLLY: Governor's Lady, hell—I'm going to be governor!

It's in the songs, as when Calhoun reproves Pompey with "What made you do this to me?" and Pompey is already singing "What makes the gopher leave his hole? . . ." It's freedom, of course. It's "The Eagle and Me." It's Why We Fight.

Arlen and Harburg were clearly trying to challenge Rodgers and Hammerstein in their *Bloomer Girl* score, so precisely coordinated with the action that scarcely a number could suit another show. Maybe Evalina and Calhoun's love song, "Right as the Rain." But note that their first duet, "Evalina," is an ironic courtship of north by south that finds her sarcastic and morally superior and him bewildered, the music a slithery wisteria jazz. Where but in *Bloomer Girl*—at that, quite early in Act One and no later—could we fairly hear such a piece? Feminism claims a number ("It Was Good Enough for Grandma"), the radical's impatience is heard from (in McCracken's "T'morra, T'morra," which closes with a classic Harburg rebus: "I'd rather have somethin' to remember than nothin' to forget!"), and Evalina's five brothers-in-law, traveling salesmen, have the bawdy "The Farmer's Daughter."

If Irving Berlin loved race numbers, Harold Arlen preferred race shows, as we'll soon see. In *Bloomer Girl*, he wrote but a few spots for black characters, mainly "I Got a Song," in which balladeer Richard Huey, in a jail scene, offered to extemporize upon any topic thrown at him. He claims to have a "Railroad Song," a "Woman Song," a "Sinner Song." "I got 'em! I got 'em!," he cries, disarmingly. Indeed, he does, as the liberal and the poet in Harburg collide, deviously diverting. When he and Arlen go anthem on us, as in "God's Country" from *Hooray For What!* (1937), they're dealing in agitprop. But give them a single person to lend expression to and they do really conjure up a singing Americana.

"Let's face it," wrote Wilella Waldorf in the *Post*. "We are in for several seasons of intensely old-fashioned quaintness, most of it with choreography by Agnes de Mille." It's remarkable how many reviewers did in fact see that a cycle was in progress, though only Waldorf and George Jean Nathan resented it. They liked the bracing nonsense that the musical had mostly been serving up before. To Nathan especially, the notion of an intelligent musical was not only an oxymoron but an outrage.

A public educated by *Oklahoma!* could not have disagreed more. *Bloomer Girl* ran for 654 performances, a mammoth showing that was possibly extended by Nanette Fabray's assumption of Evalina: for where Celeste Holm had a fetching weird presence, Fabray had genuine, classic charm. Some are born to musical comedy (Ethel Merman, say), some achieve musical comedy (Barbra Streisand), and some have musical comedy thrust upon them (Robert Preston). Nanette Fabray *was* musical comedy, and only bad luck in the 1950s kept her from making the alltime pantheon along with Marilyn Miller, Merman, Mary Martin, and Gwen Verdon.

More on Nanette later. Our next stop is *Sing Out, Sweet Land!* (1944), "a salute to American folk and popular music" that had started out at Catholic University in Washington, D.C. The salute ran wide, from "Oh, Susannah" and "Big Rock Candy Mountain" through spiritual and blues to "My Blue Heaven" and "I Got Rhythm." There were as well three new numbers, by Elie Siegmeister and Edward Eager, but this was no mere concert. Theatre buffs who know the piece by its title or even the cast album assume that it's a revue. It is in fact a book show, following the adventures of ageless Barnaby Goodchild through an epic of American history that starts in Puritan New England and takes in the Oregon Trail, the Civil War, and twenties speakeasies till it ends on an aircraft carrier in the Pacific in the audience's present day.

With a book by Walter Kerr and the arranging of the music by Siegmeister, *Sing Out, Sweet Land!* begins darkly, with Barnaby in the stocks, his archfoe Parson Killjoy gloating, and a chorus of Puritans intoning a sixteenth-century hymn, "Who Is the Man That Life Doth Will." Barnaby unrepentant, the Parson curses him, giving the show its concept: "Ye must wander the desolate roads with thy singing and dancing forever!"

This leads to the first of the original numbers, "As I Was Going Along," with which Barnaby launches his tour. Traveling through the years and a kaleidoscope of American music, ever stalked by Killjoy, Barnaby ends up three centuries later as a sailor in the navy. Surrounded by the cast, costumed to review all the eras and places visited by the show, he leads them in the stirring "More Than These," whose lyrics include the show's title phrase.

Some loved it: melodious, inspiring, moving. Others shook their heads: banal, insistent, pretentious. The Theatre Guild produced, moving Alfred Drake out of the *Oklahoma!* troupe to play Barnaby. It's offbeat casting, for Barnaby is a naif and Drake a kind of mock-Shakespearean ham. Indeed, he was to spend the rest of the decade wasted in other misadventures (including playing the stupefyingly noble Larry Foreman in a revival of Marc Blitzstein's class-war piece *The Cradle Will Rock*) till he at last found a truly identifying part: Fred Graham, the mock-Shakespearean ham hero of *Kiss Me, Kate*.

Still, Drake was in effect the evening's emcee, there more to introduce than perform. It was the large ensemble that really put the music into *Sing Out, Sweet Land!*. Burl Ives's folk style gave him an opportunity that *This Is the Army* didn't; here was the start of a strong career as both singer and actor. Juanita Hall, Bibi Osterwald, Jack McCauley, and Alma Kaye gave first-rate assistance, and the non-singing Philip Coolidge was wonderfully hissable as the censorious parson.

Whether one calls it a book show without a plot or a revue without comedy, *Sing Out, Sweet Land!* was a celebration of the vitality of American song, a true outpouring, from Anonymous to Gershwin. *That's* why we fight: to make music. Unfortunately, the Guild had to take a bad booking, at the International Theatre, up on Columbus Circle. When E. D. Stair and A. L. Wilbur built it (as the Majestic), in 1903, they reckoned that the theatre district, which had been expanding northward at a suddenly frenzied rate, would continue to expand. It never did, and the seven houses clustered around Columbus Circle were last-resort venues from the start. This poor big barn of an International had opened in glory, with the sole American musical to rival the success of *The Merry Widow* in the first decade of the century, *The Wizard of Oz*, immediately followed by the best-remembered American musical title of the decade, *Babes in Toyland*. But *Sing Out, Sweet Land!* gave 101 performances to two-thirds-empty houses, then closed.

Oddly, one of the season's biggest musical hits opened in one of those seven marginal theatres. Wartime theatregoing had swelled Broadway; virtually every dormant house was being refurbished and reopened. The Messrs. Shubert reclaimed one of their own nestlings, the Jolson, on the west side of Seventh Avenue between Fifty-eighth and Fifty-ninth Streets. As the New Century, it was refloated with *Follow the Girls*, and, when that runaway hit moved downtown to a handier location, hosted Sigmund Romberg's fifty-fifth Broadway score, *Up in Central Park* (1945).

You remember Romberg—*The Student Prince*, *The Desert Song*, *The New Moon*. The Hungarian of the two operetta guys. The other guy, the Czech, Rudolf Friml, had given up when operettas (especially Friml's) started bombing in the early 1930s. Romberg simply readjusted his style. After all, he had begun in musical comedy and could return to it, gentling down the high notes, waltzes, and finalettos for an era that sometimes tolerated and sometimes disdained that stuff. Romberg could even sample the jazz idiom, as for instance in the honking, strutting "Eleven Levee Street," written for (but cut from) the aforementioned New Orleans musical, *Sunny River*. And what's a New Orleans musical without a taste of the blues?

Up in Central Park, set in little old New York, didn't inspire many pastiche numbers from Romberg; he wrote largely in forties Broadway style.* His co-authors were Herbert and Dorothy Fields on book and Dorothy on lyrics, and his producer was the canny Michael Todd, who made it a point of honor to build a big production budget and a load of PR into an irresistible smash. With or without stars, using the likes of Cole Porter or unknown writers, Todd—like Florenz Ziegfeld, David O. Selznick, Ted Turner, and certain other Great American Showmen—believed that the only way to make money is to spend money. A Michael Todd musical was lavish, prominent, and a major hit.

That *Up in Central Park* was, lasting fourteen-and-a-half months in a season, that of 1944–45, teeming with smashes: *Song of Norway, Bloomer Girl, On the Town,* and *Carousel.* Set in the New York of the early 1870s, when the corrupt political machine of "Boss" Tweed ran New York City, *Up in Central Park* was just historical enough to be Americana, just class-conscious enough to be socially aware, and just operetta enough to be a musical comedy by Sigmund Romberg.

Here's a chance to learn what folks liked in between the classic shows, so let us pause for some detailed examination. *Up in Central Park*'s opening recalls those of *Sunny River* and *Carousel*, a pantomime to music, though, as in *Sunny River*, it's plotless, pictorial—and set, of course, in the park: kids playing "hoops," a

---

* Faced with a similar setting on *Sweet Adeline* (1929), Jerome Kern got the "atmosphere" out of the way in the overture, a medley of familiar old tunes from the turn of the century.

rider on one of those old outsized bikes, a balloon seller, a cop, newsboys. A long book scene follows, almost daring the audience to wonder whatever happened to that Good Old Opening Number. We finally get a song, "Up From the Gutter," for heroine Rosie (Maureen Cannon) and comic sidekick Bessie (Betty Bruce), establishing a major element in the show, one that had been insistent in all American show biz for almost a century and was just about to die out: Irish stereotype humor.

Rosie and Bessie both have father characters (Charles Irwin and Walter Burke), emphasizing the Irish stuff. But the principals are hero John Matthews (Wilbur Evans), a *New York Times* reporter, his buddy (and real-life crusading cartoonist) Thomas Nast of *Harper's Weekly* (Maurice Burke), and their nemesis, Tweed himself (Noah Beery Sr.). Tweed is grafting a fortune out of a massive redesigning of the park, John and Nast want to expose him, and John and Rosie get romantically involved. The catch: Rosie's father works for Tweed.

Okay, it's not intense enough to have interested Rodgers and Hammerstein. But it does have more possibilities than the prep-school dances and spy rings we met in earlier chapters. And, like Rodgers and Hammerstein, these authors take their characters seriously and love the way democracies can bring down pigs like Tweed. Remember, too, that there was a time when one of Broadway's most successful teams was Romberg and Hammerstein.

So we can expect at least a little intelligence and even experimentation here, those formal surprises that dolled up *Oklahoma!* and *Carousel*. For instance, the "heroine's wanting song," a sentimental waltz called "Carousel in the Park," illustrates her wish to be a professional singer even as it provides some geographical atmosphere, not least in an orchestral ritornello scored as a carousel's tinkly piping. Note, too, that we get spoken dialogue between the choruses, now de rigueur in any top-of-the-line musical.

Similarly, John and Rosie's first love duet isn't about love. "It Doesn't Cost You Anything To Dream" cleverly moves around the subject while drawing the two characters closer together, at that in a delightfully confidential fox trot, very up-to-date. Even Tweed, like Jud Fry, must be brought into the score, here in a lengthy scene concerning backroom politics that is delivered entirely in song, the ensemble building to Tweed's entrance and solo. It's a touch of operetta, but it works because the quaintness of the procedure helps frame Tweed as a comic villain.

By now, we've been in the park, we've met the lovers, and we've had a taste of political corruption. All this storytelling is getting dangerously serious for a Mike Todd production, so we repair to the lounge of the Stetson Hotel, where John reaffirms his interest in Rosie in the ebullient "When She Walks in the Room." Isn't this about time for a Big Ballet? Sure enough, Bessie and her vis-à-vis, Joe (Fred Barry), cue it in with a comic number, "(Let me show you my) Currier and Ives," a nineteenth-century take on the couch artist's old line, "come up and see my etchings." Helen Tamiris' dancers render still-life versions of Joe's collection, which includes "The Husband's Revenge" and "The Highwayman's Luck," till the Stetson Hotel set flies up, freeing the playing area for Tamiris' tour de force, a "Skating Ballet" on the icy park lake. As with "Laurey Makes Up Her Mind" and the "Civil War Ballet," this dance became so identified with the show that, when Universal filmed it for Deanna Durbin in 1948, it thought nothing of junking almost all the score but carefully filmed the ballet. (Today, it is generally called the "Currier and Ives Ballet" because of its fidelity to the look of period halftone printing technology.)

More love plot gives us John and Rosie's second duet, "Close as Pages in a Book," a ballad with slithery chromatic harmony and a soaring climax that again brings Romberg to his golden days as one of Broadway's two operetta kings. Next, Tweed keeps the political subtext—and the era—in trim, leading an ensemble number called "Rip Van Winkle," in salute to actor Joseph Jefferson, perennial in that role.

Now it's time for love trouble. A rich businessman (Paul Reed) offers to finance Rosie's singing career, to John's fury:

ROSIE: The best people in New York will be at my debut.
JOHN: They aren't the best people in New York! They're the worst!

By the first-act finale, everything is coming together—the romance, the exposé underplot, the secondary couple, the Irish texture. In the grandest set that Mike Todd's money and designer

Howard Bay's imagination can erect, the entire cast appears in yet another spot in the park for a celebration. Tamiris brings on can-can girls, and Rosie goes wild with "The Fireman's Bride," a raucous number in the style of "Meet Me in St. Louis" and other strophic comedy waltzes (Romberg's one attempt all evening to recall period genre). Rosie ends up standing on a table, the center of attention as she has always longed to be: but now she is also the businessman's fiancée and John's enemy.

Then John comes in, confers excitedly with Nast, and takes his glass just as Rosie turns to see him—and, at that moment, the choral reprise of "The Fireman's Bride" cuts off in embarrassment. The orchestra cuts out, too. The theatre is absolutely silent as John ironically raises his glass to Rosie, puts it down, and exits. *Absolutely silent.* In that silence, the curtain falls.

A first-act curtain without musical punctuation! Even Rodgers and Hammerstein never thought of that one. However, *Up in Central Park*'s second act is much less intrepid, as if its authors' revolutionary sympathies have been exhausted. The curtain rises on the usual pointless choral number, "When the Party Gives a Party For the Party," and, as Tweed feeds plot suspense by alternately threatening and bribing his foes and even trying to buy the *New York Times* to kill its crusade against him, John gets a "Stouthearted Men" number, baritone with male chorus in march tempo, in praise of the show's major locale, "The Big Back Yard," complete with baritone's wordless descant over men's main strain, and ladies at the close. Good old Romberg. John and Rosie try to mend fences in "April Snow," their third and least interesting duet, whose at any rate intimate feeling is eradicated by more Irish comedy, as the two fathers and Rosie try to enlighten Bessie about "it" in "The Birds and the Bees." For a scene change, Bessie keeps the audience occupied with a specialty dance to an organ-grinder's solo. It's atmospheric, true, but it's awfully pre-*Oklahoma!*.

Worse yet, the story simply collapses at this point—just when it should be tightening up. At the comparable moment in *Carousel*, the two romantic plotlines—Billy and Julie; Carrie and Mister Snow—undergo extremely drastic development, as Billy becomes involved in an attempt to rob, and even murder, one Mr. Bascombe, a Mister Snow figure, in effect. Thus, the character interplay and the sociological undercurrent meet violent confrontation, virtually stabbing at each other as Jigger attempts to knife Bascombe and Billy uses the knife on himself.

Up in Central Park has the social background and, somewhat, the motivated characters, but it never blends them meaningfully. Tweed is a cardboard villain, with none of Jigger's sociopathic intensity or manipulative finesse. John and Rosie make it up with little ado, almost as if they had glanced at the clock and seen that it was time to wrap up the romance with a reprise. The spendthrift Todd did at least throw a novelty onto the stage at the finale, set at the bandstand in the Mall: a fully uniformed, real-life, playing band for a last runthrough of "The Big Back Yard." To top *that*, Todd sent the critics and selected first-nighters in hansom cabs to a midnight supper with the cast at Tavern-on-the-Green.

"As big as its namesake," declared Lewis Nichols in the *Times*. But "pretty dull." Most of his colleagues thought it a lot better than that; but it wasn't reviews that sold the show to an adoring public. It was the nostalgic American thing, the Mike Todd PR thing, the Big Ballet thing, the new-moony-Sigmund-Romberg-hooked-up-with-sassy-Herbert-and-Dorothy-Fields thing. It was the mid-1940s, when the wrong musicals were all terrible but the right ones were extremely popular, despite their flaws. In other words: you didn't have to write a great musical to score a huge hit. All you had to write was a *new* musical, one In the School of the Revolution. Drop your first-act curtain on No Music, and you Had Something.

Black shows, too, looked to nostalgic subjects. *Memphis Bound!* (1945) actually took place in the present, but its tale of a showboat troupe staging *H.M.S. Pinafore* had a nineteenth-century spirit. Bill Robinson took above-the-title billing, Avon Long (Sportin' Life in the Cheryl Crawford *Porgy and Bess*) was strongly cited below the title, and the original Porgy in DuBose and Dorothy Heyward's play that was the source of Gershwin's opera, Frank Wilson, was also on hand. Billy Daniels, Sheila Guys (later Guyse), and Thelma Carpenter, each of whom later distinguished him- or herself in at least one other black musical, filled out an impressive card. And, as always in black shows, the dancing ensemble was primed to dazzle, under choreographer Al White.

Something more: *Memphis Bound!* was not merely about a performance of *H.M.S. Pinafore*, but mostly *was* a performance of *H.M.S. Pinafore*. The score was credited to Don Walker (one of Broadway's top orchestrators) and Clay Warnick, but it was more truly a combination of pure Gilbert and Sullivan, adulterated Gilbert and Sullivan, and original work. Thus, "The Nightingale, The Moon and I" sang right off the *Pinafore* sheets and "Growin' Pains" was brand-new, albeit in the Duke Ellington mode. Well, *here's* talent: Bill Robinson, Avon Long, and the virtual founders of the English-speaking musical. But Albert Barker and Sally Benson's book was terrible. Sample joke: "Remember, I am a ranking star!" cries one actor; and the comeback is "You are rank, all right, but you ain't no star."

By curious mischance, exactly a week after *Memphis Bound!*'s opening came another *Pinafore* retread, this one written and directed by George S. Kaufman, with Shirley Booth, William Gaxton, and Victor Moore. *Hollywood Pinafore* (1945) was even worse than *Memphis Bound!*, which at least had the vitality (and stereotypical humor) of the black musicals of the 1920s. What *Hollywood Pinafore* had was Moore as Sir Joseph Porter, a movie mogul; Gaxton as Dick Live-Eye, an agent, sneaking into a bit of *The Pirates of Penzance* for "An Agent's Lot Is Not a Happy One"; and Booth in the Buttercup role as gossip maven Louhedda Hopsons. Puns! Stupid puns! The score was faithful to Sullivan, and even the Big Ballet, "Success Story" (choreographed by Anthony Tudor), was drawn from other Gilbert and Sullivan scores. But the normally droll Kaufman here turned feckless. Sample joke: "What's a naturalist?"* asks someone; and the answer is "One who behaves naturally." *Memphis Bound!* was a sad failure, but *Hollywood Pinafore* was a ghastly bomb.

One nostalgic black show, *St. Louis Woman* (1946), held on in memory because of its outstanding Harold Arlen–Johnny Mercer score. The superbly imaginative Mercer, a poet of the everyday, wrote seven Broadway shows without scoring a single hit (usually because of book problems, as here). Arna Bontemps and Countee

---

* A forties euphemism for "nudist."

Cullen wrote the libretto, based on Bontemps' novel *God Sends Sunday*, on the black subculture of late-nineteenth-century St. Louis. A first mistake was the authors' reliance on atmosphere rather than plot and on breaking the evening into three acts, which sapped the narrative energy from an already enervated storyline.

This is a three-couple event: Della (Ruby Hill) and jockey Li'l Augie (Harold Nicholas); Della's castoff lover, Biglow Brown (Rex Ingram), and *his* castoff Lover, Lila (June Hawkins); and comics Butterfly (Pearl Bailey) and Barney (Harold Nicholas' brother and dancing partner, Fayard). The last couple covers scene changes with songs in typical forties style, while Biglow menaces Della and Li'l Augie. But that's nearly all that occurs: not enough for a musical. It's a favorite joke that *Oklahoma!* is merely about Who Takes Laurey to the Dance—but *Oklahoma!*'s script relentlessly shifts plot direction as the central triangle positions and repositions itself, the second triangle gracefully dissolves into a couple, and the social background ever more strongly asserts itself.

St. Louis Woman is about Who Takes Della to the Dance—the Cakewalk Ball, actually—and that's all it's about. The social background of ghetto St. Louis highlife is no more than background. Moreover, the Della–Augie–Biglow conflict comes to a climax too violent for the rest of the show:

> BIGLOW: (*to* DELLA) Every man has the right to beat his own
> woman. You left me; I ain't left you.

He does beat her, but Augie intervenes, just as Lila skulks on with a gun to shoot Biglow. As he falls, thinking himself *Augie's* victim, he puts a curse on Augie's riding luck, which is supposed to provision the third act's plot playout when Della guiltily leaves Augie, hoping thus to defeat Biglow's curse. Then she simply changes her mind and returns to him, and his luck holds. It makes for a rather empty third act.

A second mistake was letting the set and costume designer, Lemuel Ayers, also direct this difficult show. He was replaced in Boston by *Oklahoma!* and *Carousel* wiz Rouben Mamoulian; you see how, again, these two titles overwhelm all that follows. Mamoulian could do little to improve the composition, but he did create some nifty tableaus, his stock-in-trade. The show took off in darkness, with a spotlight on a trainer named Badfoot (Robert Pope) polishing a bridle. A bit of song led to Badfoot's coming downstage to sing "Li'l Augie Is a Natural Man." Then, as Badfoot said, "Maybe I ought to tell you what he's doin' now," the backdrop rose on Biglow's honky-tonk filled with people frozen in place, the only motion the smoke filigreeing up from their cigarettes. A shocked and wonderful moment as the audience takes in Darktown's Saturday night finery, then a burst of music as the stage comes alive.

St. Louis Woman was one big burst of music, with Arlen and Mercer utterly conjoined in the feel of a one-of-a-kind show. A funeral scene and the vaguely Crown-like Biglow reminded some critics of *Porgy and Bess*. No way. With its swaggering vamps and matter-of-fact colloquialisms—"Come Rain or Come Shine," the main love duet, is virtually concocted of clichés—this score recalls nothing. Pearl Bailey, in her Broadway debut, was the cast's standout, armed with two solos in what was to become her trademark style of Slow and Lazy, with Plenty of Space for Ad Libs, "Legalize My Name" and "It's a Woman's Prerogative (to change her mind)." But Della and Li'l Augie each had an ideal establishing song, her "Any Place I Hang My Hat Is Home" and his "I Feel My Luck Comin' Down." And of course the Nicholas Brothers, specialty dancers in Hollywood musicals almost since infancy, had their turn, in "Least That's My Opinion."

It's the same sad story: if the score were all that mattered, *St. Louis Woman* would have succeeded. That old canard about the soul of musical comedy being "music and girls" never seemed more wrong; no one knows what the soul of musical comedy is. Maybe it changes from show to show. *St. Louis Woman* was also short on dancing, despite having two choreographers, ballet's Anthony Tudor, replaced by MGM's Charles Walters. A 1998 Encores! concert staging at New York's City Center, with Vanessa Williams, Stanley Wayne Mathis, Charles S. Dutton, and the very fetching Yvette Cason (in Bailey's role, with refreshingly faster tempos), alleviated some of the 1946 problems by rebreaking a very cut-down script into two acts and emphasizing a production number, "Cakewalk Your Lady." Still, Helen Goldsby's grimly stalking Lila revealed how limited this character is, except in her songs, "I Had Myself a True Love," so extravagantly bluesy that it sounds like the center of the show, and, cut in 1946 and here restored, "I Wonder What Became Of Me."*

The songs and the staging were *St. Louis Woman*'s glories. As the show reached finale, the entire cast (except, of course, the by-then dead Ingram) posed for a photograph and, in the style of the 1890s, had to stand immobile before the camera's open shutter, thus mirroring the freeze that launched the show's first big scene. Such lovely touches made some theatregoers strong partisans of the piece, and it became one of the first of the modern-day "cult flops," the kind of show its supporters never tire of mentioning. For many years, meeting Harold Arlen in some social context, strangers would say, "When are they going to revive *St. Louis Woman*?" But Arlen didn't revive it: he recomposed it, as a "blues opera" called *Free and Easy* (after the first line of "Any Place I Hang My Hat Is Home"). It appears to have been staged but once, in Amsterdam in 1959.

Of all the nostalgic Americana shows, the most successful after *Oklahoma!* and *Carousel* was not a musical play but a musical comedy and not an ensemble show but a star turn. It was a Rodgers and Hammerstein show, but they didn't write it. They produced it: *Annie Get Your Gun* (1946).

Some readers may find this baffling: Rodgers and Hammerstein moving in on Mike Todd territory? But there were predecessors in George M. Cohan, Vincent Youmans, and Irving Berlin (a silent partner with Sam H. Harris). Anyway, Rodgers loved the theatre so much that he became a producer simply to be near his inamorata; and he and Hammerstein had it in mind to drop the Theatre Guild from their masthead, so to say, and present their shows

---

* Goldsby was particularly hampered on the Friday night of the 5-performance run, in the shooting scene that originally ended Act Two. Goldsby's gun failed to discharge, but Dutton crumpled all the same, leaving the audience to surmise that he was expiring of a heart attack. One doesn't get a lot of those in musicals. What Goldsby *should* have said, before her precipitous exit with the recalcitrant gun, was "Good! The silencer worked!"

themselves. And, given that they wrote but one show every two years, it made sense for them to produce other writers' shows as well, to keep their production office occupied.

Well, of course, one thinks—they'll present a string of musical plays to secure their hold on their new colony, Broadway. No: except for *Annie Get Your Gun*, they produced only straight plays, most notably *I Remember Mama* (1944) and *Happy Birthday* (1946). Both enjoyed very long runs, and *Mama* went on to a supreme film version with Irene Dunne and even a television series, with Peggy Wood. Nevertheless, *Annie* was Rodgers and Hammerstein's outstanding production written by others: not only because it was the most expensive musical yet seen, not only because it ran three years (even longer in London), not only because it gave the Queen of the Musical, Ethel Merman, her breakthrough role from caricature into portrayal, not only because its score almost immediately enjoyed a popularity to rival that of, yea, *Oklahoma!* itself, but mainly because it marked musical comedy's transformation by the musical play.

We've seen this already, of course, in *Bloomer Girl*'s Agnes de Mille and social panorama and in *Up in Central Park*'s formal tinkering and semi-serious look at political corruption. These are musical comedies with a musical-play flavor. *Annie Get Your Gun* presents a different case, for while it, too, is a musical comedy, it hasn't the remotest hint of the musical play. However, when we set it next to major musical comedies of the early 1940s—*Louisiana Purchase*, say, or *Let's Face It*—we find in *Annie* an emancipated genre. It is not suddenly adult and idealistic. Yet it's more than "music and girls." It's rational, consistent. And it doesn't need Agnes de Mille or formal novelties to be so. It's not musical comedy turning into another form: it is simply correcting the mistakes long inherent in its own form's traditions. To put it another way, it's musical comedy without the de Marcos.

Let us consider *Annie* first as a star show, the latest, one might think, in that line of *Hold On To Your Hats* or *By Jupiter*. Except it wasn't. By the mid-1940s, Ethel Merman was literally the biggest star on a Broadway that reacted to stars with extraordinary warmth. Sure, *Oklahoma!* and *Carousel* didn't have stars; but they made a few. Remember, stars were not merely how a production sold a show; stars were how the audience *understood* a show. Mary Martin would eventually rival Merman, but not before *South Pacific* in 1949. In 1946, Martin was still minor/major enough to head *Annie*'s national company, to tour while Merman reigned in New York.

Merman was major/major, as we've seen; but a curious interlude precedes *Annie*, when Merman signed to play the lead in a musical version of *Rain, Sadie Thompson* (1944). A minor producer, A. P. Waxman, had corralled Vernon Duke and Howard Dietz for the score, Rouben Mamoulian to direct, and Dietz (with Mamoulian) to write the book. How was this tight little piece about a hypocritical parson trying to reform a tart on Pago Pago to be opened up? With jungle dances. And was Merman, so often cast *more or less* as a daughter of joy, really right for a hot-tamale role made legendary by Jeanne Eagels and filmed by Gloria Swanson, Joan Crawford, and (albeit later, in 1953) Rita Hayworth?

As Merman tells it, she left the show during rehearsals because she didn't like Dietz' lyrics in general and one couplet in particular, because it mentioned a brand of lipstick, Mal Maison, that Merman never heard of. Nor did Merman's informal survey of, she said, "between fifteen and twenty-five girls" light a single spark of recognition. "The lyric goes, or I go," says Merman. "The lyric stays," says Dietz. Merman goes.

Okay, stop the music. Merman leaves a show because of a single lyric? A lyric, by the bye, that sounds exactly like the kind of thing that Merman was always happy to sing when Cole Porter wrote it?

Far more likely is that Merman took a good look around her and smelled a bomb. Remember those Three Essentials? *Sadie Thompson* was earnest post-*Oklahoma!* writing, short on fun. The cast was nobody; the one name an expert could place was that of the Trader Horn, Ralph Dumke, the utterly forgettable Captain Andy of the 1946 *Show Boat*. And the score was a problem, lovely in "When You Live on an Island (you love a boat)" and "Sailing at Midnight" but dire in its comedy numbers and lacking strong-sell ballads. Nor, strangely, was there anything like a typical Merman number. June Havoc assumed the role and, indeed, the show bombed.

So Merman wasn't just a great star, but a smart one. Her very appearance in a show was a guarantee of quality: she had never been in anything less than a hit, usually a smash with songs by Broadway's most prominent writers. So now we have to consider *Annie* as an Irving Berlin show, because Berlin was in a certain way as unique as Merman. Unlike all his songwriting colleagues in this Golden Age, Berlin alone kept open a pop shop. Yes, he wrote for both Broadway and Hollywood, but what he mainly did was write songs. You know, like "Alexander's Ragtime Band" and "What'll I Do?" and "Blue Skies." The other guys wrote shows; Berlin wrote music. As an immigrant from eastern Europe, an early proponent of the dance craze in American song, a sharp master in the art of revue scores in revue's heyday and movie scores when the talkies came in and the movie musical was being invented, Berlin seemed a kind of pop icon, very famous and very central. Yet he had written only three book shows when he set to work on *Annie*—at that, shows of the Aarons–Freedley school. Remember how casually *Louisiana Purchase* dealt with character and believability.

Annie's script was the work of Herbert and Dorothy Fields, musical comedy journeymen but suddenly now, in the mid-1940s, Rodgers and Hammerstein adherents. And of course Rodgers and Hammerstein were producing. "Shouldn't this be a country score?" Berlin doubtfully asks Hammerstein. "What do I know about country music?" Hammerstein ponders sagely, then says, "Just drop the 'g' off of words ending in 'ing.'" Like "Doin' What Comes Natur'lly."

It worked. Berlin's "country" sound took in the boogieing "Moonshine Lullaby," Merman's solo backed by a trio of black Pullman porters; the pointedly stupid harmonies of "Natur'lly"; and the vaguely ethnic "I'm an Indian Too." Otherwise, it was the typically melodious Berlin grabbag of go-everywhere tunes—except this time he really dug into the script. Not that this hampered his lifelong facility. He simply lifted his lyric hooks and character profiles *out of* the script instead of pasting pop tunes *onto* the script, creating his most distinctive but also most popular score. He tossed off what became the American entertainer's anthem, "There's No Business Like Show Business," blithely began "I Got the Sun in the Morning" on a C diminished seventh 6/4 chord, sired the mother of all challenge duets in "Anything You Can Do," and essayed a ballad, "The Girl That I Marry," of such purity that it utterly disarms criticism.

Berlin's major assignment was the reinvention of Ethel. Heretofore, her customary numbers identified her as tough urban broads, but Annie was a rural kid with a gift, her unerring marksmanship. A typical Merman entrance would be timed to a risqué joke or a line of biting slang. In *Annie*, Merman entered having unwittingly shot a bird off a woman's hat. Later, her comically slackjawed look of infatuation in her meeting scene with her vis-à-vis, Frank Butler (Ray Middleton), established a new concept of Merman, all unknown to the ways of love. So this directly led to a new kind of Merman comedy song, correcting *Panama Hattie*'s "I've Still Got My Health" and "I'm Throwing a Ball Tonight" with "You Can't Get a Man With a Gun," so . . . well, yes, *country* that its vamp sounds like a Hatfield stalking a McCoy. Then, in her first duet with Middleton, "They Say It's Wonderful," Merman truly hit a new note, so hesitant and innocent after all those Cole Porter penthouse torch songs. Annie had a torch song, too, "I Got Lost in His Arms," of a touching vulnerability and not the sort of thing you'd sing in a penthouse.

No, "I Got Lost in His Arms" opens the second act on board an ocean liner, when Annie is separated from Butler because his ego can't handle her superiority with a rifle. Oddly, only three new numbers follow it in the entire second act: the first act has eleven. But the long first act was an inevitable outgrowth of the Rodgers and Hammerstein influence on narrative structure: exposition, development, conflict, then an intermission, then pacification. Using very round numbers, forties musical comedy tends to seventy-minute first acts and fifty-minute second acts. Shows under The Influence run to hundred-minute first acts and fifty-minute second acts, putting a tremendous strain on the first-act's entertainment. Clearly, it must be filled with strong characters and plenty of background color.

Annie isn't. It has two strong characters and almost nothing else. The background is oldtime America, but only in a general way, though the backstage material of the wild west rodeo show adds some color, especially in *Annie*'s finale, in which the entire cast posed before a giant poster advertising the merged Buffalo Bill and Pawnee Bill shows, featuring Chief Sitting Bull and starring Frank and Annie, the principals set into the poster in cutouts. Then, too, Sitting Bull and his Sioux bring in some frontier atmosphere when they adopt Annie into their tribe as "Little Sure-Shot." The other characters are no more than functional: a pair of comic kibitzers from the rodeo show (Marty May, Lea Penman) and the time-honored second couple (Kenny Bowers, one of the "three men on a date" in *Best Foot Forward*, and Betty Anne Nyman), who cover scene changes with "I'll Share It All With You" and "Who Do You Love, I Hope?" This duo was so inconsequential that later, when stage technology allowed for instantaneous set changes, a 1966 Lincoln Center *Annie* revival with Merman simply dropped the pair from the script.* This pleasantly shortened the first act for an age that no longer enjoyed three-hour theatregoing; but now the second act was a little skimpy. So Berlin wrote the last hit of his life, "Old Fashioned Wedding," one of his trademark quodlibets, with a romantic chorus for Frank and a naggy one for Annie, capped by the pair in combination and an encore or two.

Among the nothing else that *Annie* features besides its two central players is a complete lack of surprise in its musical dramaturgy. *Oklahoma!* and *Carousel* in particular emphasized that a unique show must begin uniquely—and we've seen this countless times since. In *Guys and Dolls, The Music Man, Cabaret, A Little Night Music, A Chorus Line, On the Twentieth Century, My One and Only, The Mystery of Edwin Drood, Rent, Titanic*, we look for the smart show that makes instant lasting contact.

Once more, *Annie* doesn't. It opens picturesquely in a bland sort of way, on a lawn outside a hotel in Cincinnati, to the usual musical noodling. Action: the wild west gang irrupts onto the scene, leading the male kibitzer into the first number, "Colonel

---

* They were restored, in one of many ennervating revisions, for the 1999 revival with Bernadette Peters. The two were, if anything, even more inconsequential than ever.

Buffalo Bill," which is simply his spiel with choral perquisites. It's the kind of thing one might have heard in a thirties show.

So, in all, *Annie Get Your Gun* wasn't a musical play, but a musical comedy: silly and impulsive rather than rich and questing. Still, it was almost always true to itself and to its characters. *That* was where musical comedy so often went astray, untrue: in seeking the easiest entertainment rather than the correct one. Berlin slips here and there in *Annie*'s lyrics, giving her such words as "furrier" and the French "sou" that are culturally beyond her vocabulary. Remember, folks are dumb where she comes from.

However, at heart, *Annie* honored musical comedy by giving it the rightness of the musical play—and Rodgers and Hammerstein honored *Annie* with a Big Production. The playbill set apart fifty-four characters by name or description, and Jo Mielziner's sets were so grand that while they were being hung the over-structure of the Imperial Theatre showed signs of collapsing. Having had Word From Boston that New York was about to receive one of the biggest hits of the age, the town had to hold its horses while *Annie* spent an emergency two-week layover in Philadelphia and the Imperial underwent restorative surgery.

Finally coming in on May 16, 1946, *Annie Get Your Gun* turned out to be one of those shows that some critics take for granted. All the reviews were good, but a few struck odd poses—Louis Kronenberger thought that, "of the real songs, only one or two are tuneful." (Real songs? What's a fake song?)* Nevertheless, the public kept the show going for 1,147 performances, making it, at its closing in March 1949, the second-longest-running book musical in Broadway history, *Oklahoma!* being the first.

Thus, the very conventional yet up-to-date, reformed Rodgers and Hammersteinian *Annie*, so typical of forties trends, also typifies the new ability of hit musicals to go for huge runs where

---

* Actually, *Annie* does have a flaw, though certainly not in the score. Three years after *Oklahoma!* had made imaginative dance the Fourth Essential, Annie made do with the hoary dance-after-the-vocal hoofing, plus one Big Ballet, for the Indian adoption ceremonial. But then, it's the musical play that seeks *clarity* in dance. Musical comedy seeks *zing*.

record-holders had been lasting around fifteen months for decades. Of course, the theatre's economic recovery in the late
1930s created straight-play marathons in *Tobacco Road* (eight
years), *Arsenic and Old Lace* (three-and-a-half years), and *Life
With Father* (eight years, mostly in the 1940s), not to mention
the goony revue *Hellzapoppin* (three-and-a-half years). But these
were one-set, small-cast plays with a relatively small running cost,
and *Hellzapoppin* compares with the average musical as a kazoo
and a pair of finger cymbals compare with Mahler's Eighth Symphony. For a show like *Annie* to last three years, with its gigantic
cast, populous stage crew, and the highest-paid performer in musicals—who stayed with the company, remember, at full salary,
for the entire run—tells us just how imposing the Big Show had
become.

Where *Annie* proved most successful, however, was as an ex-
port. It's not just that the London *Annie* (a replica staging in 1947
with Dolores Gray and Bill Johnson) ran even longer than the
Broadway original and at a much larger theatre, the Coliseum
(where the English National Opera now plays). It's that the so
nostalgically American *Annie* turned out to be far more universal
in appeal than *Oklahoma!* and especially *Carousel* in Europe,
South America, and even the Far East. Of course, the two earlier
shows are bound up in national folkways, while *Annie* relates very
loosely to its setting. How is a public to appreciate *Oklahoma!*
without comprehension of the thesis (let's herd cows anywhere
we choose), the antithesis (farming depends on property lines),
and the synthesis (so much for you, and so much for me: democracy)? What's *Carousel* without the American's instinctive understanding of the crushing placidity of the New England burzhui?

Well, they're musical plays. *Annie*, a musical comedy, charms
anyone. It's about a girl and a guy. Along with *Kiss Me, Kate*,
Annie Get Your Gun remains by far the most successful forties
musical in global appeal.

Interestingly, the current trend in the American film to gross
grandly worldwide by giving up literacy and cultural honesty never
infected the musical. Some shows were conceived so parochially
that even a national tour seemed unlikely. Our next chapter fea-

tures a title that in fact took New York by smash but imploded
on the first booking of its tour (after four weeks in a hostile Chicago). This was an era focused not only on Americana, but on
New York City, where people talk fast, know much, and exist as
if life really were a musical comedy.

6

The Dance Musical

Here's another view of the wartime musical: visualize an escapist low-class audience of soldiers trying to impress their dates with the glamor of Broadway, meanwhile lowering standards as they bray at the dumbest jokes and especially anything even faintly smutty. Then, too, there is a sensitive public, anxious about husbands, fathers, brothers, sons in action. There is the usual jingoism, the waving of the flag and the singing of anthems and the flourishing of uniforms.

This is all true, but only part of the story. The dumb and smutty humor was all over musical comedy in the 1930s, when the risqué was "sophisticated" and, also, when Depression-pinched producers would do anything to attract ticketbuyers. And it was less the war than Mayor Fiorello La Guardia's closing of New York's burlesque houses in April 1942 that sent an infusion of low comics and showgirls into Broadway fare. Scarcely two months later, Mike Todd unveiled *Star and Garter*, a revue starring Bobby Clark and Gypsy Rose Lee that lasted 609 performances, one of the biggest runs to that time.

As for jingoism, except for *This Is the Army* and the odd choral number here and there, there was strangely little. The war made itself felt in all those jokes about ration books and Japan, in all the characters suddenly in uniform. *Panama Hattie, Let's Face It, Something For the Boys,* and *Follow the Girls* (and for that matter *By Jupiter*) had few males on view who weren't playing soldiers. But until *On the Town* (1944) there had not been a musical to define America's wartime in its *subject matter.** The previous chapter's trove of Americana was metaphorical: what America means. *On the Town,* a contemporary servicemen's tale, was realistic and self-explanatory: how Americans feel *right now.*

It was set designer Oliver Smith's idea. With composer Leonard Bernstein and choreographer Jerome Robbins, Smith had worked on a short piece for Ballet Theatre (as the American Ballet Theatre was then known), *Fancy Free,* about three sailors on shore leave trying to pick up girls in a bar. Smith thought the premise ideally expandable into a full-length piece, a musical comedy that would serve as the launching opus of the producing office that Smith intended to open with his partner, Paul Feigay.

Maybe Smith was inspired by the fact that *Fancy Free* actually begins with a song, "Big Stuff" (heard on a recording on the bar's jukebox† as the curtain goes up), as if the dance had wanted to burst into song right from the start. Smith planned to carry over Robbins and Bernstein, to be joined by lyricist John Latouche. But Bernstein brought in his friends Betty Comden and Adolph Green, who wrote both book and lyrics.

They were all twenty-somethings, and *On the Town* is a famously youthful work: energetic, innocent, and radiant with hope. These youngsters were invigorating collaborators. Comden and Green not only wrote but played leads. Bernstein thought up some of the lyrics. And Smith's highly mobile sets helped narrate, as when a subway car pulling into Coney Island suddenly split apart

---

* A few passages in this chapter first appeared in my liner notes for Deutsche Grammophon's *On the Town* recording and were extensively quoted in the program given out at the show's 1997 revival in Central Park.

† The number was to be sung by Billie Holiday, but the recorded soloist at *Fancy Free*'s premiere, on April 18, 1944, at the Metropolitan Opera House, was Billie's sister Shirley. Billie recorded the song on the ballet's first recording; whenever the A.B.T. presents *Fancy Free,* we hear it yet today.

to reveal the panorama of a roller-coaster ride at night, its runway lights twinkling like stars.

Not only did Bernstein, Robbins, and Smith retain nothing of the music, choreography, or design of *Fancy Free*; they and Comden and Green turned the original inside out. *Fancy Free*'s sailors are highly competitive; they court women by outdoing each other. *On the Town*'s sailors are supportive friends. One of them has saved the lives of the other two at sea, and they in turn spend the show helping him locate the girl of his dreams. *Fancy Free* is a burlesque. *On the Town* is a valentine. It embraces life, it embraces love, and it embraces lowdown, highfalutin New York. But mainly it embraces the naive determination of three sailors and the women they meet to stuff the adventure of their lives into a mere twenty-four hours.

So it is a carefree but also a desperate show—and this is exactly the quality of music we hear as Gabey (the idealist), Ozzie (the make-out king), and Chip (the tourist) hit the pier in the first scene. The show's opening minutes, starting with one pluck on high strings over a deep and prolonged bass note, conjure up something sudden and chancy yet illuminating—an insight amid chaos, a close-up in a great empty space. It is in fact the Brooklyn Navy Yard at three minutes to six in the morning. As a drowsy laborer yawns through "I Feel Like I'm Not Out of Bed Yet," we get the sense of time standing still all over town.

It will be the last such feeling we get, for this is perhaps the fastest-moving show of its day. Another laborer has been repeatedly asking a man for the time, and as the clock hits the hour—to the man's famous reply, "Aw, *six* o'clock, *will ya!*"—the music jumps into a frenzy as our three heroes leap onstage to plan their twenty-four hours in New York City. The confidently expectant tone of the verse to "New York, New York" ("We've got one day here and not another minute . . .") is utterly contrary to the opening's empty stillness. It is as if the music had given birth: to a strutting cacophony and then, after the vocal, to a capering woodwind canon on the "New York, New York" theme as the traveler curtain of a Typical City Street closed us off in one, the three sailors began their tour, and the audience got its first taste of *On the Town*'s unique musicale: Philharmonic hoofing.

For this is a stew that spills all over itself in warring ingredients: now jazzy, now classical; now zany, now tender; now surreal, now quotidian; now a play, now a ballet. The script takes the form of a picaresque farce unified by certain structural ties (chase sequences in one, as various authority figures pursue the sailors; one abused character's pathetically repeated "I understand"; the three appearances of working-class Flossie and her friend, Flossie forever quoting one-sided conversations with her boss ["Furthermore, Mr. Gadolphin, nylon stockings are not as important as a girl's self-respect . . ."]; and of course the throughline of Gabey's impulsive attempt to meet Miss Turnstiles, Ivy Smith.*

A farce is filled with not only action but eccentrics. Gabey is the only ordinary guy. Ivy is ordinary, too, but she makes her living as a cooch dancer in Coney Island. Everyone else in the show is terminal: the solipsistic Flossie; the alcoholic singing teacher, Madame Maude P. Dilly; the interfering Old Lady who starts the chase by calling a cop when Gabey adopts the Miss Turnstiles poster; a fussy paleontologist named Waldo Figment; Ozzie's date, the impetuous Claire de Loone; Claire's fiancé, Judge Pitkin W. Bridgework; Chip's date, the pushy taxi-driver Brunhilde Esterhazy, known as "Hildy"; her roommate, the awkward Lucy Schmeeler.

The show's one minor flaw is revealed in those names: Comden and Green aren't invariably as funny as they think they are. They can be obvious, especially in the delivery of exposition. The relationship of the three sailors and Ivy's difficult economic situation are telegraphed from front and center. The jokes are hit-or-miss, Madame Dilly forced to get too much mileage out of liquor bottles hidden in the piano and Hildy often less invigorating than overbearing. Still, both score epically, as in:

---

* Only older New Yorkers will remember the promotional placards for the real-life monthly Miss Subways, bearing a photograph and a character sketch. One of *On the Town*'s charms is its blending of the natural with the bizarre, as when a sailor falls in love with a photograph, vows to find her *that day* . . . and does. But it would be for nothing if the show took place in Oz. The show's New York is real, and, unnervingly, its Miss Turnstiles is real as well. One can prove a dream.

MADAME DILLY: Sex and art don't mix. If they did, I'd have
gone right to the top.

or, when Hildy boasts of her cooking skills:

CHIP: What's the specialty of the house?
HILDY: Me.

Only half of *On the Town*'s score suits this rapid-fire hunt-and-
peck action: the vocal numbers. Like the setting and characters,
the songs are sheer pop. True, "New York, New York" is unusually
well-built for a pop tune. But the ballads, "Lucky To Be Me" and
"Lonely Town," are simple melody, "Ya Got Me" is the Latin
rhythm number typical of the time, "I Can Cook Too" is boogie-
woogie, "(I Get) Carried Away" is the opera lampoon that music
buff Adolph Green liked to sneak into his shows, and "Some
Other Time," for all its "quartet" feeling, its subtle part writing,
is Schubertian in its purity.

Then, as always with this show, comes a slashing moment, right
in the middle of this achingly wistful song, delivered as Ozzie and
Claire, and Chip and Hildy, ride out to Coney Island to catch up
with Gabey and his dream girl in the last hour of this *folle journée*.
As the number gains climax in the release of its second chorus
("But let's be glad for what we've had . . ."), the singing stops as
the conductor calls out, "Coney Island—all out." It's an almost
Brechtian moment, hurling us out of the romance as we realize
that this is the Last Stop, the end of romance. So the songs are
simple, but their situations aren't.

Then, too, the extremely elaborate dance music enlarges *On the
Town*'s artistic perspective, gives it its identifying noise. *Fancy
Free*, though still performed today, is not as distinguished. The
two works share some atmosphere, especially in the establishing
music right after "Big Stuff"—but note that this one vocal piece
is generic, another of those ghetto doubles entendres. (Big Stuff
is invited to ride on the woman singer's "gravy train," where the
"door's open wide," the kind of thing Bessie Smith was doing in
the 1920s.) And there is that novelty of a ballet's raising its curtain
on an empty stage populated by one non-dancer (the bartender)
as a jukebox cut lazily spins out.

However, *Fancy Free* is predictable. *On the Town* is out of control, its aesthetic as dizzying as its plot because it uses so many
conventions so unconventionally. The most obvious example is in
its dances. Of course, a musical of 1944 would dance. But this
much? There's almost half an hour's worth, far more than in either *Oklahoma!* or *Carousel*, and it was composed by the show's
composer, not by some dance arranger, in that funky-passionate,
jangly-piano mythopoeia that American classical musicians had
been exploiting for decades. Now it's rustic: Aaron Copland's *Ap-
palachian Spring*. Now it's urban: George Gershwin's *An American in Paris*. In *On the Town*, it's urban but also imaginative, New
York as Neverland, a map not only of how the city looks but how
it feels.

"That Prokofyef stuff," George Abbott called it.* The youngsters who wrote *On the Town* wanted a veteran to guide them,
and Abbott, strangely, agreed to direct the show. It's strange because Abbott made many hits but rather little history. That is, he
preferred shows that exploit convention—however imaginatively—
to shows with crazy music in them. That Prokofyef stuff: edgy,
unruly, powerfully rhythmic and somewhat shrill, like New York
itself. This is astonishly brilliant writing, giddy with sudden, ridiculous fame in "Miss Turnstiles," jazzily elegiacal in the "Lonely
Town" pas de deux, jaunty and then riotous in "Times Square,"
and driven by erotic hunger in "The Great Lover." Moreover, these
dances develop the show's vocal themes with great ingenuity, unifying the ditties with the Prokofyef stuff.

Never before in a musical had such care been taken over the
composition of the dance music. True, Richard Rodgers and Kurt
Weill distinguished themselves in, respectively, *On Your Toes*
(1936) and *One Touch of Venus*. But does Rodgers' "Slaughter on

---

* One odd credit on the production team is that for the orchestrations. Elliott
Jacoby scored most of the nightclub sequence, Don Walker the Chip–Hildy numbers and "Carried Away," and Ted Royal "Lucky To Be Me." But Hershy Kay
arranged virtually everything else—apparently including the ballet music. Bernstein and Kay are credited with the orchestrations, but it is not clear precisely
what the composer scored. It is possible that he simply directed the show's entire
scoring through indications in his manuscript, leaving the actual writing out of
the parts to these others. Kay also orchestrated Bernstein's *Candide* (1956).

Tenth Avenue" or Weill's "Forty Minutes for Lunch" evoke New York as dynamically, *omnivorously*, as Bernstein?

Of course, Bernstein had the advantage in that virtually all of *On the Town* is about not character but place. Or, rather, it functions as two different shows at once: the New York show containing the character show till, at the very end, the shows merge as Gabey gets Ivy: the Character, in effect, conquering the City.

"Imaginary Coney Island—The Great Lover Displays Himself—Pas de Deux" is the title of this sequence. Yes, another dream ballet. But this one has a twist. Unlike the What If? dream ballets in, say, *Louisiana Purchase* and *Pal Joey*, or the Neurosis Revealed dream ballet in *Oklahoma!*, *On the Town*'s dream is really just the climax of a story too short on time to show us what we need to see: the union of Gabey and Ivy. So we get a fantasy.

On the nightclub tour with his friends, Gabey has picked up a doll, dressed in white topped by a red scarf that turbans her head and reaches down across the torso to her waist. Now, as the ultimate dream begins, Miss Turnstiles herself enters Gabey's subway car, a living replica of the doll in red and white. It is not so much Ivy as an image of her: Ivy as Celebrity. This is what makes *On the Town* the ultimate New York City musical comedy. Other New York shows are really just urban shows using a bit of New York flavor—*Irene, Good Boy, Face the Music, One Touch of Venus, Street Scene, Bells Are Ringing, Promises, Promises, Annie* (despite proposing an anthem, "N. Y. C."), *The Life*. Really, almost any list will do. *On the Town* has the New York atmosphere, the New York characters, the New York sights, but it also has the concept of aspiring young people using the cultural capital as an instrument of their destiny. To Gabey, the city is Romance. To Ivy, the city is glamor, fame, that American thing of making it, up from nothing to the top. Today the place of that event is usually Los Angeles; in 1944, it was New York. True, *On the Town* spoofs this notion, for Ivy does not appear especially talented and Gabey's obsession is based on a photograph for PR use by the Metropolitan Transit Authority. From Dante's Beatrice and Faust's Gretchen we come to . . . Miss Turnstiles?

But the story itself is so zany, the characters so blended of farce and sentiment, and the music so varied, that by the last half of Act Two we no longer disbelieve. Gabey's final confrontation with his dream girl is, on the contrary, the beating heart of *On the Town*, all spoof foregone. As Robbins laid it out, the pas de deux was not a make-out party but a love fight, staged in a boxing ring as Miss Turnstiles catches Gabey in her red scarf and forces him to submit.

Again, what makes this show outstanding is not its lack of conventions but its reimagining of convention. Somehow, the classical Bernstein, the ballet Robbins, the fresh Comden and Green, and the commercial hitmaker George Abbott created something Broadway had not yet known: a fresh classical commercial hit. A ballet show. You say *Oklahoma!* and *Carousel* were also ballet shows? But *Oklahoma!* and *Carousel* were not zany musical comedies, and their emotional thrust feels very different from that of *On the Town*. Rodgers and Hammerstein's characters grip one from the start; *On the Town* deviously offers musical-comedy cartoons, only to fill them out realistically. Then there's all that dancing, which in Rodgers and Hammerstein is generally an expansion of what is at least implicit in the script. *On the Town* dances to express what the script doesn't even know about. Look at it this way—the dance arrangements in *Oklahoma!* and *Carousel* are about the *Oklahoma!* and *Carousel* scores. *On the Town*'s dance arrangements are about the imagination that figures out what New York City is.

Yet is there not something incoherent in the warring sound styles of the symphonic ballets and hit-parade vocals? No: for there is always that touch of the classical in the songs, the sound of the Master tickling the rules; and that popular edge in the dances, as when the piano's striding bass of alternating minor and F Major 7 chords ushers in a sexy saxophone solo on the ubiquitous "New York, New York" theme. More precisely, Bernstein affiliated the entire score early in the evening in the number "Gabey's Comin' (to town)," in which Ozzie and Chip coach their shy buddy in the art of the street pickup. Though the three sailors are of equal importance as characters, Gabey's quest is obviously the show's essential content, and Bernstein created for this quest a leitmotif, introduced at the very start of "Gabey's Comin'" in a frisky triplet phrase of strings and woodwinds, sardonically answered by a falling major third on brass and piano.

The motif runs through the show both vocally and orchestrally, like the consecutive rising fourths of "New York, New York." But *that* theme is a go-everywhere hook: the Excitement of the City. The "Gabey's Comin'" theme (really, two themes in one) is dramatic, specific: the American Musical's Unshakable Belief in Romance. Gabey himself sings the second theme at the start of "Lonely Town," and the first theme dominates the second half of the following pas de deux, launches (on bass clarinet) the "Subway Ride," develops into a string theme of keening desire a few minutes later, and turns up, brisk and chipper, in "The Great Lover." Finally, the second theme confronts a melody from "Miss Turnstiles" in the "Great Lover Pas de Deux," creating a musical equivalent of what is happening on stage—the coming together of Gabey and his fantasy.*

On the Town's blending of effortlessly tuneful vocals with densely textured ballet music typifies the show's rich aesthetic: its mating of the absurd and the passionate. Yes, it's smart and spunky; but it's also wise, forgiving, transcendent. It pokes fun at the mating rituals of horny sailors, yet comprehends Gabey's vast yearning for a woman who is an invention of PR. It gives us an enchanted New York, but also a real one, in its rudeness, color, speed. Even the hoary convention of the chase sequences, staged deliberately in an echo of the flickering tumult of the early silent movie, maintains the show's crazy sense of balance. The slapstick is not chance fun but integral, highlighting, through irony, the vulnerable attachments being formed at the show's center. Gabey and his pals are bonding with women they may never see again, so, for all the comedy, something sad dwells at the core of this tale. "When you're in love, time is precious stuff," runs a lyric in

---

* Unfortunately, George Abbott insisted on cutting "Gabey's Comin'," because it stopped the action after the conclusion of the lengthy "Miss Turnstiles" ballet—exactly where Abbott felt the show must *move*. Two recent *On the Town* recordings include it, and stagings have begun to restore it.

"Some Other Time," and the answering line says, "Even a lifetime isn't enough."

As with *Oklahoma!*, *On the Town* sounded like a long shot while it was being put together, and producers Smith and Feigay at first had trouble attracting investors. True, George Abbott was a dean of directors. But he had been suffering through a string of disastrous flops—a Saroyan play that lasted two weeks; a twee Scots fantasy that almost lasted a month; *Beat the Band*, the sole musical in this series; and a one-week comedy called *Sweet Charity* that rose to its peak in a scene in which four society matrons unwittingly get high on marijuana. Then, at least, came a smash, F. Hugh Herbert's comedy *Kiss and Tell*. Still, there was the feeling along The Street that Abbott might have Lost His Touch.

Then, too, Bernstein and Robbins were Wunderkinder of some note, but in strictly classical realms. And the show's cast was made up almost entirely of unknowns: John Battles as Gabey, Sono Osato as his Ivy, Green and Comden as Ozzie and Claire, and Cris Alexander and Nancy Walker filling out the sextet, with Alice Pearce as Walker's amusingly obnoxious roommate, Lucy Schmeeler. Of them all, only Osato was hot news, because of her recently acclaimed dancing in *One Touch of Venus*. Walker, too, had been well-received on her debut, in another Abbott musical, *Best Foot Forward*. But she was returning to New York from Hollywood after an inconclusive three-picture stint at Metro-Goldwyn-Mayer.

It was MGM, in fact, that enabled Smith and Feigay to start rehearsals, paying a quarter of a million dollars for the film rights—about fifty thousand dollars more than the capitalization of most big-budget musicals then. Oddly, the studio bought the show more on a hunch than anything else, for at the time of purchase the completed numbers of the score were either minor ones like "I Feel Like I'm Not Out of Bed Yet" and the "Carnegie Hall Pavane"; a torch number for the nightclub sequence called "Ain't Got No Tears Left" that was dropped in favor of the comic "I Wish I Was Dead"; the lovely ballad "Dream With Me" that was in turn replaced by "Some Other Time"; a boring choral scene to open Act Two, "The Intermission's Great," also dropped; and a few other titles that never made it into the show. Of *On the Town*'s major numbers, only "Lonely Town" had been written, at that in an early version as "Lonely Me."

MGM's investment obviously gave the creative team a lot of freedom. Yet an unusual number of holdover hits, supplemented by new shows, created a booking jam.* That, plus *On the Town*'s veritable festival of obscure first-timers, forced it to settle for Broadway's ultimate hard-luck house, the Adelphi.

Built as the Craig, it was the last of the theatres erected before the Depression contracted the theatre industry. Way off center on Fifty-fourth Street and Seventh Avenue, it attracted only the most feeble bookings, all bombs. Worse, it was a sizable house, suitable for spectacles. Although it survived as a host of the Federal Theatre (Franklin Roosevelt's program to subsidize thespians in hard times), it had never had a hit. Indeed, it almost never had a show.

Even *Oklahoma!* had snagged the desirable St. James. One wonders what the critics were expecting on December 28, 1944, as they trudged the unfamiliar path to this unfamiliar auditorium to one familiar thing: a George Abbott musical stuffed with Nobody Whatsoever. Perhaps they had misgivings—was this a classical *Beat the Band?*—and that's why they were so enthusiastic, for they mainly raved, allowing the show to move to more amenable bookings closer to the epicenter. Few reviewers seemed to appreciate the show's ambitions, however. Louis Kronenberger called it "one of the freshest, gayest, liveliest musicals I have ever seen" and was sharp enough to realize how well Smith's sets empowered the whirlwind plot to keep abreast of itself. "Somehow . . . integral," Kronenberger put it, which is close enough. But Bernstein's ballet music "had no particular distinction"—a judgment comparable to Clive Barnes' later suggestion that the cast album of *Follies* be issued on 78s.

On the Town lasted thirteen-and-a-half months as a town trea-

---

* *Oklahoma!, One Touch of Venus, Carmen Jones, Mexican Hayride,* and *Follow the Girls,* all from previous seasons, had been joined by *Song of Norway, Bloomer Girl, Sadie Thompson, Rhapsody, The Seven Lively Arts, Laffing Room Only, Sing Out, Sweet Land!,* and a minor revue called *Star Time,* all playing when *On the Town* was to open—and four big shows had reserved major houses for the following months, with yet another four titles to follow them.

sure, then, oddly, faded somewhat from the revival repertory even as its reputation remained solid. The City Center never included it in its spring season of classic shows, nor was it given on television in the 1950s, when so many classic forties titles were seen. One problem was the strangely popular MGM film, which vulgarized the property with an almost entirely new score. Another problem was all that dancing—could it be faithfully restored? By 1960, when Bernstein conducted a recording (with four of the original leads and himself, billed anagrammatically as "Randel Striboneen," taking the cameo of Coney Island's Rajah Bimmy), On the Town was legendary but not entirely real.

Then, too, Fancy Free was always around, confusing people who thought it a little On the Town. Why revive a musical whose ballet version is still running? Yet On the Town was revived, off-Broadway at the Carnegie Hall Playhouse in 1959, with Harold Lang, Joe Bova, and William Hickey as the sailors and Wisa D'Orso, Pat Carroll, and Evelyn Russell as their girls.* Joe Layton choreographed, and it was he who staged the London premiere, in 1963, with Don McKay (London's Tony in West Side Story), Elliot Gould, Franklin Kiser, Gillian Lewis, Carol Arthur, and Andrea Jaffee. Neither production re-established On the Town as a worthy perennial, and a superb Broadway revival in 1971, staged by Ron Field, with Ron Husmann, Remak Ramsey, Jess Walters, Donna McKechnie, Bernadette Peters (riding about in a tiny motorized cab), and Phyllis Newman, ran only 65 performances.

Bad notices killed it, but it was in fact one of the most impressive revivals Broadway has ever seen. No one "improved" the book,

---

* Note an important procedural change: Lang was a dancing Gabey. In the 1940s, ballet was still new enough, undigested enough in the overall integration of integrated musicals, to be entrusted to anyone but a ballet dancer. In the original On the Town, Gabey's part in the dream ballet was performed by a dancer, Ray Harrison. In the 1950s, partly because of the emergence of dancing actors such as Gwen Verdon, Helen Gallagher, and Lang himself (in the 1952 Pal Joey), and partly because Jerome Robbins cast West Side Story entirely with an all-dancing, all-singing, all-talking ensemble, characters could no longer drift away as the dream misted in and be temporarily spelled by a ringer. A telltale moment: in one of the last of the official dream ballets, that of Flower Drum Song (1958), Ed Kenney had to play himself, though he was not a dancer and simply moved as gracefully as possible among the terpsichorean cohort.

breast-implanted the score with interpolations, or played a role in inverted commas, commenting upon rather than portraying the characters. It was *On the Town* literally *revived*: vital, big-hearted, and above all what everyone said it was in 1944: new. Perhaps the male leads were on the merely acceptable side, but the women were excellent, knowingly eccentric to balance the three sailors, eccentric but thinking they've hidden it. Everyone loves to call *On the Town* "of its time," but that's true of all popular art. What it also is is universal, a comedy of humors, a parable, a romance, a trip.

Oddly, in Europe the show is a favorite, especially in Germany, where it is regarded as central to our culture. The going translation struggles to accommodate Comden and Green's abundant slang, but the choreographers have a field day with the "Great Lover" dance, stripping Gabey and Ivy to the minimal to uncover what American musical comedy has really been about all along: boy *gets* girl.*

The 1997 Central Park revival could have used a German choreographer. The dances, by Eliot Feld, were strangely pointless, reflecting none of Feld's gifts as a ballet champ. Director George Wolfe smartly reinstated "Gabey's Comin'," exploited the obvious opportunity to add Central Park to the show's scene plot for "Lucky To Be Me," and moved "Some Other Time" from a subway car to a great empty subway station, an interestingly isolating effect (though we did lose the "time-keeping" train conductor). Wolfe chose an unusually youthful cast; but their performances ran to caricature. The enthusiastically received Lea de Laria made Hildy less lovable-tough than sheerly tough, in a funny but not charming performance (though her scatting on "I Can Cook Too" was swank). Worse, the Ozzie (Robert Montano) and Claire (Kate Suber) played the museum scene as lusty freaks. No: she's a man-chaser with a conservative facade that is *always on the verge* of slipping; and he's crudely outgoing, not sex-crazed. As so often today, when the staging staff is too young to know how these

---

* In fact, amid all the chasing and goofing around, all three sailors "score" their dates in the traditional usage of servicemen on leave, though of course Gabey does it in a dream.

shows worked when they were new and disdainful of the musical in the first place, the production becomes dislocated: untrue to what the material represents and unable to become something vitally reinvented.*

Wolfe did take occasion to improve his *On the Town* when it moved to Broadway in 1998. The book scenes continued to be shouted and paused and rumbled, without a trace of the throwaway delivery that forties show biz doted on. (And of which Nancy Walker was a reigning mistress.) But the new choreography, by Keith Young, amended by an unbilled Joey McKneely (though this insider's secret was such open knowledge that bag ladies in Rego Park could be heard discussing it), was now anchored to the story. The first-act finale followed the leads on a travelogue of dives, and "The Great Lover" was played as a nightmare in which High Society in red and black separated Gabey and Ivy till he ran across the stage to fling himself into the air at her for the blackout. A great deal more scenery—the Central Park that backed "Lucky To Be Me" was now a stage-filling postcard—helped place the adventure, and a new Gabey (Perry Laylon Ojeda), Ivy (Tai Jimenez), and Claire (Sarah Knowlton) worked out well. Still, as the bungling of a classic, the show was bad history. Even worse history was the large number of critics' remarking on Wolfe's "decision" to go without the original choreography. Wolfe had no choice, for the original dances are lost: as Robbins himself pointed out when putting together *Jerome Robbins' Broadway*.

Of course, as a musical comedy *On the Town* is harder to restage than, say, *Carousel* or *Brigadoon*. As musical plays, they are protected by powerful characterizations. *On the Town* is character vaudeville: bashful sailor, couch-artist sailor, tourist sailor, cab-driving broad, la-di-da lady with hidden manias, and so on, right down through supporting lead Madame Dilly on to Flossie, Rajah Bimmy, and every other person on stage. *On the Town* is too deranged to hold together easily. In fact, it's an Aarons–Freedley

---

* It must be one or the other: a stylish resuscitation or a wholly reinstructed edition. The Walter Bobbie–Ann Reinking *Chicago* is an instance of the former, and the Hal Prince *Show Boat* and Sam Mendes *Cabaret* are instances of the latter.

show with an *Oklahoma!* dance plan: nonsense, but artistic nonsense. It's greater than it should be, silly yet magnificent. Is it those dances? That bifurcated music? The sorrow in the joy? *Oklahoma!* is the decade's central show, where the history happened. But *On the Town* may well be the central musical of all time: so rich, so bonkers, so tuneful, so ready to admit how deeply love may cut into one's very being. "The subject matter was light," Bernstein later remarked, "but the show was serious."

Billion Dollar Baby (1945) was not. This "musical play of the terrific '20s" was designed to recall the crazy doings and types that were by then just old enough to get the public's nostalgia going all tingly. Texas Guinan, revue annuals such as the *Follies*, the Charleston, celebrity gangsters, those sobby confessional songs with "recitation" interludes, dance marathons. But something went wrong: Serge Koussevitsky had a talk with Leonard Bernstein during *On the Town*'s Boston tryout.

Koussevitsky, the revered émigré Russian conductor of the Boston Symphony and Bernstein's mentor, was unhappy that Bernstein was throwing time away on pop when he should be Composing and Conducting. Moreover, Bernstein knew that Koussevitsky was entirely right, if not more so. He must abandon Broadway, if only temporarily, for High-Maestro Art.*

So Bernstein was not available for *Billion Dollar Baby*, though Smith and Feigay produced, Comden and Green wrote the book and lyrics, Robbins choreographed, and Smith designed the sets, all as on the previous show. Morton Gould came in as composer, and there's the problem. Like Bernstein, he wrote his own dance music; Gould even wrote his own orchestrations. But this is a dud of a score, busy and jazzy and, yes, intelligent and daringly harmonized. But it's virtually tuneless.

The 1920s is "What'll I Do?," "Fascinating Rhythm," "Indian

---

* Bernstein was indeed to leave his mark as a conductor, most importantly as the archon of the Gustav Mahler Revival. However, even the best of Bernstein's classical compositions—the Serenade, the "Jeremiah" Symphony, the *Chichester Psalms*—are not remotely as distinguished of their kind as are *On the Town*, *Wonderful Town*, *Candide*, *West Side Story*, and the score alone of *1600 Pennsylvania Avenue*.

Love Call," "Yes, We Have No Bananas," "Tea For Two," "Who," "The Best Things in Life Are Free." Gould's music, much too forties in sound to support a dip into the past, gives us the drearily ruminative "Bad Timing," the obsessively blue-noted rhythm piece "One-Track Mind," the worthless "I'm Sure of Your Love"—and those are the three main numbers. "A Lovely Girl (is like a bird)," an onstage number in the *Jollities* revue, with the girls costumed as birds, recalls the 1920s visually but not melodically, though it sings along nicely enough. The title song even provides a taste of twenties pop, though it is heard but briefly, on radio as the curtain rises. (Technically, its title is "Million Dollar Smile.")

Robbins of course got to lay out a Big Ballet on the Charleston, and "Make My Dreams Come True," the heroine's Wanting Song early in the show, provisioned Robbins' sleek send-up of silent-screen matinee idols to Gould's takeoffs on twenties piano styles. But all the chorus numbers were boring, the comic tango "Faithless" was a tango but not comic, and nowhere did one hear the equivalent of "Lonely Town" or "I Can Cook Too," much less a "Some Other Time."

The cast was better than the composition. The heroine, Joan McCracken, was one of the musical's treasurably odd talents, a dancer with great stage looks and a raucously clear voice that could send lyrics into the farthest rows of the balcony. She hadn't a trace of warmth, but neither did her character, Maribelle Jones, a Staten Islander who schemes to Get There in the very era of Making It. She must rise. She *will* rise. From beauty contest to speakeasy, from Broadway to PR stunt to love and death among the criminal classes, Maribelle rises till she at last marries a billionaire—just in time for the 1929 Crash, which occurs during (and interrupts) her wedding finale.

Clearly, *On the Town*'s people were thinking Different. They would not remake *On the Town*. One clear protagonist, a period setting, a hard-edged story, dance at the service of the narrative rather than in control of it, pure pop sound: this was indeed all different. In *On the Town*, the principals are (or become) devoted to each other. In *Billion Dollar Baby*, Maribelle hooks up with crook Dapper Welch, cheats on him with his bodyguard, Rocky, then turns Rocky in to the cops, who shoot him dead. There was one cliché: another of those dream ballets with a title, this one being "A Life With Rocky," an opportunist heroine's version of "Laurey Makes Up Her Mind."

Billion Dollar Baby's cast was fine. Mitzi Green, the former Hollywood child star famed for her celebrity "impressions," played the Texas Guinan figure, Georgia Motley, in a zesty recreation, armed with two barely acceptable solos, the plangent "Broadway Blossom" and the lively "Havin' a Time." David Burns played Dapper Welch in the middle of a four-decade career that took him from Cole Porter's *Nymph Errant* (1933) in London into the age of Sondheim and Jerry Herman (and on to the Philadelphia tryout of Kander and Ebb's *70, Girls, 70* [1971], during which he collapsed on stage, dying shortly after). The Rocky was William Tabbert, who was to create Lieutenant Cable in *South Pacific* and Marius in *Fanny*. (He, too, suffered a fatal collapse, before my eyes, during a rehearsal for a revue chronicling the history of the American musical, in 1974.) Danny Daniels and Shirley Van danced "One-Track Mind," punctuating the music between the lyrics with their taps, and dancer James Mitchell stepped in for Tabbert's Rocky in the dream ballet.

In fact, the entire show was fine, if one believes some of the critics. "Even better," said John Chapman of the *Daily News,* "than *On the Town*." "More ambitious," said Louis Kronenberger, though he did think it less enjoyable. The reviews were interestingly divided: no one disliked the show, but some couldn't figure it out. Why was it so scornful of its own characters? Was this satire or a miscarriage of craftsmanship? *On the Town* was daffy; this one was *mean*. The *World-Telegram*'s Burton Rascoe got it without getting it: "The music by Morton Gould is stunty without being melodic."

Yes, but the entire show was stunty without being melodic: smart but devoid of feeling, aimlessly parodistic, a twenties setting with a forties sound. Though it was a minor hit, it hurt Joan McCracken badly, for she had been on a comet-like rise ever since her debut as a featured dancer in *Oklahoma!* and her "T'morra" role in *Bloomer Girl*. Chorus in 1943, principal in 1944 . . . now, in 1945, she was starring in a misfire.* *Billion Dollar Baby* was a bad idea well executed, yet it somehow never centered on one great number (like, say, "Once in Love with Amy") or one great dance (like the so-called Mack Sennett Ballet) that kept two other forties shows in memory even when they weren't much revived. A musical can run on jokes and a look when new, but it needs more than that to survive.

---

* The tragically underused McCracken appeared only twice more on Broadway: in the revue *Dance Me a Song* (1950) and, back in a supporting role, in Rodgers and Hammerstein's *Me and Juliet* (1953). Hers is a fascinating story, so forties in her jump from ballet into musicals, like Sono Osato, James Mitchell, and countless others; so bohemian in her marriages, to Bob Fosse but also to Truman Capote's lifelong lover, Jack Dunphy. She died before reaching forty. The curious can catch McCracken on film, as one of the many guest performers in *Hollywood Canteen* (1944) and, more prominently, loud and weird and delightful, in MGM's 1947 remake of *Good News!*.

7

OPERETTA

Operetta culture imploded at the end of the 1920s, when the genre had become so dependent upon lavish production that a Depression economy couldn't sustain it. Still, the 1930s hosted the odd title, and then by the 1940s the classics were continuously showing up for short Broadway runs, usually after an obscure national tour. The year 1943 saw a week's worth of a *Student Prince* with wannabees and has-beens (including *Scandals* dancer Ann Pennington), not only produced by the Messrs. Shubert in their usual thrift-shop ermine but directed by Mr. J. J. Shubert himself. There was also a *Vagabond King* with Met baritone John Brownlee, a *Blossom Time* with early-talkie stalwart Alexander Gray as Franz Schubert, and a *Merry Widow* with Jan Kiepura and Marta Eggerth, in heavily Slavic English, that lasted 322 performances. By far the champ in this field, in the early 1940s, was a new version of *Die Fledermaus* called *Rosalinda* (1942), a fifteen-month smash with Balanchine choreography, staged "after" the famous production that Max Reinhardt had created in Berlin in the 1920s, already brought to Broadway in 1929 by the Shuberts. One rather expects an amazing cast for such a hit, but even experts will recognize only the heroine, Dorothy Sarnoff (later the original Lady Thiang in *The King and I*), possibly the Adele, Virginia McWatters, and the Orlofsky, refugee Oskar Karlweis, a comic in for a contralto. Falke was, believe it or not, the future television star Gene Barry, and a very young Shelley Winters played Adele's cousin Ida, here sensibly renamed Fifi.

So operetta was mostly revivals, and bombs at that, though a classic title hit made it big here and there. These successes seemed to secure public fancy by "removing" themselves from the form, remarking on it rather than presenting it. By camping, even. But why not, when straight revivals so often failed? A perfectly acceptable staging of Oscar Straus' *The Chocolate Soldier* in 1947 collapsed in 69 performances. Balanchine choreography, Mielziner settings, a refurbished libretto by Guy Bolton, and a few further Straus interpolations . . . nothing availed. The cast, though not compelling, had appeal: Keith Andes as the pacifist hero, Frances McCann as the heroine, Billy Gilbert giving his patented stuttering bumbler, Henry Calvin (the future Wazir of *Kismet*) as the Bulgarian captain, and Ernest McChesney as the pompous "hero" whom Andes supplants. The producers even troubled to hire Bernard Hanighen to improve the awful old lyric translations of Stanislaus Stange, in use since the American premiere of *Der Tapfere Soldat* (The Gallant Soldier), in 1909.

Six weeks earlier, Victor Herbert's *Sweethearts* (1913) had returned to Broadway, though this was not so much an operetta revival as a Bobby Clark show. John Cecil Holm expanded the comic role of Mikel Mikeloviz for Clark, but Clark essentially extemporized his bits in rehearsal, doing what he always did in his painted-on glasses with his cane and live cigar. As with most comedians, you loved him or you didn't get it; in a typical gag in *Sweethearts*, Clark entered pulling a cart, got to center stage, turned to the audience, and in his businesslike squeal called out, "Has anyone seen a horse?"

I don't get it. Nevertheless, Clark still had a public, and they made *Sweethearts* a hit. When Clark was offstage, the public enjoyed what remained of the original show; about a prince who loves a laundry maid who is in fact a . . . oh, you guessed? Mark Dawson and Gloria Story played these two, with June Knight and

Robert Shackleton as the vivacious second couple and Marjorie Gateson matching Clark's capers with tough-old-dame shtick. Half the reviews were pans, which usually spelled doom for an operetta, but nothing starring Bobby Clark could be called an operetta. *The Chocolate Soldier* was an honest revival and a failure; this *Sweethearts* was a hit at 288 performances.

The most successful of the operetta revivals was another Herbert show, *The Red Mill* (1906), which opened at the Ziegfeld Theatre in 1945 and was quickly moved down to the more central 46th Street (today the Richard Rodgers) for a total run of nearly sixteen months.* *Sweethearts* is an operetta with an operetta plot; *The Red Mill* is an operetta with a musical comedy plot: about two penniless Americans trapped in Holland who help two thwarted young lovers. But where the 1947 *Sweethearts* built up a minor role into the star part, *The Red Mill*—which contains roles for a star *duo* (originally Dave Montgomery and Fred Stone)—cast two unknowns in the slots, Michael O'Shea and Eddie Foy Jr. Foy, of course, had a star for a father, and was to earn Broadway stardom himself. But in 1945 he was no more than a journeyman. Nor were the production credits or performing support anything to herald in gold leaf. Billy Gilbert directed, which sounds strange: since when was this Hollywood buffoon a director? Aida Broadbent choreographed, Adrian Awan and Walter Isreal designed, Edward Ward orchestrated . . . excuse me, but who *are* these people? At least Fred Stone's gifted daughter Dorothy took the soprano lead and her sister Paula co-produced. And let us note longtime operetta stalwart Odette Myrtil in a cast of principals that was otherwise filled with names out of a phone book: Edward Dew. Ann Andre. Frank Jaquet. Charles Collins (Dorothy Stone's husband).

It sounds like a flop. But one point in its favor was Milton Lazarus' revision of the 1906 book, basically a rationalizing rather than a remaking. Lazarus dropped everything that had dated—the "Dutch" comedy, the crazy little dance following the song capped by a crazy little exit that then has the characters scurrying back

---

* This broke, by 10 performances, *Rosalinda*'s record as Broadway's longest-running musical revival.

onstage during the applause to restart the action, the hero's name (Doris, here changed to Hendrik; in London in 1919 it was Boris, which is even worse than Doris, at least in Holland), one of the more overtly operetta-like ensembles, a stereotypical Italian novelty number, and a load of puns. Lazarus put some earthy bounce into 1906, as in Myrtil's entrance:

> EDDIE FOY JR.: Can I interest you in a trip through the mill, Madame?
> MYRTIL: (*soignée, ironique, moqueuse*) I've been through the mill.

As with *The Chocolate Soldier*, some of the composer's other music swelled the score. The orchestral piece "Al Fresco" was turned into a vocal duet, the piano solos "Badinage" and "Punchinello" were given orchestral versions; and the dancing now favored the forties ensemble rather than eccentric solos and such. But the original show was still there—all there, even unto the typical "Fred Stone special" Act One finale, in which the acrobatic Stone sailed up one of the mill wings, caught the imprisoned heroine in his arms, and sailed down with her to freedom. Stone himself was in the audience on the revival's opening night, beaming (I trust) as Michael O'Shea and Dorothy Stone pulled off the same stunt.

Clearly, what worked for *The Red Mill* was the score, one of Herbert's most enduring, with the Bowery waltz "The Streets of New York," the love songs "Moonbeams" and "The Isle of Our Dreams," the duet with intertwining lines "Because You're You," and the march so long favored by baritones crossing over from opera, "Every Day Is Ladies Day With Me." Certainly, composers of the new operettas could have used such a wealth of melody. Europeans Fritz Kreisler, Emmerich Kálmán, and Robert Stolz all suffered humiliation with, respectively, *Rhapsody* (1944), *Marinka* (1945), and *Mr. Strauss Goes to Boston* (1945). Even Chopin and Tchaikofsky were defamed, in the pastiche scores of *Polonaise* (1945) and *Music in My Heart* (1947).

If Kálmán can't put an operetta over, no one can; what went wrong? Let's try his *Marinka*, an interpretation of the Mayerling incident, in which the Austro-Hungarian crown prince was found dead in a hunting lodge with his (dead) mistress. George Marion wrote the lyrics to Kálmán's music, with a book by Marion and Karl Farkas. It was well produced, under Hassard Short's direction, with choreography by Albertina Rasch and orchestrations by Hans Spialek, so there's more than a little continental experience on the production staff. We hope for something truly *operetta*: exotic, fragrant, melting. And look—the show is booked into the Winter Garden and not the Century, where so many operettas go when everyone expects them to fail.

Marinka's failure wasn't destiny: the show worked hard to flop. *Song of Vienna*, its original title, tells us how out-of-tune it was in a post-*Oklahoma!* age. "Meet me in Mayerling," the chorus blithely warbles. "My Prince Came Riding" is the establishing song of the heroine (*Oklahoma!*'s Joan Roberts). A comic number, Roberts' "Treat a Woman Like a Drum," is in bad taste even for the incorrect 1940s, with its helpful reminder, "Ten or twenty whacks should be the maximum." And the hero (Harry Stockwell) and heroine prepare to expire in "One Last Love Song." We wish.

Actually, in this retelling the lovers do not die, but end spirited away to Connecticut on the Emperor's order. As he explains:

> FRANZ JOSEPH: Leave—and don't waste my time! I have to start concocting a fiction story about you two, which I shall bungle, which nobody will swallow, and which will no doubt lead to a writers' free-for-all, as far as your legend is concerned, for years to come. . . .

Perhaps the authors felt that they had made operetta contemporary in the use of a modern frame—schoolgirls gaga after a drive-in showing of the *Mayerling* film are then told the Real Version by one Bradley (Romo Vincent), who becomes the show's comic, Bratfisch, in the flashback action, and who at last caps the show with an ironic wink as a vision of the two lovers lights up the background. For nostalgia's sake, however, George M. Cohan's ex-wife and former partner, Ethel Levey, put in a cameo appearance, smoking a cigar and leading a leashed bulldog, as the proprietor of the Hotel Sacher.

Oddly, at a time when the operettas kept failing, opera tried to gain a foothold on Broadway. I mean *opera*—Gian Carlo Menotti's double bill of the buffa *The Telephone* and the guignol *The Medium* (1947), Benjamin Britten's *The Rape of Lucretia* (1948), with Kitty Carlisle and Giorgio Tozzi, and Marc Blitzstein's brilliantly dramatized but melodically ill-equipped *Regina* (1949), from Lillian Hellman's *The Little Foxes*. The Menotti and Britten are opera-house pieces, out of place on The Street. But Blitzstein was one of those typically American talents that spans mediums, and here we should pause.

Briefly, though: because *Regina*, even with its bits of spoken dialogue, is truly an opera and not a musical. Still, it was staged and performed mainly by folk associated not with the concert hall or opera house but with Broadway: producer Cheryl Crawford, director Robert Lewis, singers Jane Pickens, Brenda Lewis, Priscilla Gillette, and Russell Nype. Most important, Blitzstein's approach to Hellman was, however faithful, very creative, expanding and tightening the play, always looking for a chance to turn talk into music. It is worth remarking that a host of opera adaptations of dramas—from Robert Ward's *The Crucible* through Pizzetti's *L'Assassinio nella Cathedrale* (Murder in the Cathedral) and Rossellini's *Uno Sguardo dal Ponte* (A View From the Bridge) to Poulenc's *Dialogues des Carmelites*—simply set the spoken text to music.

What Blitzstein sought was something new: music as alchemy. The operas mentioned above were never new. They're old plays plus new music. *Regina* is something new; a play excavated so that music can flood it. Its big first-act party ensemble finds the chorus addressing the audience, as they couldn't have done in Hellman's naturalistic play; and the best number, the so-called Rain Quartet, has no basis in *The Little Foxes*. *Regina* was a reinvention. It's notable, too, that critics didn't find opera aberrant on Broadway, as they had done in the previous decade with *Porgy and Bess*. Reviewing the Menotti evening, Brooks Atkinson noted that the musical play had "pushed the dramatic stage in the direction of ballet and music . . . [so] there is no reason why [Menotti] should not bring music over in *our* direction."

The italics are mine. What Atkinson is saying is that Rodgers and Hammerstein, by installing the musical story as a tight unit, have unleashed music as a power. Yes, dance, too. But the key thing here is that American musical theatre is re-establishing itself at a point somewhere between musical comedy and opera.

That brings us to our old friend Kurt Weill, slightly comparable to Blitzstein, though Weill had vastly greater success in his lifetime and continues to do so today. They meet in Blitzstein's *The Cradle Will Rock* (1937), very much in the line of Weill's *The Threepenny Opera* in both style and politics—and of course Blitzstein translated it for the famous Theatre de Lys revival with Lotte Lenya in the 1950s.

There the resemblance ends. Weill was a melodist and an artist, who happened for various complex reasons having to do with the nature of the precarious Weimar Republic, to have collaborated on artwork with Leftists. Blitzstein was a braying stooge of the Communazi Red Front whose work never succeeded and who is virtually forgotten today.*

Weill enjoyed two smash hits and a number of almost-made-its. *The Firebrand of Florence* (1945) is his one disaster: an operetta so roasted by the critics that it closed after forty-three empty houses. Adapted from Edwin Justus Mayer's play *The Firebrand*, on the doings of Benvenuto Cellini in the last days of the Medicis, *The Firebrand of Florence* had a book by Mayer and Ira Gershwin, with Gershwin also writing the lyrics to Weill's music. Only four numbers were published, and nothing caught on even momentarily—not surprisingly, for the score makes its points not in songs but in gala musical scenes reminiscent of the dreams in *Lady in the Dark*.

For instance, the opening is eighteen minutes of local Florentine color, plot exposition, and a celebration of the volatile, irreverent Cellini (Earl Wrightson), artist, rogue, and lover. In fact, he is not only celebrated but almost executed ("The hanging of the season!" cries a souvenir hawker), getting off only through deus ex machina, a ducal pardon. ("The pardon of the season!") Thereafter Cellini pursues the virginal Angela (Beverly Tyler) while fending off the amorous Duchess (Lotte Lenya, Weill's wife)

---

* *Regina*, which is still performed here and there, usually by opera companies, lasted only 56 performances, despite some admiring reviews. The *World-Telegram*'s William Hawkins likened it to Richard Strauss' *Der Rosenkavalier*.

of the ridiculous Duke (Melville Cooper), an amateur poet also after Angela. For a throughline, the Duke's cousin Ottaviano wants Cellini to assassinate the Duke, but Cellini prefers battle with his natural enemy, Count Maffio. (These two are dueling once again as the show ends.) Throughout, Weill uses operetta's powerful musical structures in his own way, in his unique voice, ultra-modern, of Broadway yet finer than Broadway. He creates operetta out of not bosomy waltzes but bite and seduction.

A five-week failure with a brilliant score and an eye-filling Max Gordon production? Scapegoats must be found, and historians invariably blame the cast. Was the stodgy, inexperienced Wrightson, for all his baritone velvet, an apt Cellini? Who's Beverly Tyler? Wasn't the batty old Brit Melville Cooper simply out of place? Critics slaughtered Lotte Lenya so thoroughly that she temporarily gave up acting in musicals.

Weill himself had wanted Don Ameche, Walter Slezak, and of course Lenya, his favorite performer. Producer Gordon tried Wilbur Evans and Alfred Drake for Cellini and Susanna Foster as the ingenue. But show biz was booming, and everyone was busy. There is no question that, while Gordon was lucky to sign John Murray Anderson to supervise the production, and Jo Mielziner and Raoul Pène du Bois to design it, he did have to compromise on his cast.

But hold. Wrightson and Tyler were singers rather than singing actors, true. However, the Duke in Mayer's original play was Frank Morgan, whom we know from his many MGM roles (not least in the title part of *The Wizard of Oz*) as a dithering-booby comic. This was precisely the type that Melville Cooper specialized in, so how wrong could Cooper have been?

Then, too, wasn't Lotte Lenya not so much miscast as simply too continental for American taste? Today, after her eternal Jenny has become essential in any invocation of Weill's German theatre music, and after a number of spiritedly lurid cameos in movies of the 1960s and 1970s, Americans know how to relish this enchanting hag. However, back in 1945 she was a jolt, perhaps most particularly on her entrance in a closed sedan chair, which she popped out of like a showgirl exiting a cake at a smoker. The reviewers were so unprepared for Lenya and even the very part she was playing that John Chapman thought her solo, "Sing Me Not a Ballad," "would be a wow for Ethel Merman." Oh, please. This is an insinuating number, a hot tease in your ear. Maybe Lucienne Boyer or Liane. Even Zarah Leander. But Merman?

I think it was not the cast that sank *The Firebrand of Florence* but the clumsy script. The second worst thing about it is its lack of genuine story. Everyone runs around like crazy, but nothing happens; no one learns anything. The *worst* thing is the banal wording, weighty with decades of operetta makeweights. Cooper's entire role is irritatingly stupid, as he mixes up his words. Complimenting Angela's "virgin style," he instead comes out with "sturgeon vile." After talking his way through "A Rhyme For Angela," he maintains a ghastly running gag:

> PETITIONER: My Lord, I beg you to pardon my brother!
> DUKE: What's he done? Zangela . . .
> PETITIONER: He shot his mistress. But it was an accident!
> DUKE: Accident? Cavangela . . .
> PETITIONER: Yes, he was aiming at his wife!

It's a naughty show, at least. (The out-of-town title was *Much Ado About Love*.) The first-act curtain finds Lenya and Cooper sourly regarding each other on a terrace as their expected dates— Wrightson and Tyler—tryst. But it's too silly when it isn't naughty and silly even *while* it's naughty. It's the kind of show that deserves a complete recording but should never be revived.

Weill's following work, *Street Scene* (1947), was more of the same: another adaptation of a play from the 1920s, with the playwright (here Elmer Rice) on hand to see his piece ennobled by Weill's genius. But where *Street Scene* also failed commercially, it has lasted. Both as Rice's play and as adapted into "dramatic musical" (so it was billed), *Street Scene* is, literally, its title: an action set entirely "on a sidewalk in New York City" in front of a brownstone.*

* Why the vague location? For universality? (Rice's play is similarly unclear as to neighborhood, citing only "a mean quarter of New York.") But the piece unmistakably takes place in the East Sixties, for at one point a young resident of the brownstone is seen after graduation from Julia Richman High School (we even hear the alma mater), still in use, on Second Avenue between Sixty-seventh and Sixty-eighth Streets.

Well, this is no operetta, surely. Operettas are set in exotic places—ballrooms, or at least Poland. *Street Scene* is made of working-class life. So we see, as the "contents" of the brownstone are gradually made intimate to us: the Maurrants (Norman Cordon, Polyna Stoska), he so brutal and she so crestfallen; their kids (office worker Anne Jeffreys, schoolboy Peter Griffith); the Jewish family (father Irving Kaufman, daughter Norma Chambers, son Brian Sullivan), the son in love with Jeffreys; the young couple anxiously awaiting their first-born; the Italians, the Irish, the Germans, the Swedes, the black handyman; and so on. The building becomes a box of stories as Jeffreys and Sullivan seek to bond; as Jeffreys' frustrated, romantic mother also seeks a bond, adulterously; as the other women gleefully gossip about the affair; as Maurrant shows up to catch his wife and her lover together and murders them. All this within a span of twenty-four hours, as we look on.

The swashbuckling and humorous *Firebrand of Florence* could easily dazzle with music, for the lack of storytelling freed it to sing about . . . well, Florence, rhymes, sex, laughter. Anything. *Street Scene* must limit a composer: to narrow-cultured nobodies getting nowhere. Yet *Street Scene* is Weill's masterpiece—and, incidentally, his first American score to throw off, to the last note, any echo of the jagged sound that he invented for his German works.*
But then, this so very American subject matter—immigrants and their children battling the destructive forces of poverty and intolerant ignorance—marked the culmination of the immigrant Weill's determination to Americanize his style, a move that would take him to the one-act, folk-song pastiche *Down in the Valley* (1948), and to an adaptation of Mark Twain's *Huckleberry Finn*, with Maxwell Anderson, aborted on Weill's death, in 1950.

Some writers accuse Weill of selling out to the American Bitch Goddess in virtually all his work for Broadway, decrying it as greatly inferior to his German catalogue. This is usually said by

---

* There is one Weimarisch memento, the use of a page or two of Weill's music for Erwin Piscator's pageant *Konjunktor* (1928) to open *Street Scene*'s second act. Originally a baleful nocturne, it has in its new context a "dawn and church bells" quality.

people who hate musicals in the first place, or by those who resent
Weill's abandonment of political art after *Johnny Johnson* and
Knickerbocker Holiday in the 1930s. How can one blame Weill
for being the Weill that *he* wanted to be; and how can anyone
think of a faithful adaptation of Rice's ultra-grim *Street Scene* as
a sellout?

In fact, Weill's *Street Scene* is less an adaptation than Rice's
script set to music by Weill and lyricist Langston Hughes (and an
unbilled Rice). Of all plays made into Broadway musicals, *Street
Scene* underwent the fewest changes I know of. *Oklahoma!* and
Carousel, while retaining much of their source works, modified
characters, added scenes, and even changed the spirit of the originals—nothing in *Green Grow the Lilacs* or *Liliom* anticipates
Oklahoma!'s title song or *Carousel*'s ecstatic finale.

Street Scene went unchanged, save a bit here and there: the
loss of the self-righteous social worker in charge of the evicted
family, the addition of that high-school graduation, to provide
"Wrapped in a Ribbon and Tied in a Bow," a charm tune to
lighten the dark atmosphere. Even the apparently extraneous jitterbug number, "Moon Faced, Starry Eyed," which gave Danny
Daniels and Sheila Bond a dance specialty in a show that otherwise had no formal dancing ("Wrapped in a Ribbon" climaxed in
a brief street prom), caps a scene that was part of the 1929 script.

Is there really music in this moody piece? Adultery and murder?
But what has opera ever been about but that?—and, make no
mistake, for all its dialogue, Weill's *Street Scene* is "an American
opera" (as the published score finally admitted, a year after the
1947 premiere). Virtually every major and minor principal is an
opera-weight singer; the original cast could have sustained an evening at the Met. Soprano Stoska, tenor Sullivan, and bass-
baritone Cordon had sung leads there, and soprano Jeffreys could
have. Even tenor Sydney Rayner, as Mr. Fiorentino, had been a
Met Radames and Turiddu.

That unfortunately made possible the score's one mistaken
number, the "Ice-Cream Sextet," an unmotivated opera spoof that
fails as spoof. It edges *Street Scene* dangerously out of its otherwise consistent tone. This is a momentary lapse, for just as Rice
binds many disparate characters by the simple fact that they live

in one building, Weill gives the building a style in his very sound, sprawling yet constricted, just like the narrative. He does this partly through three ubiquitous *ur-Motiven* of no certain designation, through constant reiterations of vocal melodies, and through extensive underscoring, to bridge the distance between life and lyricism.

It's strange how much beauty Weill found in Rice's play. The supplementary people color in the background: Rice's Scandinavian janitor became black so Hughes could write him the bluesy "I Got a Marble and a Star"; the expectant father chimes in with "When a Woman Has a Baby"; three building women shrill out the evil Gossip Trio, "Get a Load of That." But the leads mark out *Street Scene*'s true action: in Sam Kaplan's tortured "Lonely House"; Mrs. Maurrant's elaborately wishful "Somehow I Never Could Believe," the very center of the work, as she pours out her heart to insensitive listeners; and Rose's response to her boss' lascivious "Wouldn't You Like To Be On Broadway," the idealistic "What Good Would the Moon Be?"

Filling out the quartet of leads, Mr. Maurrant offers the brutally threatening "Let Things Be Like They Always Was." There is no beauty in this tyrannical bigot. Indeed, he murders beauty. But it is interesting that, in Rose's last scene with her father, before the police take him away, Weill set Maurrant's repeated "I loved her, too" to an unmistakable reminiscence of the *Wolfserzählung* theme from Eugen D'Albert's opera *Tiefland* (The Lowlands). A kind of German *Tosca*, wildly popular in the Germany that Weill grew up in, this piece tells of a Mexican shepherd who marries a rich man's mistress, then kills the man when he tries to force himself on the shepherd's new wife. The *Wolfserzählung* ("Wolf Tale") theme first notes his killing of a wolf, but then figures dramatically in the climactic murder scene. Thus, the intruder upon a marriage becomes a kind of wolf, evil, killable. Is Weill trying to reinstruct Rice, encouraging us to see Maurrant as not the attacker but the *defender*? Certainly, Weill did nothing with poor Sankey, Mrs. Maurrant's lover. He doesn't sing a note: and, in opera, the non-singers are of no importance.

"Love and death have gone away together," the chorus sings, in elegy after the murders. *Street Scene*'s house of stories shows us new life given, old life taken. It's the familiar cycle, made ironic by the use of a framing device, "Ain't it Awful, the Heat?," an ensemble number. What could be more cyclic than the seasons—yet what more irrelevant to the fortunes of men and women than the day's weather? Weill's restless introduction to the show eventually finds the curtain rising to a radio's pop tune (an anticipation of "Moon Faced, Starry Eyed"). It's a punishing summer day for residents and passersby alike, styled by Weill's "heat" music: "slow, dragging," a trilling flute over drooping strings, brass chorus, and monotonous tympani, typical of this intricately orchestrated score. A few lines between Mrs. Fiorentino and Mrs. Jones suddenly find the two singing their dialogue as the number evolves and more voices join in, making it a septet.

Oklahoma!'s opening introduces a major character; *Carousel*'s opening jumpstarts the narrative. *Street Scene*'s opening does neither, because no one of its characters is individually major and its narrative isn't as important as how it feels to live in this building. We don't realize how brilliant "Ain't it Awful, the Heat" is till *Street Scene* is ending, after Rose has left the despairing Sam behind in the emotionally strangling "lonely house," the address of not entirely living. Life Goes On is all one says at this point. Even: Vacant Apartments Must Be Rented. As a couple inquires about the evicted family's flat, "Ain't it Awful" starts up again, passersby again dress the stage . . . life goes on, right. And, as the song reaches its conclusion, the orchestra intones one of the *ur-Motiven*, and the curtain falls on the most breathtakingly heartless stage picture till *Cabaret* and *Follies*. As Brooks Atkinson suggested earlier, Weill was Bringing Music in our Direction. Not operetta, but a play that is sung. It was a form that Weill had in fact been working in from the beginning, whatever his critics say. Indeed, *Street Scene* is one of the few great musicals after 1943 that would have existed without Rodgers and Hammerstein.

Song of Norway (1944) existed *despite* Rodgers and Hammerstein. This, too, brought music in our direction, unfortunately with no book whatsoever. This may be just as well, for when the book is on people say things like, "Don't cry, little Grima; it's only a fairy tale, and has a happy ending," or (to Henrik Ibsen) "Come and visit me, Henrik, at my villa in Rome."

"An operetta based on the life and music of Edvard Grieg," *Song of Norway* had no pretensions as a forties musical play, no *Up in Central Park* musical-comedy humor, no *Rosalinda* staging tricks. *Song of Norway* was an old-fashioned, faraway-place, pretty-costumes, one-clown-handles-all-the-jokes, Big Sing operetta. It also had a lot of Big Ballet, by George Balanchine. In fact, *Song of Norway* was virtually a dance piece interrupted by theatre. The endless stream of *faux*-folk ballet is at first dizzying, till one figures out the key: there will be a dance, *one*, every time a ball or festival is in progress; *two*, every time someone mentions Norway; *three*, every time there is a set change; and, *four*, every time there isn't.

But first things first. *Song of Norway* was not a Broadway project; it originated on the West Coast. Edwin Lester, who ran the Los Angeles and San Francisco Civic Light Opera, was an adherent of twenties operetta. In fact, he invented a sub-genre, known as the floperetta: because if it didn't bomb it deserved to. Floperettas almost invariably did bomb, but this time something else happened. Lester conceived a show that would tell the Hans Christian Andersen story to Grieg's music, a true Scandinavian romance. However, Hollywood mogul Samuel Goldwyn had a rival Andersen project in the works, and could have caused legal trouble. (Goldwyn did eventually film the Andersen saga, with Danny Kaye, to a Frank Loesser score.) Now Lester wondered if if he should perhaps tell the Edvard Grieg story, to Grieg's own music.

Fabulous! Except it turned out that there was no Edvard Grieg story. The guy was a minor composer of songs and piano pieces who turned out two warhorses: the Piano Concerto in a minor and the stage music for Ibsen's *Peer Gynt*. He lived and died blamelessly; where's the story? But one Homer Curran worked up a treatment that centered on Grieg and his two childhood friends—his best pal, the real-life composer (here turned into a poet) Rikard Nordraak, and his future wife, Nina. An Italian opera singer comes between Grieg and his friends, Rikard dies, and a repentant Grieg returns to Norway and writes the concerto.

Sensing the mother of all floperettas, Lester carefully selected his ingredients—Milton Lazarus to flesh out Curran's scenario, Robert Wright and George Forrest to wheedle songs out of Grieg's catalogue and to write the lyrics, and Arthur Kay, the Civic's music director, to supervise and orchestrate.* And Balanchine, of course. But maybe the most elemental of Lester's choices was impulsive, tempestuous Irra Petina as the opera diva, for Petina became Queen of Floperetta. She had her rivals—Brenda Lewis was thought more impulsive, Joan Diener more tempestuous. Nevertheless, Petina—a former second-line Met mezzo who sang Carmen on quiet Tuesdays but got shunted into Mercédès for the Saturday afternoon broadcasts—was a marvelous singer, a sharp comedienne, and a star in the grand old sense. A *presence*. The rest of *Song of Norway*'s cast was adequate: nicely musical, but short on oomph. Robert Shafer, who played young Rikard, was so near retirement that, scarcely a decade after, he played old Joe Hardy in *Damn Yankees*. It was Petina who gave the show its energy when Balanchine's corps weren't going into their eighteenth Spring Dance.

Song of Norway needed that energy, for Lester really did order up a bygone piece. The diction is that of the "raiment" school; the comic (Sig Arno) is another of those little European guys who gets pushed around by women, which we're supposed to take as quite the most riotous joke ever; the Norwegian characters sustain folk atmosphere by constantly referring to "trolls"; and everything occurs according to that operetta logic in which, as long as the music makes sense, nothing else has to.

For example, near the end of Act One, at some local pageant, Edvard and Nina decide to get engaged:

> EDVARD: Let's tell them. May I?
> NINA: Yes, Edvard!
> EDVARD: Friends, here is something really to celebrate—Nina has consented to be my wife!

---

* Kay was a phenomenal musician, but, because he worked on the Coast (at first in Hollywood and then for Lester) and not in New York, he is never named on the short list of great orchestrators—Frank Saddler, Hans Spialek, Robert Russell Bennett, Don Walker, Jonathan Tunick, and perhaps four or five others. But listen to the cast album of *Kismet* (another Civic project) and note how Kay makes a Broadway pit sound like a symphony orchestra. *Song of Norway* is even more remarkable for its loving detail—the sparing use of vibraphone, so unusual in theatre pits, or the use, say, of three *soli* violins and harp to bring out a single phrase.

The orchestra swings into a version of that bane of piano students, "Wedding Day at Troldhaugen" (which actually can be useful, as it gets syncopated and thunderous and sounds very difficult, but isn't), as the crowd lets out thrilled noises. Then we get a harmonic transition on the dominant seventh as a big old gal in peasant dress solemnly comes into view.

A MEMBER OF THE ENSEMBLE: Shh! It's Mother Grieg!

And, lo, without even asking, "What's going on?," this woman raises her arms over the kneeling Edvard and Nina and launches a "Hymn of Betrothal." The chorus joins in, Rikard has a short solo addressing the "midnight sun," and the whole thing comes to a sudden stop as Petina storms in to drag Edvard on to the fleshpots of Europe.

On one level, Petina functioned as the antidote to all the quaint stuff, the very notion of a folk betrothal in folk dress led by a vatic contralto. Maybe Petina was *Song of Norway*'s secret. Balanchine, too, was a relief from the nonsense of the book. But what really built *Song of Norway* big was its score. As with the various versions of the Franz Schubert musical that is known in America as *Blossom Time* (1921), there is no way to dismiss a show with music this good.

Of course, Wright and Forrest had a lot to work with. Grieg's output was limited, favoring small works such as songs and piano sketches.* He was a born melodist, no question—but simply to plot a set of lyrics around a bunch of unrelated tunes would not have created a theatre score, and the authors, apparently working closely with Kay, were ingenious at adapting and inventing. They even gave the whole a sense of structure, using that pervasive concerto. Because the evening was to arch inexorably toward a finale for which Balanchine would set the concerto into dance, it seemed logical to draw on the same music for the first two vocal numbers, thus framing the story with the same material, first as song, last as dance. There would be no overture; the audience would hear the famous downward-driving piano figure that begins

---

* Besides the piano concerto, there is the Symphony in c minor, an early work that was performed rarely in Grieg's lifetime and not thereafter till 1981; Wright and Forrest did not use anything in it.

the concerto and about a minute more of the work, whereupon the curtain would rise, prematurely as it were (just as *Carousel*'s was to do later that same season), thus hurling the audience into the action.

But what odd action. We see a group of young people—kids, adolescents, and Rikard—scaling the summit of the Hill of Trolls. It's a haunted place. Here is where North Wind imprisoned beautiful young Norway, and Rikard recounts the tale for us in the first number, "The Legend." It can't be easy to fashion a tenor narrative out of the first theme of the first movement and the last theme of the last movement of a piano concerto (while adding in original themes), but Wright and Forrest created something wonderful here, an opening that breaks a cardinal rule of craftsmanship in the musical: tell the public what the show is about or at least give it a sense of the show's spirit during the first five minutes. Rikard tells us no more than The Legend: Norway mocked North Wind when he came wooing, so he turned her heart to ice and locked her in a cave as a hollow echo, never to be freed till a great minstrel warmed that frozen heart.

Well, okay. But after *Louisiana Purchase*'s attorney warning of the risk of satire, *Pal Joey*'s show-biz loser running through his audition, and Curly's bright golden entrance, this is a puzzling number. It's also a brilliant one, very gratefully written for the singer and restless, moody, pulling off a nifty stunt when the picture of Norway merrily dancing away from North Wind lands just as the merrily dancing strings-and-woodwinds figure from the concerto giggles in.

In a book scene after the number, Grieg and Nina join Rikard, and now comes another number that doesn't tell us what the show is about, "Hill of Dreams." This trio concerns . . . well, this trio. Again, it's beautifully made of beautiful music, impish and loving where "The Legend" was visionary. But that contrast is essential— the two numbers *together* tell us what *Song of Norway* is about: a friendship among three characters, all of whom want one of them, Grieg, to become the voice of his people. *He* will melt Norway's heart, not to mention provisioning the Biggest Ballet in the entire decade when we finally arrive at the concerto. And note that, at the very end of "Hill of Dreams," after the singers have hit their last note, we get one final taste of the concerto-opening theme that launched "The Legend," further binding the two numbers.

Wright and Forrest were this clever throughout the piece. Only Nina's "I Love You" comes straight from Grieg. Everything else is not only adapted but filled out with lovely new strains, especially when the authors reach the release of a song and can't find anything in Grieg that works. A number in Grieg's *Haugtussa* cycle, rippling with the play of brook water, becomes "Bon Vivant," the comic's ode to the life of the *flâneur*, assisted by the chorus, who pull off a stunt at the end as the music fades and they all drift offstage, only to dive back into view for a smashing coda. "Freddy and His Fiddle" has more Grieg, "Now"—the captious lament of the bored soprano—has less. Throughout, Kay made sure that there was plenty of piano, making *Song of Norway* a concerto in itself; "Midsummer's Eve" and "Three Loves," both the romantic waltzes that operetta thrived on, feature Grieg at the piano keyboard. In fact, "Midsummer's Eve" is a musical scene, Grieg playing offstage as the diva hears All About Him from Rikard.

By far, Wright and Forrest's triumph of adaptation was "Strange Music," adapted from that "Wedding Day in Troldhaugen" that summons the "Hymn of Betrothal." This theme is in fact *so* adapted that it is a new work; and the release is entirely original. It's one of the outstanding love duets in all operetta, right up there with "Deep in My Heart, Dear" and "Indian Love Call," and it tells us why operettas constantly bombed in the 1940s. It wasn't that they were operettas; it was that their scores were limp. This score springs.

One odd note: no dream ballet. But then, dream ballets were by the mid-1940s very psychological, and Balanchine wasn't interested in psychology. "Don't act, darling," he would tell his people. "Just dance."

Robert Helpmann choreographed the London *Song of Norway*, in 1946, and it, too, was a hit, though not on the same scale as in New York. There, at 860 performances, *Song of Norway* remains the longest-running outright operetta in history, though it had none of the staying power of the classic Romberg and Friml titles of the 1920s. *The Student Prince, Rose-Marie,* and *The Vagabond King* were given major film remakes in the 1950s; *Song of*

Norway was hiding out in summer tents and at the Jones Beach Marine Theatre, where the concerto ballet could be climaxed with the appearance of a Viking ship on real water.

Yet *Song of Norway* was filmed, in 1970. Seeking a follow-up to the spectacular success of the *Sound of Music* movie, pro-ducer–director Andrew Stone seized *Song of Norway* as potentially comparable: dirndls, European scenery, interpolated puppet-show sequence, and Florence Henderson, Maria in the Rodgers and Hammerstein show's national tour.

The movie bombed, though it has an arrestingly international cast: Toralv Maurstadt, Frank Poretta, Harry Secombe, Edward G. Robinson, Oscar Homolka, and Christina Schollin, with pianist John Ogden filling in as Grieg on the soundtrack. Incredibly, the New York City Opera included the piece in its operetta revivals in the 1980s. By now, we have surely heard the last of it. Yes, it was bringing music in our direction, but in union with a silly story and with wonderful dancing that cannot be reproduced. *Song of Norway* was the exception that proves the rule: operetta was over, because the musical play had absorbed it: *Up in Central Park, Carousel, The Firebrand of Florence, Kiss Me, Kate.* If a musical comedy can sound like Puccini, who needs operetta?

8

FANTASY

It is not clear why fantasy, long considered unsuitable in the musical, suddenly blossomed in the 1940s. It is not even clear why it was thought unsuitable, unless the strong use of it in the musical's nineteenth-century forms made fantasy feel obsolete when American musical comedy began to invent itself circa 1920. Certainly, by 1925, musical fantasies were unheard of. Rodgers and Hart's *I Married an Angel* (1938) indeed included an angel in its cast, but this was less a fantasy than a social comedy with one extraordinary character.

Cabin in the Sky was the first genuine fantasy of this era, with its parable-like atmosphere and warring armies of God and Devil; and *Lady in the Dark*'s three musical dreams suggested what could be done with surrealistic song and dance. Then, too, ballet—now an official obsession—favors fantasy, with its weirdly dumb eloquence. And presiding sages Rodgers and Hammerstein gave fantasy their seal of approval in the last five scenes of *Carousel*. Indeed, the sight of the dead Billy Bigelow, getting to his feet to Go Beyond while his widow grieves unseeing—this after one-and-a-

157

half acts of strait realism—must have been a jolt to first-time audiences.

But by then other fantasies had begun to pepper the decade, usually one or two a season. The lavish *Dream With Music* (1944) was actually more of a fancy than the "musical fantasy" it called itself: a soap-opera writer (Vera Zorina) dreams that she is Scheherazade in old Baghdad, where her real-life acquaintances turn up as Aladdin, the Sultan, and so on. However, the dream itself was a fantasy, complete with flying carpet, a genie, an enchanted forest, and Balanchine choreography. Clay Warnick culled, to Edward Eager's lyrics, the music of Schubert, Beethoven, Saint-Saëns, Weber, Chopin, Wagner ("The Ride of the Valkyries"), Haydn, and Stephen Foster (the genie materialized to "I Dream of Jeannie With the Light Brown Hair"), among rather many others. Like Wright and Forrest, whose *Song of Norway* was playing its pre-Broadway run in California, Warnick would generally borrow for a song's A-strain and compose the release himself. He was clever at it, fashioning, out of the triplet solo violin figure that runs through Rimsky-Korsakof's *Scheherazade*, a wonderful jazz ballad called "I'm Afraid I'm in Love (with you)." But the critics thought it all an expensive mess, and it quickly closed.

The year 1946 saw two flop fantasies play back-to-back in the same month in the same theatre, the Century. *If the Shoe Fits* was a vulgar Cinderella spoof, and *Toplitzsky of Notre Dame* saw an angel come to earth to play football while comics Jewish (J. Edward Bromberg) and Irish (Gus Van, half of the old singing duo Van and Schenck) traded ethnic quips. Of *If the Shoe Fits*, John Chapman of the *Daily News* said, "I won't go into the book by June Carroll and Robert Duke, and they shouldn't have, either. Mr. Sillman,* an incurable amateur of the stage, should be . . . cautioned not to go near the professional theatre again."

That bad? Three fantasies, however, were not only smash hits but classic titles: one somewhat elusive now, one very famous but

---

* This was Leonard Sillman, the show's producer, June Carroll's brother, and the begetter of one good idea, the *New Faces* revues, a showcase of new talent. As a judge of book musicals, however, Sillman was reckless.

lately under one of those "political" clouds, and one revived as often as *Oklahoma!*.

The first of the trio was to have provided Marlene Dietrich with an American stage debut. Set in Victorian London, it centers on a statue of the goddess of love that comes to life and makes a lot of trouble. Bella Spewack couldn't make the book work, so S. J. Perelman and Ogden Nash took over, resetting the action in contemporary New York. Dietrich then declined the part, claiming that Perelman's script was lewd; more likely, she feared risking her career in a new form, or was too used to Hollywood microphones to try to project into a theatre. Vera Zorina and Gertrude Lawrence also turned it down; but Mary Martin was free. Her starring vehicle *Dancing in the Streets* (1943) had closed in Boston, and she in fact at the time played glamor goddesses rather than the male and female Peter Pans she later specialized in. Martin said yes, and thus saved a working profile that had faded after her bright debut in Cole Porter's *Leave It To Me!* (1938). Based on F. Anstey's novel *The Tinted Venus*, *One Touch of Venus* (1943), with music by Kurt Weill, lyrics by Ogden Nash, direction by Elia Kazan, and choreography by Agnes de Mille, was ready to go.

"Spurns the easy formulas of Broadway," said a not entirely smitten Louis Kronenberger. There were no ballroom dancers or irrelevant numbers, and of course the greatly creative de Mille was on hand, with, Kronenberger thought, "even bolder ideas about dancing" than in *Oklahoma!*, a bit more than six months earlier that year.

Nevertheless, *One Touch of Venus* gets off to a strangely conventional start, with an opening chorus ("New Art Is True Art") and traditional exposition, as basic in its data as a weather report. We meet rich art connoisseur Whitelaw Savory (John Boles) and his wisecracking secretary, Molly (Paula Laurence); he has imported a fabulous statue of Venus, which duly arrives. It must be time for the second number, for six cute young women float on. They're art students:

> SECOND STUDENT: A classical statue's going to look pretty wacky against this modern stuff!

MOLLY: Look, kids—forget that routine Savory's been dishing
out. If you've got what Venus had, you're all set!

and the six place themselves around Molly to sing backup to the
title song, on the erotic power of womankind.

It's a routine beginning for what turns out to be an agile show.
Obvious. Familiar. But once Savory's timid barber, Rodney Hatch
(Kenny Baker), accidentally brings the statue to life by placing a
ring on its finger, the show finds itself. It's partly a runaround
farce, as everyone chases Venus and Rodney and, after Venus
sends Rodney's pushy fiancée to the North Pole, even suspects
Rodney of her murder. But it's also partly a development of the
message of the title song. This really is a tale of the Ultimate
Woman and her positive effect on men, which is why producer
Cheryl Crawford went right, so to say, to the source, Marlene
Dietrich. We're talking gender candy on the Goethean level: *Das
Ewig-Weibliche zieht uns hinan.**

Indeed, Venus transforms the barber. Some of this lies in her
songs, a rich lode of information, in the jazzily seductive "I'm a
Stranger Here Myself," in the vulnerably waltzy "Foolish Heart,"
in the fatalistic—for the gods never do tarry long with mortals—
"Speak Low (when you speak love)," the show's hit. And note that
the doting "That's Him," which Martin sang way downstage on a
chair *en negligée*, follows an act of lovemaking. This is Venus in
all her wonder—erotic, yes, but also sentimental, also rash. Rash
as well were Martin's outfits: "fourteen complete costume
changes," each costing "between fifteen and twenty thousand dollars," according to the show's star dancer, Sono Osato.† Whether
it's the songs or the clothes or just Her Power, Venus is clearly
making a man out of the barber, as we learn when Venus confronts the evil fiancée, Gloria:

* "Eternal Woman draws us ever upward"—really, *inspires* us, the last line of
Faust.

† So she states in her memoirs, *Distant Dances*. Even limiting the cost to
fifteen thousand, that's $210,000, just about what a show the size of *One Touch
of Venus* cost, period. I count eight different dresses, at surely a thousand or two
at the most each. The designer, for Martin only, was Mainbocher, a rare case
of a trendy couturier's working on Broadway.

GLORIA: You led Rodney on! He never had any nerve till you
showed up!

when Venus comforts Rodney:

RODNEY: You're so nice to touch.
VENUS: Does it make you happy?
RODNEY: I—I never felt like this before.

and after Gloria storms off:

RODNEY: (*to* VENUS) To think I've been taking that for five
years, and if it wasn't for you, I'd be taking it for the rest
of my life.

He's a changed soul, and that gives the story substance. It's
pure musical comedy, yet it has subject matter. It also has plenty
of comics—big loud Harry Clark and tiny Teddy Hart as Savory's
hirelings, a detective and his assistant; and of course Paula Laurence's Molly, a link between Savory's elegance and the real world,
with her sarcasms and slang catchphrases. She's the only reasonable person in the whole play, and she helps ground the fantasy
in that she's the sole character to figure out that Martin is the
missing statue. She isn't even shocked: she's amused. "You're the
nicest goddess I ever met," she tells Venus, typically exiting with
"Keep 'em guessing."

The one element in *One Touch of Venus* that rose above musical
comedy was the choreography. *Of course.* Agnes de Mille wasn't
going to follow *Oklahoma!* with tap routines. As Kronenberger
remarked, success made her daring, and her work here was dark.
There was some hoofing here and there, yes, but, mainly, there
were two Big Ballets. Act One offered "Forty Minutes For Lunch,"
following and using the music of "I'm a Stranger Here Myself,"
in which Martin wandered through lunch-hour businessville amid
groups of grimly hurried New Yorkers. Their footsteps punctuate
the music like the stamping of breathless soldiers; but Martin
creates love in the city, bringing together a secretary and a French
sailor, who then cap the dance with a duet in one while the Radio
City set is changed. It's *l'amour* versus modern life: when love
wins, we see how influential this goddess really is. As in

Oklahoma!'s "Many a New Day" dance, de Mille deals in character. The second-act ballet, "Venus in Ozone Heights," pits love against another kind of uniformity: that of suburbia. Venus on Staten Island? No way: and, as the ballet closes, her compatriots, who have been harassing her throughout the act, spirit Venus off into legend once again, leaving modern life, Savory, and the poor smitten barber behind. And there the play ended.

In Boston. Well, that's what Sono Osato says. But how were the authors to leave the audience without a conclusive meeting between the lovers, even a sad one? In any case, by the time the show opened in New York, the ballet was followed by a last book scene. Gloria having been retrieved from the North Pole, Rodney is off the hook legally, and we find him staring at the statue to the strains of "Speak Low." Then comes perhaps the most unexpected and delightful last minute in any musical of the decade: Venus comes back. Or, rather, Martin does, now in the person of a young New Yorker:

> GIRL: Can you tell me where I register for the art course?
> RODNEY: (*doing a take*) Why—sure . . . Where do you come from?
> GIRL: Ozone Heights.
> RODNEY: Do you like it there?
> GIRL: I wouldn't think of living any place else.
> RODNEY: My name is Rodney Hatch.
> GIRL: My name is—
> RODNEY: (*Going quickly to her*) You don't have to tell me. I know.

Curtain. So Lady Love made arrangements to replace herself, an intriguing idea comparable to *Carousel*'s suggestion that God interferes in human affairs for everyone's good. Maybe wartime promotes such credulous affirmations, whether Christian or pagan. But *One Touch of Venus* was not a "wartime show" in any other sense: an escapist show. Yet of course its composer was a Hitler refugee, writing during a war conducted to destroy Hitlerism. This gives some pertinence to Weill's position.

As we know, he was a classically trained Weimar grad, composing operas in Germany, a Balanchine ballet while on the run in France (*The Seven Deadly Sins*), and now musicals in the

United States, which he loved despite his earlier participation in Leftist German America-hatred. What we don't know yet is that he is the most imposing figure in the forties musical after Rodgers and Hammerstein and Agnes de Mille; I have deliberately broken up his output into as many chapters as possible to emphasize his versatility. Ignoring Weill's thirties musicals (*Johnny Johnson* and *Knickerbocker Holiday*), Weill becomes the absolute forties composer, running through all the available genres except revue:

Lady in the Dark (1941)	Straight play containing three ballet ballads and one song	Smash
One Touch of Venus (1943)	Musical comedy	Smash
The Firebrand of Florence (1945)	Operetta	Bomb
Street Scene (1947)	Broadway opera	Succès d'estime
Love Life (1948)	Concept musical comedy	Hit
Lost in the Stars (1949)	Concept musical play	Succès d'estime

I have spoken already of the detractors of Weill's American catalogue and their agenda. Let us turn tables and consider the superiority of Weill's Broadway over his German output. There is, first of all, a liberation from the insistently political drumming and cut-out characters. *Die Dreigroschenoper* remains one of the century's unique works, and no one can appreciate Weill without acknowledging the genius with which he attacked the set pieces of *Aufstieg und Fall der Stadt Mahagonny*, each next scene a little opera in itself.

However, nothing in any of Weill's German works compares to the simple humanity of Liza Elliott's journey into the center of herself, or to *Street Scene's* cluster of dead souls, or even the barber's redemption in *Venus*. In fact, Weill fell in with his various Leftist colleagues in his Weimar days more out of artist's solidarity against fascism than out of political affiliation. Weill was often exasperated with his most constant collaborator, Bertolt Brecht, who, like all Communists, was to strike humanitarian poses while gloating at the breaking of millions in Stalinist jail-countries.

Enough pleasantry. What an odd background for the composer of *The Firebrand of Florence*—perhaps, more precisely, for the composer of a show produced by Max Gordon, whose other credits include *The Band Wagon, The Cat and the Fiddle, Roberta,* and *The Great Waltz.* But in fact Weill's is a familiar story, in which an emigrant member of a gifted people enriches his adopted culture. The Broadway musical would not have been what it was without Kurt Weill.

That said, let's admit that *One Touch of Venus* is no *Lady in the Dark.* Weill is clearly trying something new to him: a commercial hit in the American style of what commercial means. So it can't be *White Horse Inn.* It can't even be *Louisiana Purchase.* By late 1943, the musical is undergoing The *Oklahoma!* Effect. No one knows what commercial *is* anymore.

Then, too, Weill's earlier partners had been either raw lyricists but worthy playwrights (Paul Green, Maxwell Anderson) or Ira Gershwin. On *Venus*, Weill had Ogden Nash, a comic pop versifier and no lyricist. Nash, now virtually forgotten, was famous in the 1940s, especially for one trick: an extension of a line to extravagant lengths while still respecting the rhyme scheme. You can't do that in music, so Nash was a non-lyricist without a trick. One can tell. Oddly, the ballads work but the comedy numbers don't. "Way Out West in New Jersey" and a Cole Porter list song, "That's How Much I Love You," fall flat. "One way to be very wealthy"—the first line of Molly's "Very, Very, Very"—runs on to "is to be very, very, very rich." It's a spiffy start, but it goes nowhere. Nash did little other work on Broadway despite *Venus's* success, and at that only with Vernon Duke, another émigré from totalitarianism.

Speaking of emigration, how did Weill arrive at his new all-American style? This same year, 1943, Weill could satirize German band music in a Drinking Song in the Valley Forge sequence in the film *Where Do We Go From Here?* (released in 1945). That is, Weill's perspective was now so replete that he could "style" his homeland. Yet some of *One Touch of Venus* bears the sweet acid of Weill's German sound, right-on, not burlesqued. One number will sound like pure American forties pop, the next like Hindemith in drag. "The Trouble With Women," another of

Nash's laughless comedy numbers, is in fact "In der Jugend Gold'nem Schimmer," from *Happy End*, written in Germany in 1929.

Still, *One Touch of Venus* gives us a taste of new Weill. He was a wonderful character writer, as in the barber's "(Waiting for our) Wooden Wedding," so patient, willing, innocent. One contrasts that with "That's Him": sated and knowing. He knew people, Weill—something you'd never guess from the cardboard icons that Brecht was always throwing at him. Better, he was the most imaginative of all composers, forever doing something for the first time that would then become cliché in others' hands, such as those shuffling footsteps that form part of the "Forty Minutes for Lunch" scoring, or in the Scary Ghost Music that launches the Entr'acte, reminding us that Gloria is in the North Pole, Rodney is suspected of murder, and Venus is haunted by her duties as a goddess.

One Touch of Venus' later life is typical of a forties hit: a bowdlerized movie with almost no score, a fifties TV version (taped live, onstage, with Janet Blair and Russell Nype), and then, in the modern era, two New York concert stagings, by Bill Tynes' New Amsterdam Theatre Company (with Paige O'Hara and Lee Roy Reams, and Paula Laurence back as Molly), and by Encores! (with an all-conquering Melissa Errico). It's such a famous title—but is it a famous show? *Finian's Rainbow* and *Brigadoon* are famous shows, without question. As Captain Andy says, "You know 'em, you love 'em . . ." Do you? Because one of them is always with us and the other is . . . not.

At first, they seemed a pair—hailing from the second half of the 1946–47 season, the one a satiric musical comedy and the other a romantic musical play (arguably an operetta), not just fantasies but very supernatural. Leprechauns, wishes come true; a Christian miracle. Both titles were extremely strong in dance, by the debuting Michael Kidd and the decade's fixture, Agnes de Mille, and both shows were sleepers. Both, too, had Celtic backgrounds, respectively Irish and Scots; and both used the European base to comment on American life. Their similarities are remarkable.

But one comparison absolutely separates them. Like *Annie Get*

Your Gun, Finian's Rainbow remains faithful to a zany tradition in a rationalist age; *Brigadoon* is so rationalized that it can't be an operetta, after all. In fact, it's a Rodgers and Hammerstein show, one of the few that Rodgers and Hammerstein didn't actually write. (Others include *Paint Your Wagon, 110 in the Shade*, and *I Do! I Do!*.) I don't mean a Rodgers and Hammerstein imitation. I mean an original show in the Rodgers and Hammerstein format. *What format?* Well, that's what I mean.

Let's take *Finian* first. The fantasy inheres in the traditional fairyland pot o' gold that Finian (Albert Sharpe) has stolen and smuggled into America, to bury it near Fort Knox, where it will, he hopes, capitalistically "grow." But a leprechaun, Og (David Wayne), follows him; and the local corrupt senator, Billboard Rawkins (Robert Pitkin), needs Finian's tiny parcel of land to complete a swindle.

The love interest is supplied by Finian's daughter, Sharon (Ella Logan), and left-leaning guitar player Woody (think "Guthrie") Mahoney (Donald Richards), and the American peasant-class racial background is supplied by a chorus half-white, half-black, a very distinctive touch. But then, this is an E. Y. Harburg show. Having subplotted racism in *Bloomer Girl*, he now thrusts it front and center, for Rawkins' turf is Missitucky, U. S. A., and his victims are poor sharecroppers who—typically for Harburg—start as victims of political profiteering and end as consumerist maniacs buying, on credit, lovely gadgets they don't need.

That's Harburg's America: capitalism means you're a crook or a stooge, but everybody lives well. Writing the book with Fred Saidy and the score with composer Burton Lane, Harburg was *Finian*'s auteur, its leprechaun after that pot o'gold that yields an understanding of how America works. The show's pot o'gold yields three wishes; unwittingly using one, Sharon wishes that the relentlessly racist Rawkins were black himself, so he can experience at first hand how it feels to be oppressed by a Rawkins. Thunder and a blackout, during which the Rawkins underwent a fast piece of makeup surgery. The lights came up on a changed man. Not repentant: black. He now has so few career opportunities that he joins a revivalist singing group.

The second wish gives voice to Woody's mute sister (Anita Alvarez), and the third bleaches Rawkins to clear Sharon of the charge of witchcraft. There's a lot of magic in *Finian's Rainbow*, but mostly there is tomfoolery, a sort of fantasy in itself. Alvarez is not only mute but a kind of pixie, a woman who only communicates through dancing steps that are "translated" by a black kid. Finian's gold instantly—but *instantly*—brings to Finian and the sharecroppers the endless credit of the Shears and Robust (think "Sears, Roebuck") company catalogue. This cues in a kind of capitalist spiritual—in the rich world of Harburg that isn't an oxymoron—called "That Great Come-and-Get-it Day." Paradoxes are Harburg's meat: the singing group that the newly black Rawkins joins is ultra-religious and obsessed with sex. "We take our text from Genesis," one of the gospellers explains, "wherein it says that Adam and Eve begat Cain and Abel." This leads to a litany of Conceptions, from that of "the rabble at the Tower of Babel" to that of the "Daughters of the D. A. R." It's Harburg giving the religion zealots what they thought they wanted: too much of a stupid thing. Harburg's jokes are always brilliant, always poetic, always witty, and always bitterly right about a wrong world.

Still, *Finian's Rainbow* tries to show a way into freedom: no racism, no more corrupt politicians, and give people *room*. They'll figure it out if you let them. Ironically, *Finian* itself has no room. It's stuffed with plot, music, dancing, jokes, and—most of all— its own throughline, which is, roughly, Rawkins versus Finian versus the leprechaun is, really: a crook can't defeat a visionary who himself can't overrule a sensualist. (For, in America, the leprechaun is turning mortal: horny.) The score is that truly forties invention, an every-number-a-delight sing; and the dancing, with no dream ballet, matches the script as fun, but pointed fun. "If the American musical stage continues to improve," wrote the *Times*' Brooks Atkinson, "it will no longer be necessary for anyone to speak dialogue on the stage. Everything essential can be said in song and dancing."

Not entirely. Yes, some of *Finian*'s best effects were musical. As Act One ended, in effect, with the celebration of industrial product, Act Two began with the consumption of product: a dance of those who Came and Got It. Choristers in mink shorts, leopard-skin pajamas, dark glasses, and other Outfits of the Arrived seized the stage and performed to a series of variations on a theme— march, waltz, polonaise—till we finally heard the theme itself, "When the Idle Poor Become the Idle Rich." It's one of Harburg's cleverest political aperçus. We *are* all the same in the race of man, regardless of cultural background, race, or whatever: only money invents differences.

But Atkinson didn't realize how solid *Finian*'s book is. Well, maybe gossamer solid, with its leprechauns and dancing mute, its stereotypical Irish humor even as its spoofs stereotypical black humor. Still, this is a show with a Weltanschauung—easy enough in the musical play (*Carousel* has more Weltanschauung than Rolf Hochhuth) but rare in musical comedy:

> SHARON: Are there no poor in America, no ill-housed, no ill-clad?
> FINIAN: Of course, Sharon. But they're the best ill-housed and the best ill-clad in the whole world.

Or:

> RAWKINS: (*who has a habit of breaking into A Speech no matter where he is*) Gentlemen, the festering tides of radicalism are upon us. But before I yield up our glorious South— and her sister commonwealth, the U.S.A.—I will lay down my life. I will go further than that—I'll filibuster. Back, you crackpots, and forward, America. . . . Forward to the sweet tranquillity of the status quo! Forward to yesterday!

Or, noting the advent of the Age of Technology:

> FINIAN: (*holding a small, jagged rock*) Inside this piece of stone is a whole multitude of gnomes, elves and fairy folk, like Neutron the Latent and Proton the Potent, ready to go to work for you and bring you all happiness.

In other words, Harburg sides with the anti-Stalinist Left in seeing democracy as the Answer, and America—despite her reactionaries and because of her wealth and power—as the ultimate Democracy.

Despite a disastrous London run, in a replica staging, *Finian* at first appeared to be another forties classic, with a popular score that demanded constant rehearings in the theatre, preferably with

Kidd's original dances. "How Are Things in Glocca Morra?," "If This Isn't Love," "Old Devil Moon," "Look To the Rainbow," and "Something Sort of Grandish" were hits of a lasting nature; and a 1960 City Center revival with Jeannie Carson, Biff McGuire, and, as the leprechaun, England's Bobby Howes, in a new staging by director–choreographer Herbert Ross, transferred briefly to Broadway. Then, in the late 1960s, when Hollywood hungered for Broadway adaptations after the banquet served up by the *Sound of Music* film, *Finian* was made into a quite faithful movie by Francis Ford Coppola. Indeed, in 1968 its hard look at southern white racism seemed more apropos than ever.

Yet now we hear that a revival would be dangerous, offensive. Blacks would bristle at the picture of a man *punished* by being turned *black*: as if black were degradation. No, you idiots. He's Himmler sent to Auschwitz. It's called Getting a Taste of Your Own Medicine.

Brigadoon, of course, has no such problems. Apolitical and timeless, *Brigadoon* is less a fantasy than *Finian* but also more a fantasy: less merrily abnormal yet more thoroughly enchanted. *Finian* has one fairy character and a number of fairy effects; *Brigadoon* is, save two characters (and, briefly, two others much later on), all ghosts. It has little plot next to *Finian*'s vehement complications, and is, in the end, a soothing show, even if somebody gets killed in it. After all, *Finian's Rainbow* challenges your moral values unless yours match Harburg's; all *Brigadoon* does is show you how lovely life is out in the suburbs. *Very* far out, in a community that exists but one day in a century. All right, it's exclusive; so was Glen Head at the time. What marked *Brigadoon* was its tribal community, virtually a fascist state without a Leader: for he has given himself to God in order to consummate the Miracle, whereby the Scots village of Brigadoon* will survive the troubling

---

* The name comes from a famous old photo opportunity, a dear little bridge straddling the Doon River: the Brig o' Doon. The show's plot also had a source, Friedrich Wilhelm Gerstäcker's short story *Germelshausen*. Lerner didn't credit it, perhaps because the mid-nineteenth-century tale was too obscure for anyone to care about—except an indignant George Jean Nathan, who thought Lerner's borrowing "strangely unacknowledged" and Lerner's excuse that Shakespeare, too, borrowed plots "comfortable."

new eighteenth-century decadence by almost vanishing. It will live for a day, disappear for a century, reappear to live for a day, and so on. It's like Cher's career, only more so.

Brigadoon, interestingly enough, was the work of men who had failed and failed till they went into the Rodgers and Hammerstein camp. Berlin-born composer Frederick Loewe had an operetta-baritone father and classical training, and claimed a Broadway credit in the unsuccessful *Great Lady* (1938), an operetta with three musical comedy stars, Norma Terris (of *Show Boat*), Helen Ford (of *Dearest Enemy*), and Irene Bordoni (of *Paris*). Earle Crooker was Loewe's lyricist then, but at some point Loewe hooked up with a young Harvard graduate, Alan Jay Lerner, who joined Loewe and Crooker to write the book for *Life of the Party* (1942), which closed out of town.

Sensing a match in Loewe and wanting to write lyrics himself, Lerner got Crooker dropped for *What's Up* (1943). This second and last show to be directed and choreographed by George Balanchine was a bomb in the Aarons–Freedley musical-comedy mode. (Premise: comic Eastern potentate cuts loose in a girls' finishing school.) Now Lerner and Loewe changed tack, with a more artistic musical comedy featuring ballets by Anthony Tudor, *The Day Before Spring* (1945). (Premise: college reunion reignites old flames.)

There was some progress. *What's Up* had a terrible score, but *The Day Before Spring* offered some good numbers, such as the boogieing "A Jug of Wine (a loaf of bread and thou, baby)," the cabaret-*intime* "You Haven't Changed At All," the dryly lamenting "My Love Is a Married Man." In both shows, the European Loewe seemed effortlessly American, devoid of the Caligari overtones that haunted Kurt Weill for so long. Yet they were of comparable age and both studied with Feruccio Busoni.

"You have to fall in love with your characters," Lerner once said. Maybe that was what had held them back till *Brigadoon*. Certainly, "Almost Like Being in Love" loves its singers, taking delight in what first-sight romance feels like, especially between an American guy and a highland spook. It's a Broadway hit tune, yet it has its delicacy, its hint of the burr under the exuberance. Then, too, *Brigadoon*'s Scots setting set loose in Loewe the environmental sound—sparingly, yes, but right up there in the bagpipe-crazed prelude—that became this team's hallmark. From *Brigadoon* on, Lerner and Loewe were minstrels of a specific place and time—gold-rush California, Edwardian England, *belle époque* Paris, legendary England: "They Call the Wind Maria," "The Ascot Gavotte," "À Toujours," "The Jousts." The scores were not overtly generical, not insistent. Yet Loewe always found what we might call Atmosphere.

Brigadoon has it to spare. After the bagpipe introduction, an unseen chorus gives us a "once upon a time" as we discover two Americans lost in a wood with, according to the map, no town anywhere near. But there *is* a town; we, and the two Americans, can hear it singing its theme song. On inspection, it turns out to be a quaint sort of place; but then, that's what Americans come to Europe for. The atmosphere, in both sight and sound, is so rich that we're still taking it in as the story pulls itself together. The romance: local Fiona and American Tommy. The comic subplot: Tommy's buddy, Jeff, and man-hungry Meg. A second subplot: a triangle involving Harry, who loves Jean, who's marrying Charlie this very night.

She'd better. Lollygag in Brigadoon and you waste a century. But can Tommy commit to Fiona and give up everything he has on one day's notice? And will Harry stand by and see Charlie take Jean? Because if anyone of *Brigadoon* tries to leave, the Miracle that sustains it dissolves, and the town vanishes forever. Sure enough, Harry assaults Jean at the wedding, is repulsed, and promptly *runs* for the exit.

It's a good story—exactly what *What's Up* and *The Day Before Spring* weren't. The production team includes Agnes de Mille, straight-play director Robert Lewis, the always imaginative Oliver Smith for sets, and David Ffolkes for costumes. However, note the very odd distribution of talent in the dramatis personae: Tommy and Fiona are a romantic operetta duo, but Jeff is a non-singing comic and Meg a belt soubrette. Charlie only sings, and Jean and Harry only dance. There is also Mr. Lundie, the village schoolmaster, and Jane, Tommy's fiancée back in New York, both also speaking roles only. Just four singers and the chorus for the entire score?

I call this pure Rodgers and Hammerstein: unusual story, unconventional choices in the telling of it, de Mille, unclear genre, long first act (the longest in the decade, in fact). It's a show that hadn't been seen before, and that was its power: no set format. *Finian's Rainbow* was comparably original in its story and characters, but not in its structure, which was standard post-*Oklahoma!* musical comedy. And while *Finian's Rainbow* outpaced *Brigadoon* in laughs, there is no denying the force of *Brigadoon*'s score: the inveigling "Once in the Highlands," "Down on MacConnachy Square," "Waitin' For My Dearie," "I'll Go Home With Bonnie Jean," "The Heather on the Hill," "Come To Me, Bend To Me," "There But For You Go I," "From This Day On," and the aforementioned extra-hit "Almost Like Being in Love." *Finian's Rainbow*'s songs are greatly pleasing, but even the evocative "How Are Things in Glocca Morra?" and "Look To the Rainbow" don't bear the emotional weight of *Brigadoon*'s ballads, which somehow combine the lilt of contemporary pop with the elegy of operetta—a blend not unknown to Rodgers and Hammerstein as well. There is one out-and-out barky number, a scene-setter called "Jeannie's Packin' Up." But counter this with Trude Rittman's brilliant dance arrangements, better even than those she did for Rodgers and Hammerstein, as, for instance, in two lovely new themes for the "Come To Me, Bend To Me" dance, a sprightly Allegretto Grazioso for woodwinds and a flowing string Cantabile that's as good as Loewe's vocal melody.

In *Oklahoma!*, the score unifies the show; in *On the Town*, dance unifies the show; in *Finian's Rainbow*, the book unifies the show. In *Brigadoon*, the setting unifies the show: this is *very* Scotland, from tartans and bagpipes and dialect to Smith's ruined Gothic kirke, shown in moonlit gloom.* The heavy atmosphere

---

* Costumer David Ffolkes felt that *Brigadoon was* its visuals. In his memoirs, director Lewis recalls the show's Boston opening, when everything went wrong during the transition from the first forest scene to Brigadoon itself. In typical forties style, a traveler closed on the forest as a few villagers came out front trying their *soli* market calls while stagehands readied MacConnachy Square behind the traveler. As the number proper took off, the traveler was to open and the soli choristers to blend into the thick of a big song-and-dance piece. *This* night, however, the traveler failed to open, leaving the audience mystified and

provides a neat *coup de théâtre* in Act Two, when the view takes
us from Scotland to a New York bar and "I'll Go Home With
Bonnie Jean" turns piano-dirty: from the pristine to the corrupt.
It in is the bar that we meet Tommy's fiancée, an objective-
correlative for all that is wrong with modern life—at least, with
modern life as Tommy sees it: empty and material. As the fiancée
rattles on, Tommy experiences a series of reprises by the Brigadoon populace (behind a scrim) in a scene reminiscent of one in
The Student Prince. The word "hill" cues in Fiona's singing "The
Heather on the Hill," "go home" cues in "I'll Go Home With
Bonnie Jean," and so on, Tommy's very real world now haunted
by his adventure into faërie. There is one dramaturgical error
here—the echoes take in songs that were performed when Tommy
wasn't around to hear them: so how could they be echoes?

Nevertheless, Tommy breaks off his engagement, grabs a
phone, asks for Room 316,* and tells Jeff, "Get plane reservations
right away!"

Back they go, and, indeed, Brigadoon is gone:

> TOMMY: To think that somewhere out there—between the
> mist and the stars—there's somebody I want so terribly . . .
> God! Why do people have to lose things to find out what
> they really mean?

That line alone tells us how different *Brigadoon* is from *Finian's
Rainbow*. The Irish show is satiric and the Scots show romantic,
yes—but, more, the Scots show is *spiritual*. The atmosphere is
not just musical and pictorial, but emotional: Tommy is a man
looking for something that modern life doesn't supply. It's very
telling that, in the first scene, when he and Jeff are lost, Jeff gets
off a gag ("Maybe we took the high road instead of the low road"),

---

Lewis and de Mille, at the back of the theatre, in despair. Suddenly, the curtain
gave way, revealing the citizens of Brigadoon in various states, a few seated "in
Degas-like positions," says Lewis, "and some in just positions." To complete this
sensory underload, the MacConnachy Square backdrop had gone up, revealing
the back wall of Boston's Colonial Theatre. It was then that Ffolkes came running up to Lewis, crying, "Bunty Kelley's got the wrong socks on again!"

  * A charming period quirk in this timeless tale: it's a hotel bar, and, like most
New York City bachelors in the 1940s, Jeff lives in a hotel.

to which Tommy replies, "There's something about this forest that gives me the feeling of being in a cathedral."

Tommy needs religion, and village *Volkstum* is to be his creed. He needs a people to join and beliefs to share, while Finian only wants to get rich. One is a sly Celt fleeing to America, the other an American fleeing to a Celtic land innocent of Americanism. Oddly, Finian gets what he wants but then wanders off to "look to the rainbow" that, we are told, is all in his head, whereas Tommy's deep need *anchors* him in the rainbow. It's so important for Tommy to stop wandering that he compels Brigadoon to reappear just for him, in defiance of the ghost town's stated rules of engagement. In one of the decade's few genuinely offbeat endings, Mr. Lundie totters over the bridge that connects Brigadoon to the real world, greets Tommy, and ushers him into fairyland: "If ye love someone deeply, anythin' is possible. Even miracles." As Jeff looks on, the two start over the bridge, and the curtain falls.

First of all, note that most musicals tended to close with a big reprise of the available hit by virtually the entire cast. *Brigadoon*'s closing chorus is of course singing offstage, at that not a hit tune but that weird town hymn thing. Well, that's not unusual for a show in the Rodgers and Hammerstein line; and we've already met a few shows that ended without a big reprise. *Pal Joey* used three people and no singing; *Lady in the Dark* didn't even use music. What's especially fetching about *Brigadoon*'s finale is that it fails to show us the musical's most satisfying cliché: boy gets girl. Fiona does not appear with Mr. Lundie (though some revivals do bring her on), because *Brigadoon* is about more than its love plot. It's about a man who finds his destiny in a place where nothing happens. It's the opposite of Finian's journey: he prefers the Place Where Everything Never Stops Going.

Like *Finian's Rainbow*'s cast, *Brigadoon*'s was an ensemble, even if they were either singers, or dancers, or actors. David Brooks and Marion Bell (who became one of the seven Mrs. Lerners) were the central lovers, George Keane and Pamela Britton the comics, and Lee Sullivan and Virginia Bosler the second love couple, with James Mitchell playing Harry. As with *Annie Get Your Gun*, the London production ran longer, though somebody worried a few of Lerner's characters' surnames: McLaren became

MacKeith, Beaton became Ritchie, Dalrymple became Cameron. If you say so, Mr. Adams.

With none of *Finian's Rainbow*'s potential for controversy, *Brigadoon* has proved the more lasting of the two, constantly reproduced in major venues. Broadway saw it again in 1980, in Vivian Matalon's somewhat reconsidered staging (there was a taste of tribal wariness about the townspeople), though de Mille's choreography was, as always, revived;* London knew a pleasantly conventional revival, now with new dances, by Tommy Shaw, though the "Come To Me, Bend To Me" ballet went missing. The New York City Opera has continually given it, again with de Mille's layout. It's looking tired.

I'd like to see a rethinking, along the lines of Nicholas Hytner's *Carousel*, in which the fascism latent in Brigadoon's confining social and religious structures is emphasized. More should be made of Jeff's nihilism, of the New York fiancée's pestering conventions. *He* could be played as Jerry Lewis, *she* as Martha Stewart. The bar scene could be reset in a television studio, where she is far too busy revealing needlepoint and eulogizing the soufflé to listen to Tommy. And consider the *Brigadoon* afterstory: Tommy has vanished, Jeff was the last person to see him alive, and his alibi will be some babble about a ghost village. Will some bold director, one day, give us a de-fantasized *Brigadoon*, with a very short final pantomime of detectives grilling Jeff in an interrogation room?

* It's a broad program, including ensemble bits during "Down on MacConnachy Square" and before and after "My Mother's Weddin' Day"; four big set pieces, one each after "Bonnie Jean" and "Come To Me, Bend To Me," one for the wedding sequence, and one to open Act Two, "The Chase" (after the fleeing Harry); and a funeral solo (to bagpipes) for Lidija Franklin over Harry's corpse. Along with de Mille's dances for *Oklahoma!* and *Carousel*, those of *Brigadoon* appear to be the only surviving choreography of the forties musical.

9

REVUE

Broadway's version of the variety show flowered around the turn of the century and developed in power till it dominated the 1920s in the famous producer's annuals—Ziegfeld's *Follies*, George White's *Scandals*, Earl Carroll's *Vanities*. Like operetta lavish as a rule, the revue nearly collapsed in the Depression, though an occasional echo of the annuals, the "intimate" (i.e., cheap) revue, and the theme revue (as in *As Thousands Cheer*, a staged newspaper, with each new scene introduced by a headline) kept the form on view even as its ground zero, vaudeville, literally went out of business.

The sad truth of it was that revue was moribund, and would soon be dead. Rodgers and Hammerstein's inculcation of the story show and television's at-home-for-free variety nights made revue superfluous on Broadway by the 1960s. In the 1940s, it was a form feeding off of thirties models while planting nothing new itself. Low comics Ole Olsen and Chic Johnson paraphrased their 1938 smash *Hellzapoppin* in the increasingly less successful *Sons O' Fun* (1941) and *Laffing Room Only* (1944). A Ziegfeld *Follies* turned up in 1943. This was a Shubert venture, the great showman's named rented from his widow, Billie Burke, as it had been for two earlier Shubert editions, in 1934 and 1936. The talent— comedians Milton Berle and Arthur Treacher, beauty Ilona Massey, dancer Jack Cole, puppeteers Bil and Cora Baird—was not as starry as that featured in the *Follies* when Ziegfeld was alive, but the show was a smash. Conversely, the Shuberts' own *Artists and Models* series of the 1920s was revived by others later that year in an expensive yet cheesy production featuring singer Jane Froman, the then still wannabe Jackie Gleason, and a bunch of nevermadeits. The show borrowed the worst of burlesque, the worst of everything. A sample: a singing trio called the Radio Aces performed "What Does the Public Want?"—"blithely unaware," George Jean Nathan reported, "that the subsequent lack of applause indicates that the Radio Aces are unmistakably not one of the things." In the end, *Artists and Models'* purpose in life was to close suddenly after three-and-a-half weeks, freeing the Broadway Theatre for *Carmen Jones*, which had had trouble getting a booking.

Some revues were simply agglomerations of self-contained acts, virtual vaudeville. No chorus, no Big Ballet, even no score: just performers in some sort of order. These shows went unnoticed. A few other revues, however, exploited this vacant format by hiring an ensemble to appear and reappear in sketches and songs, a single composer–lyricist team to supply the numbers (though interpolations were common), and a director to try to pull it together. *Angel in the Wings* (1948) is typical, originally a summer-stock touring package* called *Heaven Help the Angels*. Its stars were Paul and Grace Hartman, a husband-and-wife team who were omnivorously untalented, and Hank Ladd, a comic. Bob Hilliard and Carl Sigman wrote the score, which provided one novelty hit,

---

* Back before television occupied America's free evenings, stock was summer vacationers' Broadway: a network of tents, converted barns, and leftover legit houses presenting new and old fare by both resident companies and this-week-only touring guests. The production standards varied from amateur to frugal-but-slick, and the performers themselves tended to the unknown or to third-rank stars and has-beens. Very little history was made in this venue, but it was in fact a stock production of *Green Grow the Lilacs*, at the Westport (Connecticut) Country Playhouse, that gave Richard Rodgers the idea for *Oklahoma!*.

"Civilization" (the one beginning, "Bongo, Bongo, Bongo, I don't want to leave the Congo . . ."), sung by the one cast member with star potential, Elaine Stritch. Modest in every way, the piece nevertheless succeeded.

Most of these small and only vaguely unified revues came to Broadway from somewhere else. *Touch and Go* (1949), by Jean and Walter Kerr with music by Jay Gorney, started as *Thank You, Just Looking*, at Catholic University; George Abbott brought it to town virtually as he had encountered it, though Helen Tamiris was hired to upgrade the dancing. *Touch and Go* was amiable and spoofy, without even a shred of the elegance the revue had known in the 1930s; but then the age didn't look for elegance in its variety shows, or even wit. "Be a Mess" offered a trio of "Olivia, Barbara, Jane," as the first lyric ran. "Dumb, neurotic, insane" ran the answering line: Peggy Cass, Nancy Andrews, and Kyle MacDonell as movie stars De Havilland, Stanwyck, and Wyman, celebrating their triumphs playing *misérables* in *Sorry, Wrong Number, The Snake Pit*, and *Johnny Belinda*. A Rodgers and Hammerstein version of *Hamlet, Great Dane A-Comin'*, included such numbers as "This Is a Real Nice Castle" and "You're a Queer One, Dear Ophelia." There was also a *Cinderella* as directed by Elia Kazan in his *Streetcar Named Desire–Death of a Salesman* mode, a dance in Grandma Moses visuals called "American Primitive," Nancy Andrews and Dick Sykes in the desperate comic duet "This Had Better Be Love," and the number that every critic singled out, Peggy Cass' "Miss Platt Selects Mate."

The best of these little drop-in revues, remembered long after *Angel in the Wings* and *Touch and Go* had fallen out of mention, came from Pittsburgh before undergoing development in California. This was *Lend an Ear* (1948), almost entirely written by Charles Gaynor and almost entirely staged by Gower Champion. (Joseph Stein and Will Glickman wrote some of the sketches; and Hal Gerson directed some of them.) *Lend an Ear* was a cute show. Its score was cute, a bit conventional in such ballads as "When Someone You Love Loves You" and "Who Hit Me?" but up-to-date in "Neurotic You and Psychopathic Me." It had a cute cast, too—Carol Channing, Yvonne Adair, William Eythe, Gene Nelson, Tommy Morton, all on the rise, though Eythe, one of the show's co-producers, was hoping to put a kick into his unimposing Hollywood career with some Broadway réclame.

And, indeed, *Lend An Ear* thrilled the town—but, really, all for one sketch, a first-act finale spoofing twenties musicals, "The Gladiola Girl." Anticipating *The Boy Friend*'s deconstruction of the genres, this mini-show hit on the you-and-me-in-our-little-nest number, the New Dance Sensation ("The Yahoo Step"), the girls-and-boys-flirting number ("Join Us in a Cup of Tea, Boys"), and so on. Something about an oldtime show turning up in the Rodgers and Hammerstein era caught the public's fancy, and "The Gladiola Girl," like *Florodora*'s famed Sextet, "Tell Me, Pretty Maiden," became a Point of Consideration on what the musical was. The *Florodora* Sextet was a PR spot; "The Gladiola Girl" was a shock of historical recognition: the twenties musical no longer existed. That is, musical comedy as Americans had uniquely developed it no longer existed, because it had developed into something else. A mere five years after *Oklahoma!* had opened, *Lend an Ear* was holding a funeral: ostensibly for Princess shows and *Lady, Be Good!* but also of *Walk With Music* and *By Jupiter* and *Early To Bed*. It was happening that fast.

Best of all the revues was the theme show, with a topic or background that informs the entire evening. As always with the revue, the score, design, and performing talent were stronger than the sketches, which somehow were seldom as funny as they should be. It made the form uneven almost as a rule.*

Uneven entertainment was the curse of Billy Rose's *The Seven Lively Arts* (1944), the most elaborate revue in history: Bert Lahr

---

* One may compare the typical revue sketch to the general sort of sketches on the long-running TV show *Saturday Night Live*. Whether spoofing current events or simply running with some crazy idea, the sketch in both cases is often a promising concept poorly sustained. What helped in the revue was the star comic of the sort that could make almost anything funny just by showing up. A birthright clown. Nevertheless, the revue never offered anything as inspired as *Saturday Night Live*'s serial goofs such as Gilda Radner's Emily Litella, eternally complaining about something she misheard only to sign off, upon correction, with an idiotically benign "Never mind"; or newsman Chevy Chase's mocking of the oh-so-earnest Jane Curtin as she offers the characteristic Response From the Other Side on some political issue; or even the "land shark" takeoffs on the movie *Jaws*.

and Beatrice Lillie, Benny Goodman's band, Stravinsky ballet with
Alicia Markova and Anton Dolin, sketches by George S. Kaufman
and Moss Hart (among others), Cole Porter songs, staging by Hassard Short, and designs by Norman bel Geddes and Valentina.

It was a terrific idea, fueled by Rose's determination to become
Broadway's latest Greatest Showman. Patterning himself after
Florenz Ziegfeld, who like Rose had come up along the less pres-
tigious avenues of American show biz, Rose used the profits from
Carmen Jones to buy and refurbish the Ziegfeld Theatre, reopening it on the third anniversary of the bombing of Pearl Harbor
with something even bigger than the *Follies*: a star-stuffed cross
section of the arts.

In planning, there was to have been a bit of book organization,
tying the acts to the New York arrival and ensuing career pursuits
of seven youngsters, each representing a different art. This scenario didn't pan out, but it still opened the show as "Big Town
(what's before me?)," which introduced would-be painter Nan
Wynn, dancer Jere McMahon, pop singer Paula Bane, ballerina
Billie Worth, actress Mary Roche, playwright Bill (later William)
Tabbert, and Hollywood starlet Dolores Gray.

With comic Doc Rockwell serving as emcee, this colossus of
great names heaved itself from neo-classical *sinfonia* to jam, from
spoof to romance. Each genre was authentically presented, separate but equal: this was a congeries, not a blend, even if Rose
tried to persuade Stravinsky to let a Broadway veteran reorches-
trate "Scènes de Ballet."* Of course, with Bert Lahr and Beatrice
Lillie, the comedy had to sparkle. Critics liked Lillie especially as
an English grande dame trying to speak slang to American soldiers
in a canteen, and emphasized Lahr as a stagehand who hates
scenery. ("Did you catch me in *Our Town*?" he asks a producer.
"Played cards in the cellar all season . . . Great show!") But other
sketches were no more than adequate, Rockwell's patter (written

---

* "YOUR MUSIC GREAT SUCCESS STOP," Rose wired the composer during the
Philadelphia tryout. "COULD BE SENSATIONAL IF YOU WOULD AUTHORIZE ROBERT
RUSSELL BENNETT RETOUCH ORCHESTRATIONS STOP BENNETT ORCHESTRATES
EVEN COLE PORTER." Stravinsky wired back: "SATISFIED WITH SUCCESS."

by Ben Hecht) irritated, and it's not clear how much of the audience doted on *both* Benny Goodman and the ballet.

Most problematic of all was the score. It produced a standard, Nan Wynn's "Ev'ry Time We Say Goodbye," and offered sweet ballads in "Only Another Boy and Girl" and "The Band Started Swinging a Song." But the comedy songs—a Porter specialty, remember—were disasters. Wynn, Roche, and Gray got a cautionary number on the dangers of the preying male, "Wow-Ooh-Wolf!," that is simply dead; Lahr appeared as a period English admiral singing a would-be burlesque of drinking songs that is no more than a very long and dreadful drinking song. For Lillie, Porter came up with "When I Was a Little Cuckoo," a Lillie-like idea, but witless and boring. Worse yet were the Porter retreads that sound like unintentional parodies, such as Gray's "Is It the Girl (Or Is It the Gown?)," introducing a Ziegfeldian showgirl parade in Valentina getups and actually asking, "Which one of the two do you love?" William Tabbert's solo, "Frahngee-Pahnee," is Porter *exotique*, with the intense rhythm section and the "jingling ankles bedecked in jade." Yet we never learn what Frahngee-Pahnee even is. A flower? One's native sweetheart? A type of sarong? Is it the girl or is it the gown?

The Seven Lively Arts lasted 182 performances, a decent showing—but not on a Billy Rose budget. The show lost a fortune. Undeterred, Rose then filled the Ziegfeld with *Concert Varieties* (1945), now with Classical Guy Deems Taylor as emcee. The dancing took in Katherine Dunham's troupe, a ballet composed by Morton Gould and choreographed (and danced) by Jerome Robbins, and Rosario and Antonio in, for instance, the "Ritual Fire Dance" from de Falla's *El Amor Brujo*. The comics numbered Imogene Coca, Zero Mostel, and Eddie Mayehoff. There was no score to speak of, and this one lasted a month.

Just as there more or less *had* to be a wartime revue, namely *This Is the Army*, didn't there also have to be a demobilization revue? *Call Me Mister* (1946) ran 734 performances for the ebullience with which it caught the euphoria of peace. Produced, written, and performed by ex-servicemen and -women (or U.S.O. staff), it was the work of Arnold Auerbach and Arnold Horwitt, with songs by Harold Rome. However, *Call Me Mister*'s strongest element was the way it caught the spirit of the times—in "Going Home Train," filled with discharged servicemen celebrating their newfound liberty ("Plain civilian from now on . . .") in a medley of six contrasting melodies, heard first one by one then all together in thrilling climax; in the ballads "When We Meet Again" and "(You've always been) Along With Me," on the separation of sweethearts; in a sketch lampooning military bureaucracy by showing how ineffectual Paul Revere would have been if he'd been up against army red tape; in "Military Life," a bouncy comedy number in 6/8 time that begins, "He was a jerk before he got into the service," and then charts the effect of basic training and army discipline. The result: "Still a jerk."

That number alone may have pushed *Call Me Mister* to victory. Even today, when the very notion of a celebratory postwar revue is unthinkable—the Korean and Vietnam Wars were too unfinished or unpopular to be celebrated, and the revue is dead, anyway—people occasionally mention "Military Life" or simply quote "Still a jerk." Like many of *Call Me Mister*'s best numbers, it was performed in one, before a traveler of colored blotches against a white field; this was not a fancy show. In fact, *Call Me Mister*'s biggest number was thus presented: Betty Garrett and four GIs* singing "South America, Take It Away." Garrett had sung "Stop That Dancing" in *Laffing Room Only*, two years before. Here, she dilated upon the medical disadvantages of conga, samba, and such.

Harold Rome, a committed liberal, had filled his earlier shows with political material—"Sing Me a Song of Social Significance" is typical, the opening number of a show (*Pins and Needles*, 1937) that will sing of little else. By 1946, however, such agendas had the feel of agitprop, and *Call Me Mister* isolates its leftism. "Yuletide, Park Avenue" looked in on the rich at Christmas in a carol saluting bon-ton stores. (E. Y. Harburg and Sammy Fain were to echo this number five years later in *Flahooley*'s "Sing the Merry.")

---

* An odd note: while *Call Me Mister* emphasized getting out of war and out of the service, the men performed in uniform . . . till the finale, the title song, when the entire cast paraded forth in the latest fashions, a wonderful touch.

"Red Ball Express" saw a mixed-race group of men recalling wartime success in transport while waiting to be hired for truckdriving jobs; the black got turned down. Also, black baritone Lawrence Winters made tribute to F. D. R. in "The Face on the Dime," perhaps the most touching moment in an otherwise once-over-lightly show.

It was "Military Life" and "South America"—and the show's overall spirit—that made *Call Me Mister* such an epochal event. Without them, it would have been just another revue, and would probably have lasted as long as, say, *Three To Make Ready* (1946), which opened a month before *Call Me Mister*: Ray Bolger, Arthur Godfrey, Gordon Macrae, Harold Lang, Bibi Osterwald, Brenda Forbes . . . all talented people. Yet who wanted a pointless variety night now?

Three To Make Ready did last an excellent 327 performances, as the latest in sketch-and-lyric writer Nancy Hamilton's series that had started in *One For the Money* (1939) and continued with *Two For the Show* (1940). Still, the series ended with *Three*, because the revue as a whole was ending, especially the empty vaudeville nights.

At least the theme revues gave one a sense of structure. *Make Mine Manhattan* (1948) didn't do a great deal more than bring Danny Daniels and Sheila Bond back for another jitterbug dance, a year after *Street Scene*, but it had a New York savor and did at least give Bert Lahr a break when Broadway lead Sid Caesar declined the tour. Anticipating a stunt that he would pull off in *Little Me* in 1962 (and that Lahr would also try in *The Beauty Part* that same year), Caesar assumed multiple identities in a spoof of the fledgling United Nations, playing delegates from various countries. The sketch took place in an eatery on First Avenue, as the hapless restaurateur (David Burns) tried to cater to the sudden influx of foreigners and their wildly divergent taste in food. Other scenes burlesqued drama critics, the garment-industry background of Hollywood moguls, and Rodgers and Hammerstein's *Allegro*, with the idealistic doctor transformed into a dentist. However, *Make Mine Manhattan*'s authors, composer Richard Lewine and word man Arnold Horwitt, seemed to understand that the spoken comedy spots were the inherent weakness of the revue format, and they programmed relatively few of them. Music filled the show—"Movie House in Manhattan," about a cinema palace filled with every amenity save a good film; "Talk To Me" and "My Brudder and Me," the two Bond–Daniels spots; "Traftz," a laugh at the picturesque menu of the woman's tea shoppe; the gently tuneful first-act finale for the ensemble, "Saturday Night in Central Park"; the second-act opener, "Ringalevio," a grownups-playing-kids dance; the jazzy "Gentleman Friend," for Bond; the finale, set in Grand Central Station, "Glad To Be Back"; and rather more as well. Nothing caught on even momentarily, but Lewine and Horwitt must have guessed right, because this now infinitely forgotten show ran a bit over a year at a time when six months was a decent run.

Inside U.S.A. (1948) expanded the setting continentally, using the title of John Gunther's book to investigate New Orleans in Mardi Gras, the Miami Beach hotel strip, Broadway on opening night, industrial Pittsburgh, and even Rhode Island. Bea Lillie and Jack Haley starred, but the good news was the reunion of Arthur Schwartz and Howard Dietz after an eleven-year separation. The bad news was their more or less terrible score, a strange development for a team that helped institute the "intimate" revue in the early 1930s with their soigné style and that would reunite gloriously for *The Gay Life* thirteen years after. Each of the two stars had his moments, especially Lillie in a truly hilarious sketch (by Moss Hart) about a dressing-room maid sabotaging the star's debut with merry premonitions of disaster:

> LILLIE: I worked out your name in my numerology book yes-
> terday . . . you know what I got?
> THE STAR: What?
> LILLIE: The Titanic. . . . According to my numerology book,
> you should have been dead about three years ago. A little
> more rouge in your cheeks, dear. You look a little pale.

Whereupon, Lillie spins around the dressing room singing "Cockles and Mussels," the one about the girl who "died of the fever."

It was pure Lillie material. What, however, was Haley material? The Tin Woodman had enjoyed a pleasant second-rank Hollywood career (after launching himself, as most did then, on Broadway;

his movie debut was a filming of his De Sylva, Brown, and Henderson hit, *Follow Thru*, in 1930). Yet he was hardly comparable to Lillie, who had established a unique persona in revue. The Broadway public knew Lillie: she did the most bizarre things as if they were daily events. Her favorite stunt was to create a chaos and then find a tiny bit of disorder in it. So her half of *Inside U.S.A.* was secure, his uncertain; and the show was uneven in any case, though it ran 339 performances and paid off.

So the short of it was that, even now in its last faint gleam before television variety killed it off, the revue was commercial, attracting major talent and good houses. It was even influential, as the natural playing field for comics too special to work well in the story shows. In fact, one of the most successful book musicals of the decade *was* a revue.

Every era has its forgotten smash hits. In the 1920s, we find *The Gingham Girl, Good Morning, Dearie, Criss-Cross*, and a number of others never mentioned today in any context. The 1930s can count fewer such, for there were fewer shows—*Take a Chance, Fine and Dandy*, and especially *Flying High*, at 357 performances in the height of the Depression the fifth longest-running book show of the decade after a quartet of classics: *Of Thee I Sing, DuBarry Was a Lady, The Cat and the Fiddle, Music in the Air*. Forties-watchers will cite *Early To Bed* or *Billion Dollar Baby*. But this particular hit seems all the more obscure because it was so very successful. Fluke-successful, at that. People called it "Public enema number one" and bragged that they knew no one who had seen it. Nevertheless, when *Follow the Girls* (1944) closed, it was the second-longest-running book musical *in Broadway history*, surpassed only by *Oklahoma!*, then at the beginning of its fourth year.

The reason why so many people loathed it also tells why it was so successful. It was that Wartime Audience again, servicemen and their dates enjoying low comedy and cheap dance routines. They were the sort, it was said, who had never seen a musical before; no wonder they enjoyed it.

Set in the Spotlight Canteen, a servicemen's club, *Follow the Girls* told of a dumpy civilian (Jackie Gleason) and a hunk of a naval officer (Frank Parker) fighting for love rights to a stripper

(Gertrude Niesen). This sliver of plot was really no more than a package to contain a host of specialties—set comic bits, dancing turns, and the like, which made *Follow the Girls* virtually a revue by other means.

It was a cheap show in every way. A cast of some sixty-strong wore a lot of costumes, true, but the sets looked off the rack. The comedy especially was cheap—that old burlesque stuff. A typical scene found Gleason and cohorts trying to ace out the naval officer in a hotel room by getting him drunk and then inducing nausea by convincing him that he's in a storm at sea. Standard gags prevailed: throwing the bed up and down, swaying around in seasick attitudes, Gleason falling for his own act and running offstage to vomit, his associates squirting the officer with a seltzer bottle (thus depicting sea spray) while lifting the edge of the bed so that the officer's legs fly up and the seltzer hits him in the seat of his pants.

Even the characters' names tell us on what level of imagination the authors—Guy Bolton, Eddie Davis, and Fred Thompson, all later to perpetrate the unspeakable *Ankles Aweigh*—were working on. The stripper is Bubbles La Marr, the comic is Goofy Gale, the hero is Bob Monroe, and the comic's sidekicks are Spud Doolittle (Tim Herbert as the skinny sidekick) and Dinky Riley (Buster West as the effeminate sidekick). That was also the level of the score, composed by Phil Charig to lyrics by Dan Shapiro and Milton Pascal, the team responsible for the *Artists and Models* revue earlier that year. *Follow the Girls'* titles include "You're Perf"; the torch wailer "Twelve O'Clock and All's Well"; "Today Will Be Yesterday Tomorrow"; the ceaselessly reprised ballad written in fluent cliché, "Where You Are"; the raucously swinging comedy novelty, "I'm Gonna Hang My Hat (on a Tree That Grows in Brooklyn)"; and of course the title song, about absolutely nothing.

It sounds awful, but it wasn't. Loud and crude, *Follow the Girls* had a raw energy that redeemed all the tacky sets and meager tunes. First of all, it had Gertrude Niesen, a blond contralto of pop with star quality to rival even Merman's: a fascinator, great in jest and song alike. She was given a Star's Late Entrance, too, bouncing onstage to deliver "Strip Flips Hip" with a combination of burlesque and Broadway, strutting as she swings her handbag and not failing to bump and grind here and there. Cheesy? No, magnetic: confident, appealing, and utterly in command. It is one of the musical's great mysteries that she never did another show in New York.

Second of all, the show filled out its eventless plot with dancing—I mean, every single kind. Somewhere along the way, choreographer Catherine Littlefield decided not to let the dance simply happen but to catalogue it: a comic apache for three, a conga line, a jitterbug ensemble, a Hispanic ballroom couple, twenty types of hoofing, a schottische (no, really), and even some ballet, to service another principal with no role, ballerina Irina Baronova, who at one point pulled off a classical stunt by turning thirty-two fouettés, just as they do in *Swan Lake*. With the costumes getting wilder and wilder at each new number, the work showed flair amid all the familiar material—individuality, even. It wasn't a good show, but it was an entertaining one. Anyway, bad shows don't close as second only to *Oklahoma!* in performance tally.

Follow the Girls also had a show-stopping number. Like most of the songs, it wasn't rooted in narrative, but simply materialized: Niesen appears in a bridal gown with a "stood up" look on her face, attended by maids of honor in pink, mauve, and so on. As they advance to the apron, a white lace "wedding" traveler closes behind them, and, in one, Niesen sings "I Wanna Get Married," a suggestive comedy number. (It's tame by Cole Porter standards. The most daring moment is when, in the second chorus, we learn that a friend of Niesen's has had triplets. The doctor asks if she has anything to say. She responds with the refrain: "I wanna get married. . . .") Slow and rangy, the melody gives Niesen something to send that formidable voice into, around, under, and through, and after two choruses and a full exeunt, Niesen glides back on alone to provide several more encore verses.

A hit in London in 1945 with Arthur Askey and Evelyn Dall, *Follow the Girls* could not be filmed: a movie is above all a story, not a tour of the world of the dance. The show was a kind of "book revue," a reply to *Oklahoma!*, however unintentionally so. Despite its flash success, there were no imitations. This show really was the last of a kind, a book show that made no pretense at storytelling or character writing, and the last revue to get by without either a major star (like *Inside U.S.A.*'s Bea Lillie) or a good score (like *Lend an Ear*'s). It's a curiosity, a museum piece that got stolen before we of today could take it in. It's gone forever—but, as Jackie Gleason noted throughout the evening, bending his arm over his head and looking right at the audience in intense philosophical consideration, "What the hell!"

10

MUJICAL COMEDY II

Whoever thought that *Beggar's Holiday* (1946) would succeed? Here was a retelling of John Gay's *The Beggar's Opera* (also the source of Weill and Brecht's *The Threepenny Opera*), set in contemporary New York with a mixed-race cast and a score composed by Duke Ellington, a superb musician but always baffled by musical comedy. It failed, in any case, though out-of-town troubles had something to do with it: directors John Houseman and then George Abbott left, Libby Holman left, the scenery and ushers left . . . John Latouche wrote script and lyrics, as so often trying to habilitate Broadway to the boldest art before Broadway was quite ready.

This sounds like a sixties show to me, even a sixties hit (though the 1960s is when Ellington again failed to come up with a viable story score, now for *Pousse-Café*, based on *The Blue Angel*, with Lilo and Theodore Bikel). The 1940s didn't embrace black or half-black shows. *Carmen Jones* was too hot to pass up, but other worthy black titles struggled to survive. Where was Lena Horne at this time? Producers Perry Watkins and John R. Sheppard Jr. offered her the lead in *Beggar's Holiday*, but the race police talked her out of it on the grounds that its underworld setting was demeaning. Yet Latouche's underworld was universal, a-racial: Alfred Drake played Macheath; Zero Mostel Mr. Peachum; Rollin Smith Chief Lockit; Mildred Smith his daughter, Lucy; Jet MacDonald Polly Peachum; Bernice Parks Jenny; and Avon Long a kind of Sporting Life, here called Careless Love: in all, a perfectly mixed-race lineup that extended right into the chorus. Ellington and Latouche did come up with two latter-day cabaret standbys, "Take Love Easy" and "Tomorrow Mountain," and one number, "The Scrimmage of Life," had the bite of the Weill–Brecht reading of this material. The show even lasted 111 performances, despite truly deflating reviews. Unique? No question. But the dead score killed it.

The more typical musical comedies were . . . more typical, particularly keen on colorful backgrounds for satiric purposes. Let's try three: *Park Avenue* (1946), on society; *Look, Ma, I'm Dancin'!* (1948), on the ballet; and *Texas, Li'l Darlin'* (1949), on politics.

Park Avenue is a painful failure, because people we like put it on: producer Max Gordon, authors Nunnally Johnson and George S. Kaufman, composer Arthur Schwartz, lyricist Ira Gershwin, and director Kaufman. A spoof not of the plutocracy per se but of its propensity to marry and divorce promiscuously, *Park Avenue* may sound like a Cole Porter show: but Porter's characters tended to be working class or bohemian. His stories didn't comment on the rich: his lyrics did. In any case, *Park Avenue* was too sedate for Porter. A Porter show liked nightclubs, the great indoors, the ninetieth floor. Despite its title, *Park Avenue* takes place entirely on a suburban terrace.

Enter young Ned Scott (Ray McDonald), in love with Madge Nelson (Martha Stewart). Ned approaches Madge's father (Raymond Walburn):

> NED: I say, do you mind if I marry your daughter?
> NELSON: Not at all, my boy. Delighted. Which one do you like?
> MADGE: Me, father. Madge.
> NELSON: You! You're not divorced yet, are you?
> MADGE: Divorced! I'm not even married yet.

It takes Nelson a while to clear it up:

> MRS. NELSON (Mary Wickes): That was Eleanor that got mar-
> ried last year.
> NELSON: Who?
> MRS. NELSON: Your daughter Eleanor. In Cleveland.
> NELSON: What was she doing in Cleveland?
> MRS. NELSON: That was where her mother's money ran out.

It's not that funny. It was a tight production, too, holding to that single set in an era when musicals routinely managed five or six (or more) sets per act.

Overall, *Park Avenue*'s perception held that divorce had become so acculturated that it was now the very destiny of marriage. Ned Scott, the authors' moral spokesman, centers it all when he disgustedly likens the aristocrat's worldview to that of *Tobacco Road*: "except that you folks are dressed better." Still, the subject was of little interest and the characters lacked meat. Schwartz and Gershwin came up with a minor score, nicely jaunty in McDonald and Stewart's "For the Life of Me" and true cabaret torch in "Goodbye To All That," but, in "Don't Be a Woman If You Can," concocting a dim imitation of a number that Cole Porter had done brilliantly in *Let's Face It*'s "A Lady Needs a Rest."

Look, Ma, I'm Dancin'! was far more state-of-the-art in its rich scene plot, heavy use of singing and dancing chorus, and exploitation of choreography. This was a Jerome Robbins show—he thought it up, in fact: a Milwaukee brewery heiress wants to dance, has no talent, funds a ballet company . . . you know. With Jerome Lawrence and Robert E. Lee on book and Hugh Martin on score, it could have been a typical Adelphi Theatre floppo: but Nancy Walker starred, albeit at the Adelphi. Fans of Walker's Ida Morgenstern on *The Mary Tyler Moore Show* and its *Rhoda* spinoff know that Walker was matchless in first-rate material, but she was matchless in eighth-rate material, too, and she had plenty of it here. *Park Avenue* foolishly tried to run without stars, a good story, or even a bright young cast. *Look, Ma, I'm Dancin'!* had Walker, youngsters, and Robbins—just enough for a barely-made-it hit.

Well, it's a barely-made-it composition. Walker's vis-à-vis, Harold Lang, plays an ambitious choreographer who is egocentric, aggressive, and even dislikable.* Is this Jerome Robbins' autobiography? Yet Lang's part is clearly modeled on the typical musical comedy juvenile: ambitious, intense, restless. Or maybe he was becoming so in the Rodgers and Hammerstein age, when shows had to present someone more interesting than the guy who wins the college football game or dreams that he is Louis XV of France. It isn't only the heroine who gets a Wanting Song. What about the hero's "Soliloquy," "The Girl That I Marry," "I'm Like a New Broom," "Something's Coming," "Summertime Love," "The Way Things Are," "The End of My Race," "Sons," "One Song Glory"? Lang's Wanting Song in *Look, Ma, I'm Dancin'!* is "Gotta Dance," an ensemble number after Lang's solo, as the singers go scatting and the dancers assist Lang in sampling the Irish jig, the waltz, the conga, even square dancing.

As the story progresses, we see Lang learn humility through Walker's love. First, he blunders by tarting up a ballet with jests and sex, so much so that the company manager storms onto the stage to demand that the curtain be rung down—the first-act curtain of the very show we're attending, *Look, Ma, I'm Dancin'!* But wait: ushers are running down the Adelphi Theatre's aisle with a flowered horseshoe for Walker. "I paid for those flowers," she cries, "and, damn it, I'm going to get them!"

That's an unusual first-act curtain. Pirandellian, even. But the second act has so little plot that this might be a . . . and in fact it *is* a George Abbott show, which explains why it's so empty of content. Abbott was a capable editor of almost-there scripts, but Abbott could not create and could thus not save a show lacking in substance. Robbins' idea for a show proved, in the end, an idea but not a show.

As for the score, it's not Hugh Martin at top level, though he registered at his tense, tough best in "Jazz," a choral piece reveling

---

* It is almost certainly because of this odd part that Lang was invited to record the title role in *Pal Joey* when Goddard Lieberson made the historic recording, which of course led to Lang's playing Joey in the 1952 revival. This is an example of how one snappy break can found an entire career.

in the "Martin sound" and a fair depiction of where jazz had traveled to in the days between, say, Fletcher Henderson and Paul Whiteman in the 1920s and the countless figures who would take it into an entirely different world in the 1950s. A ballad called "Tiny Room" impresses with a tidily soaring verse in ¾ followed by a fox trot whose each A strain begins with a falling dissonance.

One real misfire is "The Two of Us," an eleven o'clocker for Walker and Lang with cutesy dance steps and throwaway comedy. Ethel Merman and Bert Lahr did it in "Friendship" (in *DuBarry Was a Lady*), classically. Walker and Lang aren't the right mix, as if one of them had blundered in from another show. The lines are okay:

> LANG: Did you put the cat out?
> WALKER: Why? Was she on fire?

They're supposed to be corny. Try this one:

> LANG: Say, I'm a little stiff from dancing.
> WALKER: I don't care *where* you're from—keep moving!

There was perhaps not enough chemistry between Walker and Lang, the comic and the dancer: she tended to overwhelm all men who weren't comics. Her best pairings were with Bert Lahr on the revue *The Girls Against the Boys* (1959) and with Phil Silvers in the book show *Do Re Mi* (1960): colleagues in the deepest sense. There was also perhaps not a good enough score to build the show on. Supposedly, there was a movie sale; it would have made a dandy vehicle for Ann Miller in that classical versus pop thing that so fascinated Hollywood at the time. Nothing happened.

Texas, Li'l Darlin' is just as forgotten as and no worse than the previous two shows. It had possibly the least promising poster credits, for only lyricist Johnny Mercer (working with composer Robert Emmett Dolan) had any reputation. The book was by John Whedon and Sam Moore, the direction by Paul Crabtree, and the choreography by Al White Jr. No George S. Kaufman or Jerome Robbins here. Worse, the producer was Anthony Brady Farrell, the most relentlessly obtuse producer on The Street.

At the center of *Texas, Li'l Darlin'* stands Hominy Smith (Kenny Delmar), a blustering no-account running for state senator, opposed by young, cute, and tall Easy Jones (Danny Scholl), a war vet who generally appears in his air force flight jacket. Easy loves Hominy's daughter Dallas (Mary Hatcher), so it's *Romeo and Juliet* and *Julius Caesar*—and even a taste of *King Lear*, for the beauteous Melissa (Kate Murtah) crowds Dallas for Easy's attentions (as Goneril rivals Regan for Edmund) while a slow-witted elder statesman looks on. Hominy is not only slow-witted but unscrupulous—yet he attracts the attention of the publisher (Loring Smith) of *Trend* magazine, a takeoff on the *Life* and *Saturday Evening Post* that were so influential in American culture at the time.

Despite Farrell's millions, *Texas, Li'l Darlin'* was a cheap show. Hominy ran his front-porch campaign on a tiny white house strikingly framed by cactus and fencing, but otherwise the sets were utilitarian. Indeed, a surprising amount of the show was performed before a plain curtain. The cast, too, lacked allure. Scholl and Hatcher (one of *Oklahoma!*'s many Laureys) were nice singers who never got anywhere; Delmar had played "Senator Claghorn" on Fred Allen's radio show, a character very similar to Hominy.

Nevertheless the Dolan–Mercer score is the least fatigued of this trio. It's third-rate Mercer, but that's still viable. He works a lot with the city-versus-country thing, especially in the haunting "Hootin' Owl Trail" and "The Yodel Blues," a duet for Hatcher and Delmar exploiting Hatcher's birthright southern yodel style. (She was raised in Florida.) "Politics," a comic duet in one for Delmar and Smith, highlights how well a magazine publisher and a hack pol understand each other, as both deal not in truth but in presentation. There's a nice plot number in "Ride 'Em, Cowboy (don't cry)," a lullaby sung by Hatcher to her nine-year-old sister, Dogie, that becomes a torch song when Hatcher believes that she's losing her man. But the big number is a bizarre one, "The Big Movie Show in the Sky," for Scholl and the chorus. Placed as entertainment at a barbecue, the song proposes that each dead soul view a film of his life, to be Judged on its balance of sin to righteousness. "Hemispheric pop corn has got to be the top corn" is a rare bad Mercer line, but the whole thing is bad: a loud and threatening anthem that, coincidentally, bears a remarkable resemblance to Vaughn Monroe's pop hit "(Ghost) Riders in the

Sky." (Both numbers were introduced in mid-1949, so it's impossible to tell which came first.)

What all three of these shows have is built-in subject matter and what they don't have is content. *Park Avenue* seems to think that it is novelty enough to show fancy folk having divorces and drinking problems. *Look, Ma, I'm Dancin'!* is no richer as a whole than its I-be-cute title. *Texas, Li'l Darlin'* is ordinary. Of course, just-okay musicals had been filling in between the hits for decades; sometimes just-okay musicals *were* hits. But the late 1940s liked its musicals on the unusual side.

One way out of the "okay" trap was to adapt an individual literary or theatrical work, or at least something that didn't "sound like" an okay musical. Today, we take *Gentlemen Prefer Blondes* (1949) for granted as an enduring title of the second rank, not a classic but all the same revivable, with a fine Jule Styne–Leo Robin score and one of Carol Channing's two Great Roles, that of Lorelei Lee, twenties gold digger. With "A Little Girl From Little Rock" and "Diamonds Are a Girl's Best Friend" for Carol, Agnes de Mille choreography, and a handsome production designed by Oliver Smith and Miles White, no wonder the show ran 740 performances. Carol Channing as dizzy Lorelei Lee? It's a natural.

Except when it isn't. The source was the first of two Anita Loos novels about the adventures of Lorelei and her more rational friend Dorothy Shaw amid a world of rich predators who never tip to the fact that they are the prey. Subtitled "The Illuminating Diary of a Professional Lady," *Gentlemen Prefer Blondes* is gleefully mad writing. Loos observes Lorelei's lack of education in voice, spelling and grammar errors, worldview, and even soul. A typical chapter title is "Fate Keeps On Happening." The book is so weird that, when Loos offered it to H. L. Mencken and George Jean Nathan, editors of *The Smart Set*, they declared it the funniest thing they had ever read but unpublishable.

Obviously not: yet it was surely unadaptable. Loos' narration is that of the picaresque, traveling around and coming into contact with various eccentrics. Musical comedy needs plot. And where would Agnes de Mille fit into a twenties spoof about gold diggers? De Mille's specialty lay in exploring the feelings implicit in stories (as in *Oklahoma!*, *Carousel*, *Brigadoon*, and *Allegro*), even in inventing feelings for a story somewhat lacking them (in *One Touch of Venus*).

Somehow, co-writers Loos and Joseph Fields worked out a narrative, in which Lorelei gets involved with a shady business deal involving a diamond tiara while Dorothy runs a romance with an American socialite. (It's actually more of a quick and busy script that *pretends* to be a narrative, though at least the characters are all from the novel, one way or another.) And even though de Mille never did find anything special to dance about,* it didn't matter. After *Billion Dollar Baby*'s joyless trek through the 1920s, *Gentlemen Prefer Blondes* was a tonic. The opening has the authority and joy that Americans used to expect of the musical—a Big Number, as Dorothy leads the chorus in "It's High Time" while passengers board the *Ile de France* for a midnight embarkation to Europe, with Hugh Martin fluting out his patented choral jazz variations on the song that at times sound better than the song. It's all about getting on for a good time—exactly the feeling we want at the top of a show. No Florentine hangings or beggar's holidays. Tragedy tomorrow. Better yet, the following number is a duet for Lorelei and her "daddy," Gus Esmond: "Bye Bye Baby," the show's hit ballad. As Channing's "A Little Girl From Little Rock" came after that, we can imagine the audience's increasing comfort. Confidence, really. And of course an expert show always *looks* easy. As the Dorothy, Yvonne Adair, had appeared with Channing in *Lend an Ear*—whose best number, remember, was a twenties takeoff—the legend was born that the little revue so to say fathered *Gentlemen Prefer Blondes*.

It is not the case. "The Gladiola Girl" is a gentle spoof of twenties musicals, while *Gentlemen Prefer Blondes* is not a spoof, and not particularly twenties in atmosphere, despite the many allusions to Prohibition and a Charleston, "Keeping Cool With Coolidge." "The Gladiola Girl" offered generic characters; *Blondes'*

---

* One dance interlude, called "Scherzo," was so inserted into the action that Columbia Records' liner notes writer, George Dale, could do no better in the show's synopsis than "When everyone leaves, Gloria Stark, a dancer, uses Lorelei's suite for a practice dance."

characters are bizarre, or at least specific: the Philadelphia scion (Eric Brotherson) so taken with Dorothy; the Englishman (Rex Evans) who flirts with her; the health nut (George S. Irving) on board ship; the scion's ridiculous mother (Alice Pearce); the "button king" daddy himself (Jack McCauley); not to mention George Dale's Gloria Stark, a dancer (Anita Alvarez, the mute sister from *Finian's Rainbow*).

Most to the point, Channing's role in "The Gladiola Girl" was supplementary, whereas her Lorelei Lee was an important creation, comparable to Ray Bolger's Sapiens in *By Jupiter*, Mary Martin's Annie Oakley in the national tour of *Annie Get Your Gun* (which led her directly to *South Pacific*), and Alfred Drake's Fred Graham in *Kiss Me, Kate*. Channing had appeared on Broadway as early as in *Let's Face It* as understudy, going on for Eve Arden, and *Lend an Ear*, her official Broadway debut, gave her nothing but good notices. *Gentlemen Prefer Blondes* invented her—or she invented it, with her dear, wide-eyed ruthlessness, her straight-leg strut—a folding ladder crossing the stage—and her scatterbrained concentration on material values. Let Brooks Atkinson say it: "There has never been anything like this before."

Strangely, *Gentlemen Prefer Blondes* didn't get to London till 1962, with Dora Bryan as Lorelei, the spectacular Anne Hart as Dorothy, and the émigrée American film star Bessie Love as the dotty Philadelphian. Channing herself revived Lorelei (as she was to revive, more insistently, her other Great Role, Dolly Levi) in a cheesy revision in fact entitled *Lorelei* (1974). But perhaps the final word on this character was said by the world's most magnificent woman, Marilyn Monroe, in the musical's 1953 film adaptation, with Jane Russell as Dorothy and a host of mollycoddles. Director Howard Hawks cut to the chase: Lorelei and Dorothy are the "men" of the tale, aggressive and executive. The biological men are womanish: helplessly deferential, or—in a famous number written for the film by Hoagy Carmichael and Harold Adamson, "Ain't There Anyone Here For Love?"—unavailable for even short-term romance. Loos was on to something that was only very occasionally discussed in the forties musical, as in *One Touch of Venus* and *Bloomer Girl*: women could rule the world. They just don't want to.

The late 1940s saw as many successful musical comedies as musical plays or hybrids. But some longtime musical comedy authors found themselves in difficulty when their shows appeared to be insubstantial. Even Irving Berlin came to grief with *Miss Liberty* (1949), which must have made one heck of a window card: Berlin, Robert E. Sherwood, and Moss Hart present a musical about the statue: democracy herself. In 1885, two newspapers war for ownership of New York, Joseph Pulitzer's *World* and James Gordon Bennett's *Herald*, while the Statue of Liberty is being delivered. A lowly reporter spikes the circulation frenzy by bringing the statue's beauteous model here from France—or is she?

Sherwood wrote the book, Hart directed, Jerome Robbins laid out the dances, Oliver Smith and Motley handled the decor, and, of course, after Ethel Merman's Annie, in Berlin's last show, there could be only one star big enough to headline: nobody.

Certainly, Berlin himself ever regretted that aspect of the show. It had a George Abbott cast: youngsters. Eddie Albert played the reporter, Mary McCarty his girl friend, and Allyn McLerie the alleged model. All right, they weren't all that young—Albert had played one of the Antipholuses in *The Boys From Syracuse*, eleven years before; and the seventy-two-year-old Ethel Griffies played McLerie's aunt. In any case, all these below-the-title billings troubled Berlin. They came cheap, at least, but they lacked the vocal power to make hits out of numbers. They weren't Merman. Still, *Louisiana Purchase* had turned out a smash with only one principal (out of five) with a dynamite voice, Carol Bruce.

Like everyone else who mattered, Berlin had got caught up in the Rodgers and Hammerstein revolution: not star shows, *story* shows. *Miss Liberty*'s cast could have played a creditable *Oklahoma!*, with McLerie and Albert as Curly and Laurey, McCarty and dance lead Tommy Rall as Ado Annie and Will Parker, sullen Herbert Berghof as Jud, Griffies as Aunt Eller, and chorus dancer Eddie Phillips, a now-and-then principal at the end of long runs, as the Peddler.

But *Miss Liberty* was no *Oklahoma!*. None of the authors found all that much story in the newspaper circulation war and the model mystery, nor even in the Albert–McCarty–McLerie triangle. I blame Sherwood: what did this playwright and F.D.R. speech-writer know about musicals? The show's souvenir book included a little piece on how Sherwood had been "deeply moved" by the expression on the faces of GIs gazing on the statue as they shipped out during World War II. Okay; that might have empowered Sherwood to create a patriotic training film, but not an Irving Berlin musical.

Miss Liberty was a total disaster. It lasted 308 performances because of a heavy advance sale, but it really was a bomb with two wonderful elements—the score and the dancing.

At this time, it seemed, Jerome Robbins could not put a foot wrong, not even when he followed "A Little Fish in a Big Pond" with a dance using the corps costumed as sharks (mimicking the Pulitzer–Bennett war). Anything in Sherwood's stupid book inspired Robbins—Parisian lamplighters at dusk, a train tour (three dancers in rolling-stock getups played the train), the policeman's ball. But then, Robbins had a lot to work with: not in the story, but in the score, one that might have served a hit had the script been up to its level.

This isn't an *Annie Get Your Gun* score, no. But it's melodious and creative and has, in the lyrics, that special Berlin quality of getting right into what most people believe, articulating it almost as they themselves would. McCarty's ruefully wistful "Homework" and energetically comic anti-torch song, "Falling Out of Love Can Be Fun," honestly style a downtown gal with no education but some independence; Albert's "Just One Way To Say I Love You" is a touchingly fumbling waltz from a guy who has the will but not the way; McCarty and McLerie enjoyed a neatly analyzed duet in "You Can Have Him," in which each starts by rejecting him and ends by trying to reclaim him.

Nothing is quite as sharp as, say, "My Defenses Are Down" or "I'm an Indian Too." Nothing's that precisely turned: how could it be, when Sherwood was so vague? But it was one of Berlin's charms to make music out of nothing—out of himself, really. For instance, the Pulitzer–Bennett rivalry clearly suggested one of Berlin's signature quodlibets, in which two different tunes are introduced separately and then performed simultaneously. This turned out to be the opening chorus of newsboys and readers, "Extra Extra!" It begins in the minor (an odd tone for the

curtain-up of a musical comedy) as the newsboys hawk their papers, then goes into the major for the breezy chorus of *Herald* readers ("I like the *Herald* filled with stock market news") and that of
World readers ("Couldn't eat a meal without the *World*"), rippling
with chat. Then, of course, the two strains run together, capped,
again in the minor, by the newsboys' call. It's antique but effective
and, given Berlin's lack of technical background, surprisingly
expert. Certainly, despite Duke Ellington's credentials as a musician, there was nothing in *Beggar's Holiday* to compare to this.

But of course Berlin was at his best when liberated to make
that music out of nowhere. In Paris, Albert wants to take McLerie
out, but they can't afford the theatre, a restaurant, anything. "In
your country," says McLerie, "when there is no money—what do
you do?"

Berlin needs no more than that. The music slips in, and soon
Albert's singing the answer: "Some people go for a buggy ride. . . ."
The verse leads on to a carefree waltz, "Let's Take an Old-
Fashioned Walk," which becomes a big number with a set change,
a big choral arrangement, and a lot of Jerome Robbins going on.
This was *Miss Liberty*'s hit tune, its identifying number, yet it was
the sort of song that could have fit into any show at all. It had to
be: *Miss Liberty* was any show at all with a period newspaper background. Its failure caused Berlin—already a wary collaborator,
holding out for the best—to be all but abstemious from then on.
With Ethel Merman as his star, he happily wrote *Call Me Madam*
(1950), and with Joshua Logan he worked on a musical based on
James Michener's *Sayonara*, finally giving up and settling on *Mr.
President* (1962). That's two productions in over a decade: and,
after that, Berlin never tried Broadway again.

Cole Porter was having an even tougher time. *Panama Hattie*,
Let's Face It, and *Something For the Boys* were all smash hits.
Then *Oklahoma!* opened, and suddenly Porter's *Mexican Hayride*
(1944) looked tacky, though it, too, was a smash. Like *Something
For the Boys*, it was a Mike Todd production with a book by Herbert and Dorothy Fields, this one built around comic Bobby Clark.
He played a smalltime crook who flees to Mexico, there to try on
the usual Clarkian disguises (including that of a tortilla seller and
a mariachi musician) while bullfighter June Havoc and American

diplomat Wilbur Evans do the romance, George Givot plays a Mexican bandit who teams up with Clark, and soprano Corinna Mura supplies local color.

"It stinks," said Porter. More accurately, it lacked strong musical values. Mura's two solos, "Sing To Me, Guitar" and "Carlotta," are superb, and Mura really went to town in them, capping each with a top B. (The one in "Carlotta" was trilled, an effect that would have been extra-special even in an operetta.) At least Wilbur Evans got the heaving "I Love You," the score's one hit. But Porter could give Clark and Havoc nothing worth Porter's while. Clark's "Girls," a typical clown-and-kickline number, was the kind of thing that Clark knew how to make work. But Havoc's "Abracadabra" must be the worst—at any rate, the least melodious—song that Porter ever wrote.

Perhaps, like Broadway itself, Porter had tired of the format he had been using since the 1920s. Moreover, all his hits since anyone could remember has been star shows, not Porter shows; and *The Seven Lively Arts*, we know, found Porter virtually floundering. The smart money, always quick to detect signs of collapse in the great, gathered close to see what Porter would do next.

And of course that's when Porter suffered the worst failure of his career, worse than that of his first Broadway show, a two-week flop: because Porter was unknown then; worse than the revue that folded out-of-town: because he was still unknown; worse than the failure of a romantic comedy that he did with the Shuberts in the late 1930s: because everyone knew that Mr. J. J. had wrecked the show with reckless tinkering during the tryout.

No, *this* title marked an out-and-out, right-in-the-center-ring bomb: an Orson Welles spectacle that couldn't get a better booking than the Adelphi yet touted itself as the show to end shows. "An extravaganza in two acts and thirty-four scenes," Welles called it, while replacing one of the leads in Boston so that Orson Welles could Make His Musical Comedy Debut. Somehow, geniuses like Welles go for make or break in everything that they do. This was break, and Porter took the rap.

Well, Welles took the rap, too. And the irony is that *Around the World* (1946), with a book by Welles drawn from the Jules Verne novel, should have been one of the wonderful events of the age. Welles put on just about the biggest show since the Hippo-drome annuals; "extravaganza," said the *Post*'s Vernon Rice, was "an understatement." The special effects took in movies, a circus (with the aerial artists working in the Adelphi auditorium), the collapse of a railroad bridge as a train raced across (all in minia-ture), the landing of the U. S. Marines (up the aisles) to rescue the hero from Indians while he's trapped in an eagle's nest (and here comes the eagle), and many other chances for Welles to reinvent the musical just as he had reinvented the Hollywood film in *Citizen Kane*.

Certainly, some of what Welles did was extraordinary. Take the opening, a Vitagraph-like silent film designed to introduce the two main characters, protagonist Phileas Fogg (Arthur Margetson) and Scotland Yard's ever-suspicious Inspector Fix (Welles). We see London, we see Fogg removing his money from a bank because of a rash of robberies—*wait!* for now we see a robbery, complete with trembling customers and agitated bank clerks as the robber, outside, breaks in through the bank's glass front . . . but we ac-tually hear the shattering glass, for the silent film has ended as the screen rises on the very same scene in its very next second. The play itself has begun.

Welles hewed closely to Verne, including the love interest, the Indian Madame Aouda (Mary Healy), though he Americanized and rejuvenated Fogg's servant, Passepartout (French and thirty in Verne) for Larry Laurence, who was later to enjoy a major pop singing career as Enzo Stuarti. Welles even added in a character, the Cockney Molly (Julie Warren), as Laurence's vis-à-vis. With all the imagination that Welles employed to transform the unsta-geable into a series of *coups de théâtre, Around the World* should have been a great spectacle: why was it a musical? Why, espe-cially, a Cole Porter musical? Porter wrote for the likes of Ethel Merman and Bert Lahr, not Arthur Margetson and Mary Healy. By the time that Welles finished placing his silent-movie spots and working out that miniature railroad disaster and timing the final scene wherein, just as in Verne, Fogg wins his bet with lit-erally one second to spare, there wasn't a lot of room for music by anyone in any case.

Porter must have been desperate for work to take this assignment. Still, with his characteristic *bonhomie* he made the best of it. An episode in which Passepartout gets high on opium led to "Pipe Dreaming." Fogg's defiance of the attacking Indians while in the eagle's nest led to "Wherever They Fly the Flag of Old England," devised to be sung simultaneously with the so-called Marine's Hymn, the one that begins "From the halls of Monte-zuma. . . ." "Look What I Found" is a joyous ballad—the sort that invokes the ringing of bells—and "Should I Tell You I Love You?" is its ironic counterpart.

So far, so good; but those four numbers are already more than half the score. *Around the World* was a freak show, another of Orson Welles' mad gambles. Porter's participation did great harm to his already compromised reputation, especially when the critics called the show dull, eagle and all. It died in 75 performances. (Actually, excepting *On the Town*, that could be an Adelphi house record.)*

The bottom line of it all is that traditional musical comedy was in trouble. Solid story content or a star performance such as Carol Channing's Lorelei Lee could protect the form, but it clearly could not go on without reinstruction. Let's get a fix on late forties musical comedy in two titles of 1947—both, for an experimental control, George Abbott shows. So now we know there'll be no Rodgers and Hammerstein hanky-panky. Right?

First is *Barefoot Boy With Cheek*, a college musical in the line of *Leave It To Jane* (1917), *Good News!* (1927), and *Too Many Girls* (1939). As always, football is the essential sport, faculty keep a relatively low profile, and students speak of classes but don't seem to attend any. Max Shulman wrote the book, from his novel of 1943 by the same title, filling it with stereotypes—the tabula rasa hick of a freshman (the protagonist), the bright co-ed (his girl), the dumb co-ed, the commies, the idiot football star, and so on. Like some of *On the Town*'s characters, Shulman's bear Tell-

---

* Oddly, earlier that same year, another "around the world" musical opened at the same floppo theatre: *Nellie Bly* (1946), a look at the real-life woman who was the first journalist to traverse the globe, in 1889. Joy Hodges played Nellie, though the show's stars were William Gaxton and Victor Moore, in their seventh and last teaming. Who can blame them, after a two-week run?

ing Names. The hero is Asa Hearthrug; his girl is Clothilde Pfefferkorn; the dumb girl, a sorority sister, is Noblesse Oblige; the commies are Boris Fiveyearplan and Yetta Samovar; the football player, a Finn, is Eino Fflliikkiinnenn. At least Comden and Green's Lucy Schmeeler was funny, evocative. These names are vulgar and implausible, even as spoof. Worse, Asa's journey from nobody to president of the Student Council provides too little story to keep the show moving.

It's hard to know why Abbott wanted to produce and direct this piece of leaden fluff. It can't have been the score, by Sidney Lippman and Sylvia Dee, which was a parade of cliché: "Here's a Toast to Alpha Cholera," "It's Too Nice a Day to Go To School," "I Knew I'd Know" (the heroine's ballad), "Everything Leads Right Back To Love" (the love duet), "Little Yetta's Gonna Getta Man," "(Promise we'll still be sweethearts) After Graduation Day," and so on.

True, Abbott loved working with newborns, and college musicals brought out the debutants. Of those later prominent, Billy (later William) Redfield and Ellen Hanley were the young lovers, Red Buttons played frat man Shyster Fiscal, and Nathaniel Frey got a bit part. But *Barefoot Boy*'s one real asset was the Yetta, Nancy Walker, in her third Abbott musical—in fact, her third musical, period. That shows trust; but *Barefoot Boy* did nothing for Walker. She had but one almost good scene, when she and Noblesse Oblige (Betty Lou Watt) fight over dating rights to the oblivious Redfield:

> YETTA: Let's have some kind of contest. . . . The one who can quote the most from Karl Marx gets him.
> NOBLESSE: No, the one who can quote the most from Emily Post.
> YETTA: No. The one who can name the most stations on the Trans-Siberian railway.
> NOBLESSE: . . . The one who can sing the most song hits.
> YETTA: No. The one who can sing the most movements from the Shostakovich symphonies.
> NOBLESSE: Don't be ridiculous!
> YETTA: Just the allegro movements?
> NOBLESSE: No, I've got it. The one who can name all of Van Johnson's measurements.
> YETTA: No, Gromyko's.

Those who recall Walker can probably hear her voice and timing in those lines—the quirky vehemence of the born bluffer who knows she can't win but would die rather than surrender. What we have here is not great comic writing but great Walker writing, yet in the end even she could not save this dismal piece, and duly moved on to her fourth Abbott show, *Look, Ma, I'm Dancin'!*.

High Button Shoes came in as obscure a project as *Barefoot Boy With Cheek*. Except for director Abbott, everyone was a first-timer or relative unknown: producers Monte Proser and Joseph Kipness; composer Jule Styne and lyricist Sammy Cahn, both from Hollywood and on Broadway for the first time; bookwriter Stephen Longstreet, adapting his novel *The Sisters Liked Them Handsome*; and stars Phil Silvers and Nanette Fabray. Designers Oliver Smith and Miles White and choreographer Jerome Robbins had already won their spurs, true. Nevertheless, this seemed an unimposing undertaking, especially when word filtered out onto The Street that Longstreet's book was hopeless and that Abbott and Silvers were heavily rewriting it. The Shuberts, *éminences grises* on the project because it was to play one of their theatres, actually okayed a jump in Abbott's percentage to include author's royalties; but Longstreet grumped. "Watch out," Silvers reportedly warned him. "One of these nights we might play *your* script."

Silvers was the last of the great Golden-Age Comics to debut, coming just about an era after Victor Moore and Ed Wynn, a generation after W. C. Fields, Fanny Brice, and Joe Cook, and a decade after Jimmy Durante and Bobby Clark. Silvers played one Broadway show, *Yokel Boy* (1939), then went to Hollywood to perfect his persona as a small-change con man who seems most gauche when most attempting to ingratiate himself. His stock phrase was a violently grinning "How ah ya?" By the time of *High Button Shoes*, Silvers had decided to change his act from pseudo-charming to pseudo-commanding. It found ultimate completion in Silvers' first television series, *You'll Never Get Rich*, about scheming, manipulative Sgt. Bilko of the peacetime army; but Silvers already had his man down in *High Button Shoes* as Harrison Floy, a "bilko" who sells fake watches and Patagonian diamond mines, puts over a shady land deal, and tries to fix a football game that he has money on. Floy is always hustling, always defeated, yet he somehow never loses that absurd fantasy of control. Nabbed by the cops, he cries, "You fools! This will cost you your pensions!" and "You've sold me your last ticket to the Policeman's Ball!"

The time is 1913 and the place New Brunswick, New Jersey, site of Rutgers University, which provides a slight link with *Barefoot Boy With Cheek*. However, a quick runthrough of the *High Button Shoes* principals reveals how much more it had in stock than Shulman's show. *High Button Shoes* is really about Floy's effect on a family, the Longstreets. Fabray is Mama, Jack McCauley Papa,* and Mama has a younger sister (Lois Lee) who's dating a Rutgers football hero, Oggle (Mark Dawson). Like Barefoot Boy's Eino Fflliikkiinnenn, Oggle is big and dumb; but Eino is implausibly infantile and Oggle sings suave baritone in two ballads, "Can't You Just See Yourself" and "You're My Girl," not forgetting his rouser, "Next To Texas, I Love You." The Longstreets also have an Uncle Willie (Paul Godkin) and a maid (Helen Gallagher), who sneak in a dance specialty by trying out the "forbidden dance"—the tango.

George Jean Nathan counted *High Button Shoes* as the twenty-eighth nostalgia musical in five years. I note considerably more; maybe he was counting only shows of nationalist nostalgia. Certainly, here was another piece of Americana, with its working Model T, its Atlantic City beachfront set forth in the era when this was the raciest resort in the world, its polka picnic, even a rendering of "On the Banks of the Old Raritan" in close harmony, Styne and Cahn's idea of an Old School Song, chimed out by the football team and led by Silvers doing pitchpipe shtick.†

Already, I can tell you, *High Button Shoes* has *Barefoot Boy* licked on the First Essential, the score. Styne and Cahn had been

---

* Fabray was ridiculously young for the role—twenty-five, to McCauley's forty-seven. The couple's son, Stevie, was played by thirteen-year-old Johnny Stewart. That makes Fabray in effect somewhat under twelve years old at the time of conception: (just barely) physically possible, but culturally unlikely, at least in 1913 in New Brunswick, New Jersey.

† There was one error in all this marshalling of atmosphere, an allusion to the silent-film vamp Theda Bara, who did not begin her screen career till 1915, two years after the time of the show.

collaborators in Hollywood, and they had tried musical comedy once before, in *Glad To See You!* (1944), which closed out of town. That show may have representd a judicious apprenticeship, however, for their *High Button Shoes* score shows a sharp ability to Integrate Just Enough, to slip in the hopeful hit tunes while observing story and character. Call it the Aarons–Freedley plan not so much influenced by Rodgers and Hammerstein as simply aware of them.

The swinging Styne of later years (as in "All I Need Is the Girl" and "Comes Once in a Lifetime") had yet to be heard; nor did Styne attempt much in the way of period flavor. What these songs have is purity, melody, point. Oggle's ballads are so persuasive that even the verses sing, and Mama and Papa get a wonderful duet of interlaced lines in "I Still Get Jealous," a paean to the joys of lifelong marriage and thus bound to please the wives in the audience. Sentimental, really, is what it is; though, ironically, it was the Rodgers and Hammerstein shows that were accused of sentimentalizing. Ironically: because something like "You'll Never Walk Alone" inheres in *Carousel* absolutely as the unavoidable climax of a tragic romance; whereas the Longstreets' marriage, as developed in the *High Button Shoes* script, does not naturally reach for "I Still Get Jealous." Rather, it's time for a number, it's Fabray and McCauley's turn, and the sets are being changed, so send them out in one to sing and clown.

Yet *High Button Shoes'* score did hold together. The reprises in *Barefoot Boy* are merely plug spots—especially when the heroine sings Act One's "I Knew I'd Know" in Act Two with the same lyrics as before, as if nothing had happened in the meantime. Indeed, little had. But *High Button Shoes'* reprises game with the songs, not least when Floy borrows Oggle's "Can't You Just See Yourself" to woo the ingenue, with a new middle section on all the traveling they'll do. All Oggle could see was the two of them on a porch; Floy sees them in Paris, Russia, the Alps. Oggle's other ballad becomes, in a second comic inversion, "You're My Boy," for Floy and his shill, Mr. Pontdue (Joey Faye). It's not Rodgers and Hammerstein thinking: too silly. But it does set up a subtext in which Floy challenges Oggle, the comic going after the quarterback. First, he takes Oggle's songs. Next, he bets against Oggle's team. Last, in the locker room at halftime, he tries to maim Oggle so that he can't go on playing. Floy is *supposed* to be warning Oggle of the opposing team's treachery:

> FLOY: Watch out for the rabbit punch. (*He demonstrates by giving* OGGLE *one. No, several.*)
> OGGLE: (*staggering*) Don't worry, I'll watch out for it.
> FLOY: And this locked-leg trip. (*Demonstrates.*) And the knee kick. (*Demonstrates.*) And—oh, the kidney attack. (*Demonstrates.*) And the clip. (*Demonstrates.*) And the straight arm. (*Demonstrates. By now,* OGGLE *is on the floor. Floy pauses. A gleam comes into his eye.*) Then there's the "dipsy doo" . . .

Styne and Cahn wrote a particularly unusual first number, "He Tried To Make a Dollar." It's something like a sketch punctuated by song, in which we see Floy and Mr. Pontdue running through their snake-oil scams. Two things always happen: to whatever Floy is pitching, Pontdue cries, "I'll take *two!*," and police whistles break up the act and Floy and Pontdue grab their gear and run. "I'll take *two!*" becomes a running gag, so of course:

> FLOY: (*reproaching* PONTDUE's *breach of etiquette*) What do you *say* when you see ladies?
> PONTDUE: I'll take *two!*

As a typical late forties musical comedy, *High Button Shoes* was bound to have a few loose ends flapping on the plot line, and Floy's attempt to steal the ingenue away from the juvenile can't be taken seriously, though the script wishes us to do so, actually trying to squeeze some suspense out of it. So the senior Longstreets on one hand, and Lois Lee and Mark Dawson on the other, remain the evening's two couples, and the show ends as it began, with Floy and Pontdue now pushing beauty powders. "I'll take *two!*" Pontdue declares, followed by police whistles and the scurrying exit as the curtain falls

Another way in which *High Button Shoes* shows its value over *Barefoot Boy* was in the dance. True, it's not fair to *Barefoot Boy*'s choreographer, Richard Barstow, to stack him up against Jerome Robbins. But it's not their respective talents I speak of, just how much more creatively the *High Button Shoes* team found the dancing places in the overall structure. *Barefoot Boy* follows the convention of building a big number out of the singing ensemble followed by the dancing ensemble, capped by the two together vocalizing one last chorus. At that, these characters have no reason to dance, nothing emotional to express—which is why the score itself is so dreary. *High Button Shoes* doesn't have a lot of feelings, but at least its characters know why they're singing—and, in this decade more than any other in the musical's history, the dance comes out of the score. Before *Oklahoma!*, the hoofing was usually so miscellaneous that it worked perfectly well with any score at all; later, when choreographers began to seize power in the 1950s, the dancing often became autonomous, on a par with and even helping to create the score, demanding certain numbers for exploitation.

In the 1940s, however, song and dance were temporarily in perfect synch. So Robbins could get a pastorale out of the picnic scene, launched by a chorale, "Get Away For a Day in the Country" (charmingly led by McCauley and young Johnny Stewart) and followed by a lively celebration of the rustic life from the dancing corps. Then the party proper gets going, and Fabray has her gala spot, "Papa, Won't You Dance With Me" (which gave Doris Day one of her first big singles for Columbia when she was about to launch her movie career). Now Robbins can throw off the "de Mille" in the scene and go for it in a show-stopping polka that is there simply to enchant the house—and does.

Not a single moment in *Barefoot Boy* compares to this one in *High Button Shoes*, when a distinctively appealing performer (Fabray) gets a hot tune ("Papa") and a presentational spot (the polka with McCauley) that sweep the audience away. Nancy Walker enjoyed such a moment in *On the Town*'s "I Can Cook, Too," but she had nothing to grow on in *Barefoot Boy*, which is why that show ran only 108 performances.

The critics were not as enthusiastic about *High Button Shoes* as one might expect, expressing misgivings at the show's inconsistency. As Louis Kronenberger put it, "For a musical that's not very good, *High Button Shoes* is a very good musical indeed." The Shuberts certainly thought so; they waited out two quick flops booked into their flagship, the Shubert Theatre, then hustled *High*

Button Shoes down from Fifty-ninth Street to Forty-fourth, where the show ran up a total of 727 performances, embarrassing Rodgers and Hammerstein's *Allegro*, which very simultaneously played two doors westward, at the Majestic, to an even more mixed chorus of cheers and jeers and a much shorter run.

But then, *High Button Shoes* had a secret weapon. It was, in all, a very funny and tuneful show with a pointless book but an attractive cast and production and, above all, the "Bathing Beauty Ballet."

Here's more of Broadway's dance history, and, as with "Laurey Makes Up Her Mind" and "The Great Lover," we find a number so basic to the very workings of the show that deleting it would render the evening incoherent. Generally called the "Mack Sennett Ballet," this seven-minute dance-pantomime covered plot action, the chase after a bag of loot. But it was, more importantly, *High Button Shoes'* one major evocation of period, a tribute to silent-film comedy. It takes in not only the show's principals, the typical Mack Sennett beachfront maidens and careening cops, but a cohort of extremely strange types, some of them almost animal in appearance and one of them in fact a gorilla. To mostly original music (by dance arranger Genevieve Pitot) but also versions of the show's second-act opening, "On a Sunday By the Sea," of Liszt's Second Hungarian Rhapsody, and of Offenbach's can-can from *Orpheus in the Underworld*, Robbins drove his cast through something the decade had not seen before: the spendthrift lunacy of surreal farce. Silent-film comedy.

The "Bathing Beauty Ballet" did not alone make *High Button Shoes* a hit, for it did have other virtues. Still, without that dance, the show might easily have made a lot of money and then vanished. It was seen on television twice in the 1950s, though it never made it to Hollywood. Nor did its score achieve lasting popularity. The ballet, of course, became legendary, though it was not properly seen again till 1988, when *Jerome Robbins' Broadway* resuscitated it.

By then, Robbins was the musical's unrivaled director–choreographer, having outlasted de Mille and out-Napoleoned Kidd, Fosse, and Champion with *West Side Story, Gypsy*, and *Fiddler on the Roof*: art musicals. Back in 1947, de Mille was everybody's senior; Robbins himself thought so (at least *said* so) at the time. Yet he was next in line. Balanchine had been the director–choreographer on *Cabin in the Sky* and *What's Up*, but he shared billing with a book director on both. De Mille was the absolute mistress of *Allegro*—and Robbins, too, got to direct after *High Button Shoes*, with its Uncle Willie, Paul Godkin, as his choreographer: a Harold Rome show called *That's the Ticket!*, with the double-take cast list of Leif Erickson, Loring Smith, and Kaye Ballard. It closed out of town, so we'll never know how it came off; but the *staging* of musicals was now to become almost as strategic as the *writing* of them. Or: what would *Oklahoma!* have been like if Robert Alton had been its choreographer? Which told more truly, *On the Town*'s ballet music or Jerome Robbins' *On the Town* ballets? If *Song of Norway* had no story, why was it such a hit? Why was *Carmen Jones* the talk of the town even among people who thought they hated opera but loved the way the piece looked and moved?

And what if some smart authors, anticipating the fifties development of imaginative production, start writing shows with the imagination built into their texts?

11

THE CONCEPT MUSICAL

Stephen Sondheim comes to Hal Prince with an idea for a show about a man who is interesting not in himself but in how his existence reveals the vicissitudes of contemporary American civilization: money squeezes, adultery, false friends, the sheer destructive tempo of modern life. Throughout, the cast will comment on the action, analyzing it as it happens; the sets will provide atmosphere rather than physical location; and the action will occur not in "real time" but in a dialogue between the work and the audience. What will be presented, in effect, is *a show about a show.*

Company? Merrily We Roll Along? Neither; nor was it Sondheim and Prince. It was Rodgers and Hammerstein, planning *Allegro* (1947), the weirdest show of the decade. Consider the opening, as the curtain rises on . . . well, on something not physically possible. On an empty stage, one saw a woman in an old-fashioned brass bed, spotlit on the right, and, on the left, eight male and female choristers in black and white robes, holding scripts. Singing, they immediately explained who the woman is, and, after her doctor husband arrived, for a short book scene,

212

added in details about the couple's newborn son. The book and the score continued to take turns as more of the cast turned up— the mayor, drunks, kids, well-wishing neighbors, all in period dress and all thrilled at the birth of the town doctor's son. Obviously, now, the town will be able to count on a follow-up doctor in the next generation.

There's something of *Brigadoon* in this: tribal, ritualized, the purity of man-sized smalltown life, where one doctor more or less makes all the difference. As *Allegro* moves on, telling of the first forty-five years of this brand-new doctor's life, we see how other systems flourish. Life in college is experimental and confusing, better for the "go-getter" than the plodder. Then comes city life, which is absolutely corrupt.

That's not the show! Rodgers and Hammerstein insisted. They never meant to assault city culture, but rather to show the distracting vexations, the social nuisances, of the fancy life, wherever it is led. More important, they wanted to tear away all the distractions of forties stagecraft and present *nothing but the show itself*—costumed actors, accompanying orchestra . . . but no sets. No stage waits while sets are changed. None of those intermittent scenes in one so extraneous to storytelling but so necessary to cover the work of stagehands. In *Allegro*, as one scene ended, the next was already beginning: the coming scene's players were taking their places even as the previous scene's players were leaving.* Props and bits of suggesting visuals—a Swedish Modern plywood desk and a grand piano for the doctor's spiffy Chicago office, for instance—would be zoomed in and out on treadmills, and projections against a blank back canvas would set mood or location. But this was to be, above all, the Totally Integrated Musical, beyond *Oklahoma!* and *Carousel* in that *Allegro* would unify not just words, music, and dance but physical production as well. For the first time, the staging of the show was *written into the script of the show*. That is, this piece was not written and then, conven-

---

* This fluid on-and-off of actors was in fact introduced in Orson Welles' *Around the World*, a year earlier, but the practice did not become famous till Joshua Logan tried it in *South Pacific*, two years after *Allegro*. It takes a hit to establish a precedent.

tionally, staged. This piece was written to be staged in an unconventional way—written thus so pointedly that it could not *be* staged conventionally.

"Torn out of the folk life of America," said Brooks Atkinson. "All the elements of theatre are so perfectly blended that the music and the ballet are interwoven into one singing pattern of narrative." Atkinson felt that, after a less compelling second act, the authors "just missed the final splendor of a perfect work of art." Robert Coleman went even further: "*Allegro* is perfection . . . a stunning blend of beauty, integrity, intelligence, imagination, taste, and skill."

Note that both men used the notion of a "blending"—precisely what Rodgers and Hammerstein were going for, all the arts in coordination as the show seamlessly unfolds. Now let's hear from Cecil Smith, the first author of a history of the American musical:

> The staging of *Allegro* consisted largely of gadgetry raised to the nth power. . . . Jo Mielziner . . . equipped the stage with a treadmill upon which bits of setting, furniture, properties, and actors rode on and off . . . with tormentor curtains at each end which rose unobtrusively as they passed through. . . . The stage was frequently monopolized by a verbose speaking chorus, reinforced by a singing chorus ready to commit itself on any subject. These imperious groups served as a combined Super-ego and Id for the young doctor, leaving remarkably little for the [actor] to do in his own behalf except respond in a chain of reflexes.

Never before had a show by emphatically established authors so divided the critics. The *World-Telegram*'s William Hawkins called it "pretentious," *PM*'s Louis Kronenberger "boring." *Allegro* also divided the public. One wonders how audiences of 1947 greeted that rise of the curtain on the "real life" that was being played at stage left as commentary poured forth at stage right from people who technically didn't exist, especially after all they had heard from their friends. "Terrible," said some; "wonderful," said others.

"Slow" and "corny" are more correct; but also "rhapsodic" and "idealistic." It's very difficult to discuss as a platonic entity a show that was, from the first, designed to be a unique theatre experience, beyond the rate of its book and score. Creating a piece that would look and move like no other, Rodgers and Hammerstein were freely giving up Control: to Agnes de Mille, the first woman director–choreographer. Rodgers later claimed that de Mille had been overparted, that Hammerstein staged the book scenes and Rodgers the songs, de Mille merely choreographing. She herself disagreed, recalling that the chaotic book changes in Boston gave her no time to consider each rewrite, let alone block it out.

However, discussion of *Allegro* as a *staging* obscures flaws built into its *composition*. The village folk are so heartwarming, celebrating the doctor's baby's birth as if a native son had just been elected president, riding up on a buckboard (the show begins in 1905), and observing outdated social niceties, as when the doctor father calls his baby "Skeeziks," or when his wife calls her mother-in-law "Mother Taylor" rather than "that interfering bitch."

It's not clear whether Hammerstein wanted to work with archetypes or just didn't ever settle on who these people are. But one of *Allegro*'s major problems is that few of its principals are in any way interesting. The authors had a marvelous idea for a staging and a slightly good story. They had no characters: it's almost a comedy of humors. The protagonist, Joseph Taylor Jr. (John Battles), is Slightly Clumsy Good Intentions. His sweetheart, Jenny Brinker (Roberta Jonay), is Scheming Vixen. Joe's parents (William Ching, Annamary Dickey) are Noble Elders. At college, Joe adopts a chum (John Conte) who fills in as Merry Wastrel With Secret Wish To Go Straight, and, in Chicago, his nurse (Lisa Kirk) silently looks on as Joe's marriage dissolves knowing that She Would Be Better For Him Than That Materialistic Wife of His. It's almost a paint-by-numbers plot, framed in cheap balsa when, at the last minute, Joe refuses a lavish promotion to return to his hometown, with chum and nurse following.

However, all *this* obscures the great thing about *Allegro*: its concept. After all, it was the first attempt since *Show Boat* (1927) to try the epic form on the musical. *Allegro* covers almost as many years (thirty-five, to *Show Boat*'s forty or so) and is far more consistent in tone and style than the original *Show Boat* was.*

---

* I repeat, the *original* Show Boat. Every revival from 1946 on has revised

And are *Allegro*'s characters *that* boring? Jenny makes a fine villain—the pretty ones always do—and the freewheeling couch-artist chum who already knows what a great big stupid hypocrisy the whole world is while his earnest friend Joe is still figuring it out is always good company. If only the parents were not so flawless, the nurse not so nobly long-suffering.

If only most of the characters were the eccentrics that the musical had always thrived on, people doing crazy things—stealing gold from leprechauns, blundering into a ghost village, tracking down Miss Turnstiles. *Allegro* is square, credulous, and, worst of all, sober. Every musical before it had had a drink or two before the curtain went up.

Worse, the score was not remotely up to what one had heard in *Oklahoma!* and *Carousel*. Not *remotely*. While taking the show to its essence, the authors scaled down even the songs, alloting most of them to minor characters. They're good songs. A college co-ed's wistful hymn to the First Date, "So Far," Joe's trio with Jenny and that omniscient chorus (Joe and the chorus sing while Jenny dances), "You Are Never Away (from your home in my heart)," and the nurse's torch song, "The Gentlemen Is a Dope," were all temporary hits. Yet it was in the nature of *Allegro* that one had to see how they fit into the show's overall flow of images in order to appreciate them.

Wait a minute. We have to *see* a song to *hear* it?

Well . . . no. We have to see *Allegro* to attend it; reading the script and playing a recording won't suffice. Perhaps that's one way of identifying a concept musical. One needs to be there—right back at the Majestic Theatre in 1947–48—in order to take in the show's all-important motion. Remember, *allegro* is Italian for "lively." That was the key to this piece. It's mercurial, busy, going.

Do those who praise *Allegro* emphasize less what it finally was than what it was intended to be? I've done it myself. Artistry this

---

the piece to reconstitute it from a musical comedy with an operetta's storyline (and a score that veers now toward operetta, now toward musical comedy) to a tonally consistent musical play. But *Show Boat* isn't about consistency. *Show Boat* is about America: diversity.

imaginative deserves proclamation. Tommy Tune once observed, of The Business, that "if you go for a five and you make a five, you get applauded for it. But if you go for a ten and you end up with an eight, you get killed."

That is, if you try for nothing more ambitious than, say, *Annie Get Your Gun* and you succeed, you win all honors. If you try for something very out of the way and are perceived to have slipped up, they destroy you. Tune was speaking of a later concept show, *Grand Hotel* (1988), a went-for-ten-got-a-ten masterpiece that, like *Allegro*, was conceived as a unique staging and got mixed reviews (but ran much longer and paid off).

Tune is nonetheless sounding a timeless theme: when experimenting, be sure to have a hit, or you'll get no credit even for *what you did that worked*. After *Oklahoma!* and *Carousel*, *Allegro* racked up the biggest advance sale in Broadway history, with literally months of sell-out houses. The advance PR had been extraordinary—*Life* magazine did a cover on three of the chorus girls, as if every bitty aspect of this juggernaut must be scrutinized. Given *modern* casting usage, *Allegro* might have been a hit, with a tight all-singing, all-dancing ensemble backing the principals. But, in 1947, no one expected singers to dance or dancers to sing; or actors to do anything but act. *Allegro* had a huge cast, and thus a huge running cost, which forced it to give up after 315 performances, a good stay for the era but not for Rodgers and Hammerstein.

Needless to say, the terminally theatrical *Allegro* could not be filmed. The bare stage appealed to amateur and stock groups, which kept it trendy almost throughout the 1950s; and it was ideal for the arena-style summer-tent production, as the show really has no stars, no center, and no proscenium. High schools loved it. The many popular classics produced in the 1950s edged *Allegro* out of this fringe repertory by the 1970s. True, Equity Library Theatre mounted it, and, twenty years later, Encores! got around to it. But E.L.T. denuded the show of its four Big Ballets—one each on Joe's childhood and first love (with Jenny), his first college mixer, the Depression's effect on marriage, and the anomie of modern life—and what's a Big Ballet show without its Big Ballets? Encores! presented a touch of the dances, and, moreover, fielded

a fine cast headed by Stephen Bogardus' perfect Joe, so affable
and bewildered. It's a hard role to fill, because it's only half-
written; Bogardus made it substantial. Christine Ebersole also
took stage as the nurse, lifting the second half of Act Two and
reminding us why Lisa Kirk won stardom in such a small role.
Nevertheless, as a concert, this Encores! staging could not even
suggest what Rodgers and Hammerstein had in mind as *Allegro's*
very *raison d'être*: a concert version of a musical. How do you
produce a concert version of a concert?

At least *Allegro* remains one of those summoning titles: a by-
word for forties experimentation, the flop that marred the otherwise consecutive run of *Oklahoma!*, *Carousel*, *South Pacific*, and
The King and I; even just the show that produced "The Gentleman
Is a Dope," a semi-standard that finds Hammerstein in an un-
characteristically after-hours mood, writing the woman's equivalent of a Frank Sinatra song.

But Broadway's second concept musical was an obscure little
work that almost nobody saw and absolutely nobody ever mentions, though it got better reviews than *Allegro*—from respectful
bemusement to outright raves. This was *Ballet Ballads* (1948),
three through-sung one-acters by composer Jerome Moross and
lyricist John Latouche. Presented for a week by a recherché thespian collective at Maxine Elliott's Theatre, *Ballet Ballads* was
picked up by producer T. Edward Hambleton and moved to the
Music Box,* where the *Journal-American's* Robert Garland saw
something "fresh and exciting, as American as a hot dog spiked
with mustard," and where Robert Sylvester of the *Daily News*

---

* Maxine Elliott's Theatre, named for its actress owner and host to such performers as Ethel Barrymore, Helen Hayes, and Jeanne Eagels (in, no less, *Rain*),
was by the 1940s a radio studio in a part of town that The Street didn't care
about: east of Broadway and south of Forty-second Street. The Princess Theatre,
where Jerome Kern, Guy Bolton, and P. G. Wodehouse had—some say—invented American musical comedy, stood just across the street from the Elliott;
it was by then a cinema. *Ballet Ballads'* week at the Elliott was considered strictly
off-Broadway. It didn't even have an orchestra, just two pianos. Hambleton retained this questionable accompaniment on Broadway, which may have contributed to its run of just two months in a major Forty-fifth Street house after mostly
glowing reviews.

found "the best song-and-dance show to reach Broadway this season."

"Song-and-dance" is key here, for in the ballet ballad sound and motion are inextricably linked. Invented by John Murray Anderson in the 1920s for the *Greenwich Village Follies* revues, the ballet ballad is stagecraft at its most ingenious, like *Allegro* a piece written to stun by the way it moves even as it sings.

"Don't let them see how you do it," movie director Ernst Lubitsch is supposed to have advised a fledgling. "Just tell the story." Yet what director better defines the art of doing it with such élan that we *must* see how he does it? That's the concept musical: showing while it's telling.

What *Ballet Ballads* showed in design was little more than an empty stage with a collection of movable parts switched about for each of the three separate works: *Susanna and the Elders, Willie the Weeper,* and *The Eccentricities of Davey Crockett.* What it showed in dance was the style of three choreographers: Katherine Litz for *Susanna,* Paul Godkin (Helen Gallagher's tango partner in *High Button Shoes*) for *Willie,* and a debuting Hanya Holm for *Davey Crockett.* The first was a revival meeting, the second a druggy *noir,* and the last a joyous folk sing combining biography with tall tales, taking the frontier hero from dalliance with a mermaid and a confrontation with Halley's Comet on to Congress and a transfiguring death at the Alamo. Although the singing and dancing choruses appeared in all three titles, the most important performers appeared in one piece only, some dividing their roles, in the fashion of the forties dream ballet, between a singer and a dancer. Katherine Litz herself danced Susanna, to Sheila Vogelle's vocalizing, Paul Godkin and Robert Lenn shared Willie, and so on. The only notable cast member was Sono Osato, of *One Touch of Venus* and *On the Town,* playing *Willie*'s Cocaine Lil. Even the authors were uncelebrated, Moross unknown and Latouche, despite Broadway credits, unranked.

They did brilliant work, customizing each third of the show by its feelings just as each choreographer controlled his or her presentation. *Susanna,* costumed in rural Sunday best, was starchy but game, very modern dance. *Willie* sounds like the wedding night of Maxim Gorky and William Burroughs, the movement a kind of dazed boogie-woogie. *Davey Crockett* looked a bit like a high-school production of *Our Town* (of course, *Our Town* looks like a high-school production in the first place; I mean even more so), with the most outgoingly happy dancing of the evening. From the sly through the eerie to the festive, *Ballet Ballads* succeeded in synthesizing what are, after all, the real Essentials of the musical: song and dance. Unfortunately, the off-Broadway feeling of the whole, the lack of headline Names, and the general apathy in the matter of mixed-bill events meant that *Ballet Ballads* had no impact—except on its authors, who with producer Hambleton went on to create an evening-length ballet ballad in *The Golden Apple*, again starting off-Broadway, then moving uptown, in 1954.

Now. What if some really smart theatre men were to borrow this notion of the work that shows as it tells—commenting on its story even while enacting it, working in a stylized chronology, highlighting spots and bits as if in a revue—but wed it to razzle-dazzle musical comedy? Something sexier than *Allegro* and more mainstream than *Ballet Ballads*?

This would be *Love Life* (1948), produced by Cheryl Crawford, composed by Kurt Weill to Alan Jay Lerner's libretto, directed by Elia Kazan, choreographed by Michael Kidd, and starring Nanette Fabray and Ray Middleton as . . . well, this being a concept show, it's hard to put this simply. They're man and wife, certainly: Sam and Susan Cooper, with children Johnny and Elizabeth. More than that, they're Mr. and Mrs. American Couple, experiencing all the social and cultural pressures of a volatile civilization over the course of one hundred fifty-seven years. *Allegro* brought characters symbolically into scenes when they couldn't have been physically present, even after they had died; *Love Life* brought the Coopers up to date without letting them age. Instead, their marriage did, riven by the industrial revolution, the women's movement, and other historical forces that overwhelm their decent natures. All the while, such variety-show punters as a magician, a black quartet, a soft-shoe act, and so on pulled off their specialty turns before the curtain to shed ironic light on the Coopers' saga. Thus, while Sam and Susan were battered yet consistent, the entertainment itself was as unpredictable as ol' man river in flood.

Yes, here's another of those rare musical comedy epics, announced as a "musical vaudeville" but, like those earlier and later epics *Show Boat* and *Follies*, a very centered narrative filled with diversions that actually firm up that center. To pick but one example from each show, what could better emphasize the realism of *Show Boat*'s tortured Magnolia–Ravenal romance than to reflect it in the play-within-the-play, *The Parson's Bride*? For here is an oldtime melodrama in which the villain (Parthy Ann, really) is easily defeated and a guardian (Julie, in effect) comes in at just the necessary instant to guarantee the happy ending that true life in fact *doesn't* provide. And how better to reveal how badly *Follies'* Ben goofed in choosing the more correct Phyllis over the more enticing Sally than to show his breakdown during a devil-may-care number in tails, his dream of the high life literally breaking down because the high-toned Phyllis was only what he needed: the lowdown Sally was what he wanted.

Of course, this is a paradigm of epics only. *Show Boat* is not a concept musical. *Allegro* was the first of the kind, *Ballet Ballads* was the statistic, and *Love Life* was the hit. Or so it appeared to be, with some rave reviews despite a titanic gripe from Brooks Atkinson at Lerner's dark worldview and the *Star*'s John Lardner's suggestion that audiences first-act the piece. It played the 46th Street Theatre, a most desirable house, and was after all a sort of combination of *Finian's Rainbow, Brigadoon,* and *Annie Get Your Gun: Finian*'s producer and choreographer give you *Brigadoon*'s librettist and *Annie*'s big baritone of a leading man opposite the Absolutely Guaranteed Next Big Star, Nanette Fabray, who stole *Bloomer Girl* from Celeste Holm in replacing her as Evalina, seized stardom in *High Button Shoes*, and was now ready to join the pantheon of Lillian Russell, Marilyn Miller, Ethel Merman, and Mary Martin. It's important to know this, because *Love Life* is almost a two-person musical in the way that *Tristan und Isolde* and *Manon Lescaut* are two-person operas. *Love Life*'s chorus handles a lot of "in between," yes. But, in the story proper, there really are only two principals in this show. Their performances give it its style, along with the exciting Kidd dances, featuring his typical *snap!* and *stamp!*, not least in the dream ballet, "Punch and Judy Get a Divorce."

Love Life ran 252 performances and lost money. Still, it claims three great strengths: its structure, its look, and its score. The structure consists of story material punctuated by commentary in the form of show-biz tropes, as if the rise and fall of a typical American marriage were to occur while the radio was on. The piece begins in 1948 during a magician's act: Sam is levitated and Susan is sawed in half. It's a picture of the Coopers' marriage, with him lacking foundation and her torn in two as nurturer and breadwinner. They are in effect trading traditional gender roles: she's got the responsibility and he's . . . confused and unsure, his protest muted in image problems.

Lerner then cuts back to when their marriage was sound: in 1791, on the day when Sam opened a furniture store in Mayville, Connecticut, and greeted his new neighbors. Thereafter, each new vignette in the lives of the Coopers centers on some new assault on their bond—Susan's increasing restlessness as a mere housewife, for instance—while the time frame jumps a generation or two and the vaudeville irrupts onto the scene in ironic reflection. Most of these numbers, heard on their own, seem contextless, one-offs, novelties, because they are not integrated into the narrative so much as snatched out of it: the deceptively soothing "Progress," "Mother's Getting Nervous," the salacious "Economics," or a hobo's "Love Song,"* a Big Broadway version of the notion set forth in "Johnny's Song," the finale of Weill's first American musical, *Johnny Johnson* (1936): why can't we all help and support each other?

By the end of Act One, when the Coopers have a brush with adultery during a cruise, they have reached 1948 and their marital situation has gained critical mass. *Love Life*'s second act has little to pursue in terms of sheer story, so the vaudeville starts to take over, first in a madrigal, "Ho, Billy O!," that is far less pointed than previous numbers, then in the "Divorce" ballet, and finally

---

* There's a glaring error in the lyric to this number that no one seems to want to correct in the revivals that *Love Life* is increasingly getting: "Spokane" is made to rhyme with "Maine," though the Washington city is in fact pronounced to rhyme with "man." I raise this point to emphasize how sharp and correct most of Broadway's Golden-Age lyric writing actually was. One never finds mistakes like this in Hammerstein or Hart.

in a big set piece of a minstrel show, with Sam and Susan as the "end men" and an interlocutor who suggests a number of reme- dies for their marriage crisis—mysticism, in a pair of fortune- telling sisters in the number "Madame Zuzu"; cynicism, in a cer- tain Mr. Cynic's "Taking No Chances"; and at last from a coloratura soprano, Miss Ideal Man, who recommends romanti- cism. "You've got to have illusions to get along in this world," the Interlocutor warns the Coopers. So these are not real solutions, but makeweights. What are Sam and Susan to do?

Let's pause for a word about the minstrel show. This nineteenth-century form, indigenously American, was a "black- face" variety show—that is, white performers in racial makeup playing in stereotypical style. The ensemble, counting dancers and singers, sat on chairs set down in rows, the front row bearing the most popular specialists, with the Interlocutor in the center and the end men, Mr. Tambo and Mr. Bones, in the last seats on either end of the row. The Interlocutor served as emcee but also played comic bits with the end men, usually a duo act of some kind. (Mr. Tambo played tambourine, Mr. Bones cymbals; thus the names.) By the early twentieth century, when blackface stars such as Al Jolson and Eddie Cantor were at their height, the min- strel show itself was outdated yet ubiquitous—not performed, but constantly referred to as an established American thing. "Sho 'nuff?" an entertainer—of any kind—might say. "Sho 'nuff," came the answer.

That's end-man cliché, retained by Lerner for Sam and Susan in the minstrel sequence. Yet by 1948 the minstrel show was more than outdated: outlandish. It hung on in the culture, more than a memory; MGM's Mickey-and-Judy *Babes* series includes several minstrel pastiche numbers, burnt-cork cosmetic and all. The hor- ror, the horror. Clearly, audiences when *Love Life* was new could relate to superannuated minstrel art as another of Lerner's games with time and genre. This by-then ancient form is a cure, a re- lease. That is, Sam and Susan get so "modern"—so screwed up by the social complications of contemporary life, in the *Allegro* manner—that only a trip back to the art of their roots (1791 is premature for the minstrel show, but close enough) can purify them.

Sam and Susan don't appreciate the Interlocutor's illusions. Ironically, however, Lerner's finale finds them back with the magician who opened the show: an illusionist. At first, *he* was floating in air and *she* was cut in two. Now they're on opposite ends of a tightrope, trying to reach each other, as the curtain falls. It's the decade's most inconclusive curtain, yet we sense that the pair will make it: because they have to. Sam and Susan have been part of history during the show; now they are history. The fate of American marriage depends on them.

A show this unusual could not look like any other show; and here, too, we need a little backstory. *Love Life*'s set designer, Boris Aronson, is comparable to only Jo Mielziner in his influence on the physical appearance of musicals. Like Mielziner an émigré from Europe who enjoyed a Broadway career in many genres, Aronson touched base with Great American Titles in Clifford Odets's *Awake and Sing!*, Thornton Wilder's *The Merchant of Yonkers* (the flop, directed by Max Reinhardt, that eventually became *The Matchmaker* and *Hello, Dolly!*), and William Saroyan's *The Time of Your Life*. Aronson had designed few musicals when he came to *Love Life*, but he was to be graduated into an archon of the concept show with *Cabaret, Zorba, Company, Follies, A Little Night Music*, and *Pacific Overtures*, after which he died.

What Mielziner gave to the musical was fluidity: solving technical problems to keep a show's narrative flowing from scene to scene. What Aronson gave was the use of abstraction, suggestion. Aronson's straight-play settings could be as realistic as anyone's— but the musical he saw as artwork, a droll testimony, *genere fantastico*. Anything can happen: so Aronson made it look that way, suavely stippling his eighteenth-century Mayville with coughing smokestacks as the industrial age kicks in, giving Punch and Judy a Greek portico and blue bunting for their divorce, and flooding the minstrel show with yellow light from a big red watching eyeball of a sun.

One of *Allegro*'s many problems was its lack of "look"—that bare stage with the bits and pieces trained on and off, the back projections that never worked properly . . . really, the high-school players club appearance for a show that garnered the biggest advance sale in Broadway history. Big shows are supposed to look big—or, better, imaginative shows should look weird. *Allegro* looked elaborately cheap. It was *Love Life* that looked weird, almost like a revue trying to turn into a book show, caught between the vaudeville facetiae and the Coopers' realistic throughline.

Actually, a book show turning into a revue is one way of defining the concept musical. Another is that, hearing its score alone, one picks up two different but related shows: one of character and situation numbers and the other of *Cliffs' Notes* on the characters and situations. Nearly half of *Love Life*'s score is *Cliff's Notes*, as the ironically shuffling octet "Progress" tells how new constructions in the culture can be destructive, just after Sam and Susan have poignantly reaffirmed their love in "Here I'll Stay" and just before they comically reminisce—because he gets everything wrong—in "I Remember It Well."* Thus, two different and even antagonistic aesthetics alternate in the songs—and one of the oddest qualities of the concept musical is its use of perfect strangers to tell us more about what's going on than the lead characters can.

Of course, if the musical's history were virtuous, *Love Life* should have been the fourth Lerner and Loewe show—the one right after *Brigadoon*—but for Loewe's exasperation with Lerner's lazy and unreliable attitude toward work. (Another collaborator whom Lerner offended was Richard Rodgers, in the early stages of *On a Clear Day You Can See Forever* [1965], which Rodgers quit, replaced by Burton Lane.) Still, it's difficult to imagine Loewe responding to the intellectual nature of a show such as *Love Life*. Madame Zuzu? Punch and Judy do what? Half the score is sung by bit players? Loewe liked a place with a sound and characters with feelings: "I'll Go Home With Bonnie Jean," "They Call the Wind Maria," "The Ascot Gavotte," *Gigi*'s Offenbachian "Gossip," "Guinevere."

It was Weill who loved composing the *pièce d'occasion*, not so

---

* Reader, you guessed right—this is the original of the number for Maurice Chevalier and Hermione Gingold in *Gigi*, on the same idea but with new lyrics and, of course, now composed by Frederick Loewe. Both versions are in slow waltz time, though the melodies scan differently and though the *Gigi* duet is more touching in that it reunites lovers who've been separated for an epoch.

much on place and characters but on an *idea*. Had he lived long enough, his final work might have been *Cabaret*; as it was, his wife, Lotte Lenya, deputized, and there's a trace of Weill's sound in the Kander–Ebb score. This is not to say that Weill's music lacks feelings. *Street Scene* alone tells us how easily this man spirited himself into his characters—"What Good Would the Moon Be?," "Lonely House," "Somehow I Never Could Believe," "Wrapped in a Ribbon and Tied in a Bow," even that see-it-from-the-villain's-eyes quotation of *Tiefland*.

The *idea* of the concept show is often encapsulated in its All-Knowing Number, which explains the show's theme and worldview and sometimes even staging plan, all at once. *Allegro*'s is "Come Home," *Cabaret*'s is the title song,* *Follies*' is "The Road You Didn't Take," *Pacific Overtures*' is "Someone in a Tree," *Side Show*'s is "Come Look at the Freaks." *Love Life* had one, but it was cut out of town—"Susan's Dream," another of those vaudeville numbers, telling how the heroine visualized the ideal American marriage. Strangely, it seems to harbor the same faults that her own marriage exhibits—uneven husband, troublesome kids. But that's as ideal as it gets. There is no ideal. "Susan dreamed," the lyric runs, "exactly what she had."

The score, overall, is wonderfully tuneful. There's Weill doing his "Look! I'm American!" thing in "My Name Is Samuel Cooper," which sounds like the child of Aaron Copland and Julia Ward Howe; and "Here I'll Stay" gives the Coopers a timeless romantic basis, while "Green-Up Time," the big dance vocal, sets up a hoedown. So this is national, even nationalistic music, but not propaganda. It's theatre music, what Weill always relished writing, despite the high political profile of his German collaborators. Naturally, Weill responds to the formal demands of the piece, strictly segregating the tone of the story numbers from that of the vaudeville numbers. The latter grin and giggle; the story songs sigh and worry and celebrate.

Why didn't *Love Life* run? Because besides its three strengths

---

* No, it's not "Willkommen," which does present the show's general behavioral pattern but gives no hint of the work's look at people who "perform" their lives, whether as thespians, hustlers, or yes-men in a no-yields-death regime.

it has three problems: too little story, too few characters, and not enough laughs. In other words: a bad book. Lerner put all his perceptions into the lyrics—for instance, in the introduction to "Here I'll Stay," where Sam claims that what he's "searching for" is "a place to live with you for ever more." A place, really, that stays harmonious and stable. That's not America. Ours is a culture constantly in flux, as *Show Boat* and *Follies* demonstrate.

Yet Lerner put very little of that into the dialogue. It reads as might a television sitcom without the laughs. It's all fill-in and buzzing. The single good straight gag in all the spoken scenes comes as Sam is about to abandon his family midway in Act One. Is he going off to war? To prison? Everyone's trying to be brave about it:

> JOHNNY: Who is going to say grace at luncheon now?
> SAM: Why, you, son.
> JOHNNY: (*proudly*) Yes, sir.
> SAM: Goodbye, Susan.
> SUSAN: Goodbye, Sam. Take care.
> SAM: Bless you.
> ELIZABETH: (*as* SAM *leaves in despair*) Mother! Mother! . . . Where exactly does Father have to go?
> SUSAN: Today is his first day at the factory.
> ELIZABETH: When will he be back?
> SUSAN: Tonight, for supper.

When we consider how many good lines we hear in *Oklahoma!*, *One Touch of Venus*, *On the Town*, and *Finian's Rainbow*, we resent *Love Life*'s lack of humor. It should have been a contender: this was a potential classic. It doesn't help to realize that plenty of unimportant and even flop musicals had no trouble getting up good lines.

Still, any Kurt Weill show arrests us, and *Love Life* does have that wonderfully imaginative structure. A place that doesn't change: what notion could be more dramatic in the great art form of the country of the culture of change? The country of *Citizen Kane*, *Gone With the Wind*, jitterbug, Elvis Presley, television, Martin Luther King, William Burroughs, *Rent*. The performance of "Green-Up Time" 's village do-si-do before Aronson's looming smokestacks tells us how rich a work *Love Life* was, bringing design and dance into order simply to present the disorder of American life. This very richness also tells us how tricky it would be to bring this work home to moderns. Life is all smokestacks now, or cell phones.

Or microphones. Imagine a musical performed without a sound system, as the players simply open their mouths and project their lines into the house. That's how theatre sounded then: one on one, with a few lines lost if you were sitting behind Row M. More than a few, in the balcony. Still, it all took place in real time. What they said on stage was what one heard, at the moment of its utterance.

Have you noticed how often Weill collaborated with playwrights rather than with veteran musical writers like Lerner? Of Weill's American shows, only *Love Life* and *Lady in the Dark* had scripts by men used to writing the texts of musicals—and these two shows were all the same radical departures from format. No, from his German works with Georg Kaiser and Bertolt Brecht and on to such American partners as Paul Green, Maxwell Anderson, Edwin Justus Mayer, and Elmer Rice, Weill liked to make musicals not with insiders but with adventurers. His plan was to create new forms *every time he wrote*; even Kern and Hammerstein never tried to pull that off, and only Stephen Sondheim has followed Weill's lead, albeit with old pros like Hal Prince or James Lapine who can hardly help but fall into familiar grooves here and there. What Weill wanted were partners who hadn't worn themselves into grooves.

That was certainly true of Maxwell Anderson, Weill's partner on *Knickerbocker Holiday* (1938), a satire on totalitarianism with Pieter Stuyvesant as the available tyrant. Anderson was political, ultra-liberal but also, unconventionally for the day, ultra-anti-communist. All statesmen were forms of Stalin to Anderson, whose outlook veered between a raging disgust to a helpless optimism. Oddly, for a political, Anderson specialized in the most outdated (one could say "conservative") of forms, the verse play.

True, his early hit, the war play *What Price Glory?* (1924), co-written with Laurence Stallings, was an earthy vernacular comedy. But such works as *Elizabeth the Queen* (1930), *Mary of Scotland* (1933), *Valley Forge* (1935), *Winterset* (1935), *Wingless Victory*

(1936), *High Tor* (1937), and *Key Largo* (1939) identified Anderson as America's "second" playwright (after Eugene O'Neill), so rhapsodic and thematic, yet scorned as so trendy and fancy and importunately highbrow. Anderson was the bourgeoisie's golden boy and the intelligentsia's whipping boy; Wolcott Gibbs wrote a *New Yorker* parody of *Uncle Tom's Cabin* as it might have been written by Anderson that is a guilty, shameful delight. Still, Anderson's writing was beautiful and theatrically canny, and it created superb roles for actors—the Lunts, Helen Hayes, Katharine Cornell, and Paul Muni were among those who played the premieres.

These works are never revived today. I mean, *verse plays?* Doesn't Shakespeare occupy that slot? Even more bizarre, then, is the notion of Anderson writing book and lyrics for a musical. Yet that's *Knickerbocker Holiday*'s charm: it knows it's strange and doesn't care. The story's good, the music's wonderful, and, even if Anderson keeps sticking too many words into the musical phrases and waxing super-poetic, the show has presence and point. With Walter Huston playing Pieter Stuyvesant, it also had a star turn—and, of course, there was a Hit Tune, still standard, "September Song."

Small wonder that Weill and Anderson maintained a friendship and sought always to reassume their collaboration. They discussed various projects, but finally a most unlikely novel, an overnight best-seller of 1948, gave them them their go-ahead piece: Alan Paton's *Cry, the Beloved Country*, on race relations in the Union of South Africa. It's lush writing—listen to the first lines:

> There is a lovely road that runs from Ixopo into the hills. These hills are grass-covered and rolling, and they are lovely beyond any singing of it. The road climbs seven miles into them, to Carisbrooke; and from there, if there is no mist, you look down on one of the fairest valleys of Africa. About you there is grass and bracken, and you may hear the forlorn crying of the titihoya, one of the birds of the veld.

It's a counterpart to John Steinbeck, perhaps: evocative, spacious, lyrical. Weill and Anderson were entranced, and, though Anderson saw it as a spoken play with incidental music and choral commentaries, Weill was not at this time in his career writing incidental music and choral commentaries for shows. He was writing shows; and this was his last, for he died soon after it opened.

Lost in the Stars (1949) would thus have been a "concept drama" if the authors had not expanded the score to take in character and situation numbers. So here is our fourth concept musical, its staging plan written into the text: a mixed-race chorus is to be omnipresent, now seated along a broad staircase rising out of the orchestra pit, now on stage, watching the action and even reacting to it.

Interestingly, while the authors brought certain characters into the music, they kept other characters out of it. *Lost in the Stars* is in essence the tale of two families to three generations; one rich and white, the other poor and black. The black senior, Stephen Kumalo, is an Anglican priest; his wayward son, Absalom, kills the white senior's son, ironically a partisan of black liberation. But while Stephen is the show's singing lead, Absalom is a speaking role, the youngest Kumalo (Stephen's nephew, illegitimately conceived) has one song, and the whites sing not at all. Two black women, one of them Absalom's girl friend, add in three numbers. Everything else is bits and chorale. So *Lost in the Stars* really is what Anderson had conceived in the first place: a play with music. Yes, it's a musical, but technically, not culturally: no dancing, no comedy, no glamor. No sex.

Yet it is the score, not the script, that distinguishes the piece. Even without access to the zany charades of *Lady in the Dark*'s dreams or the romantic eros that plays through *One Touch of Venus* or the rich cross section of humankind in *Street Scene*, Weill imbued *Lost in the Stars* with humanity, dignity, and beauty, just as Paton did his novel. Defying Paton's own warning ("they are lovely beyond any singing of it"), Weill and Anderson turned Paton's first two pages into their opening number simply by deleting lines, changing or adding virtually nothing. Like Paton's opening, the musical's is superbly inductive. There is no overture; with the house in absolute darkness, the orchestra strikes up the theme of the . . . well, the novel's title song, "Cry, the Beloved Country," and the curtain rises on an empty stage. Immediately, the chorus people enter, some up the stairway from the orchestra pit and some from the wings. One man stands at center, the Chorus Leader, who begins, "There is a lovely road. . . ."

To start a show thus is, purposefully, to announce a staging plan that will affect the narrative, a text within the text. We have seen many shows open boldly, surprisingly: *Cabin in the Sky, Pal Joey, Oklahoma!, On the Town, Carousel, Around the World*. But they were all, at that first moment, communicating from within the narrative. None began *outside* the narrative, presentationally rather than dramatically; and *Lost in the Stars* emphasizes this bifurcated structure of story told by storytellers when, after the Leader's first solo paragraph, the Chorus Answerer, sitting on the steps and gazing out into the auditorium of the Music Box Theatre, says, "But sing now about the lower hills."

Possibly inspired by the astonishing poetry of this number, which is at once an elegy on the beauty of the land and a mourning for the lost potential of its people, Anderson wrote even more lyrically in *Lost in the Stars* than he had in *Knickerbocker Holiday*. As before, he delights us with songs on topics never before thought of for a musical. But then, Anderson didn't know musicals or their usual topics. *Knickerbocker Holiday* has the book and lyrics of an author who had never seen a musical; *Lost in the Stars* has the book and lyrics of an author who had seen only *Knickerbocker Holiday*. His selection of song spots is somewhat off-the-wall, but always smart: "Thousands of Miles" for Stephen Kumalo's reflections on the relationship between father and son, a character song not only for Stephen but for the errant and as yet unseen Absalom; "Fear" for the mixed-race chorus after the murder; the disturbingly lovely title song, this time of *Lost in the Stars*, for God seems to have lost track of the destiny of men and has left us to fall helpless through the universe; "The Wild Justice," the second-act opening, another scene for the chorus and its Leader; "Oh, Tixo, Tixo, Help Me," a soliloquy for Stephen to rival *Carousel*'s; even a number about Absalom's impending execution, "Four O'Clock."

Just beginning a song with the line, "How many miles to the heart of a child?," is to bring something to the musical it seldom knew before—poetry. Could this be the best set of lyrics in all the decade? It is without question the most original, heartbreaking, stunning. "Hunt the wild justice down!" the chorus sings, of a murder trial, to pounding drums, and one thinks, "What man thought up this disturbingly accurate image?"

In keeping with the show's relatively small scale, Weill composed for a pit of just twelve players—all virtuosos, for, besides five strings, one trumpet, harp, percussion, and a pianist doubling on accordion, the three reed players had to blow among them three clarinets, three saxophones, flute, oboe, and bass clarinet. The design, too, was ingeniously threadbare: George Jenkins arranged a few iconic backdrops—the country, the city (a skyscraping Emerald City flanked by the huts of shantytown)—before which free-standing pieces would be rolled or flown in to present, in synecdoche, the places of the tale.

This is very *Allegro*. Nothing more than a railroad semaphore anchored "Train to Johannesburg," as the chorus "sang" the train, sustained chromatic keening over a "click-clack clickety" rhythmic structure. After "The Hills of Ixopo" introduces the cultural background and "Thousands of Miles" the character plot, "Train to Johannesburg" gives us the racial program: this train takes whites on a business or social journey, blacks to their doom. Wailing and click-clacking, the chorus motionlessly pulls the train in and sees it off (bearing Stephen Kumalo), but this of course is not the dancing train of *Miss Liberty*. That was zany; this is anxious, foreboding, as, again, is the warily watching chorus during "The Search," a mixture of song and dialogue as Stephen hunts for Absalom. Moving from one address to the next, from guilty citizens to government workers, he strives to hope for the best. But, at one moment, the chorus, to a man and woman, swerved their heads to stare at the action, pointing out to us a grisly plot checkpoint: Absalom is clearly involved in crime. As the number ended, the men dolorously sang, "This is heavy, heavy for me," as the lights blacked to fading spot on Stephen, Christ climbing Calvary.

This use of the chorus as intermediary between the characters and the public—another reminder of *Allegro*—was most movingly brought out in "The Little Grey House," in which Stephen tells his homeless nephew, Alex, about the village shack where the Kumalos live. Things are going ever more badly, but here is one moment of sweetness in the tragedy. "What are you thinking?" the chorus women ask Stephen, a capella. And "What do you see?" they ask Alex. There, amid the "broken boxes" and "broken hopes" of shantytown, where the two are putting up, the use of the singing women almost supplies the missing piece in the scene, Stephen's wife and, obviously, the woman who will raise Alex. This is another facet of the concept show, the imaginative "suggesting" of things and people, the anticipating and echoing that will eventually lead to *Follies'* ghosts and *Chicago's* very transformation of the story score into a series of show-biz "spots."

"The Little Grey House" itself is a ballad sung over a tender boogieing of bass clarinet punctuated by pizzicato string and harp chords. Like an old da capo aria, it has a contrasting middle section, in which Stephen briefly gives way to worry; then the soothing main strain returns, with the full chorus wordlessly helping out and the strings dominating. It turns out that the number was a lullaby, for Alex has fallen asleep in this terrible place. Not that the little grey house is anything to praise. "The only thing special is," the song concludes, "it's home!" Chorus and orchestra now present a tiny recap as Stephen puts Alex to bed and blows out the candle. Then, in the darkness, the orchestra breaks into an ugly rasp of blues as the scene changes to a honky-tonk for "Who'll Buy (my juicy rutabagas)?," a floor number, as men ogle the saucy singer. Of course, the chorus have vanished, leaving us to infer what they think of this dive. They function as the chorus couldn't in a conventional musical, serving by turns as narrators, sentimentalists, and referees in the show's moral battle between destiny and free will.

Nominally, *Lost in the Stars* was produced by the Playwrights' Company, which Elmer Rice, Sidney Howard, Robert E. Sherwood, and S. N. Behrman had founded with Anderson in 1938 out of frustration with the managers they had been giving their scripts to, especially the Theatre Guild. Weill had joined the organization in 1946, while working with Rice on *Street Scene*, and while the other members of the group freely offered advice, the casting and the hiring of the technical coterie on *Lost in the Stars* were up to Weill, Anderson, and their director, Rouben Mamoulian. They had one major problem: Paul Robeson said no. Other actors were easily found—Leslie Banks as Jarvis, the father of Absalom's murder victim; Warren Coleman as Stephen Kumalo's cynical city-dwelling brother; Julian Mayfield as Absalom; Herbert Coleman as young Alex; and Inez Matthews as Absalom's girl friend, an important role with two of the score's biggest moments, "Trouble Man" and "Stay Well."

Still, Stephen is a towering figure, one for a black baritone who can act, and Robeson, strangely, was thought to be the only one. I say *strangely* because Mamoulian had directed and Warren Coleman and another cast member, Georgette Harvey, had appeared in the original *Porgy and Bess*: didn't they think that Todd Duncan, the Porgy of that and most other *Porgy* productions to that time, could handle it? True, Duncan was more singer than actor. But he had the dignity that Stephen requires above all as he so patiently trudges roads to doom. Not inexorably—for Anderson makes it clear that Absalom could evade responsibility by lying. But just as Stephen finally finds his son, his son finds his Father: and thus will not lie. And so he condemns himself.

Todd Duncan was finally tapped, and *Lost in the Stars* opened to the same mixed reviews that *Allegro* had got, from "a soaring musical tragedy" to "pretentious simplicity." It lasted 273 performances but still lost money; worse, a generally terrible 1972 revival with Brock Peters petered out in five weeks. One problem that the revival found more vexing than the original had done was Anderson's ending. This pictures the two bereaved fathers reconciling their racial differences, though Jarvis is a conventional believer in white superiority. But they reconcile at the moment of Absalom's execution for the murder of Jarvis' son. Each says, "I have a friend." In 1972, Peters angrily waved the white man away. That doesn't work any better than the original ending did. How much more effective is the ending of Paton's novel:

> Yes, it is the dawn that has come. The titihoya wakes from sleep, and goes about its work of forlorn crying. The sun tips with light the mountains of Ingeli and East Griqualand. . . . But when that dawn will come, of our emancipation, from the fear of bondage and the bondage of fear, why, that is a secret.

As the show begins with the Chorus Leader intoning Paton's opening words, why not have this same player speak Paton's final words, letting the chorus close with Weill's coda, a last bit of "Thousands of Miles," thus putting a musical button on the evening while respecting Paton's unresolved wonder and avoiding Anderson's implausible ecumenism?

In all, the concept musical was the fourth most strategic invention of the 1940s. It did not bear much *immediate* influence, mainly because the musical was busy absorbing the third most strategic invention, the replacement of hoofing by sophisticated choreography, and the second most strategic invention, the Rodgers and Hammerstein approach to conception and composition.

However, the musical had already been undergoing transformation by a technological/cultural development from outside itself, one that would change forever how we view the musical, how its traditions are respected, and its history is told. This was the most strategic invention: the cast album.

12

THE CAST ALBUM

The word "factoid," commonly used to denote "a nugget of information," was actually coined, by Norman Mailer, to mean "a piece of common knowledge that isn't true." The classic factoid of the forties musical is that *Oklahoma!* got the first original-cast album.

No: *Florodora* did, in 1900, on twelve seven-inch Berliners.* They were piano-accompanied, and the chorus was greatly reduced. But an expanding science was soon able to accommodate a small orchestra, if not yet a true chorus. No American production was preserved at this time, save for the odd studio cut by a performer or two. By the 1910s, however, West End stagings were being recorded almost routinely, including mountings of American shows—Berlin's *Watch Your Step*, Kern's *Oh, Boy!*, Romberg's

---

* Emile Berliner invented the sound disc, patented in 1897, though the recording of sound on Thomas Edison's cylinder had already been in use for a decade. Berliner experimented widely with subject matter for his discs, for instance taking down five sides of the original cast of Victor Herbert's *The Fortune Teller* in 1898. However, the *Florodora* records constitute the first attempt to gather a selection of a show's main musical numbers in some representative quantity.

Her Soldier Boy, the aviation novelty *Going Up*, Marilyn Miller's *Sally*, with Dorothy Dickson as Marilyn Miller, Friml's *The Blue Kitten* and *Rose-Marie*, the definitive twenties musical comedy, *Lady, Be Good!* (with its Broadway stars, Fred and Adele Astaire), the biggest hits of 1925, *Sunny* and *No, No Nanette* (which didn't get as much as single original-cast cut at home), *The Desert Song*, *The Three Musketeers*, and the last of the operetta classics, *The New Moon*.

America didn't have its own show album* till 1932, when Ziegfeld revived *Show Boat* for the first of its many Broadway resuscitations, and the only one without changes. But this was not a *cast* recording. That term prefers the opening-night players and orchestra personnel performing the bulk of the score more or less as it was heard in the theatre. This *Show Boat* was anything but: two of the cast with a few ringers, new arrangements for the pickup pit (with two of the love duets remade as solos), and no chorus—not even for Paul Robeson's "Ol' Man River." Nor did the album's producer, Jack Kapp, cover any more of the score than the six hits, with an overture and medley finale (though Kapp did include a taste of "Mis'ry's Comin' Aroun'" on Helen Morgan's "Can't Help Lovin' Dat Man"). Kapp and his label, Brunswick, also saved *Blackbirds of 1928*, though this, too, was a studio creation using only some of the original performers.

Then Victor caught eight twelve-inch sides of *Porgy and Bess* on its premiere, in 1935, with the original chorus and orchestra, under the original conductor, Alexander Smallens, though Met singers Lawrence Tibbett and Helen Jepson took the solo lines. So the idea of The Album was there, now. Two shows of 1937, *Pins and Needles* and *The Cradle Will Rock*, were recorded with their original casts . . . and the little piano accompaniment heard

---

* Has anyone noticed that the word "album" is incorrect today? Albums are books of collections, as for stamps or photographs. Thus, the 78 set was an album, with "leaves" to hold the records. When the LP and its *single* sleeve were introduced, cast recordings were no longer "albums." Yet the word has hung on to the present day, now challenged by the wholly inappropriate, even illiterate, "Sound track," which actually signifies the band of audio material on film and, by extension, recordings drawn from that track. Only movies have sound tracks. Shows have cast "albums."

in the theatre. These were the first American original-cast albums: but of unimportant music and, also, of offbeat, virtually off-Broadway shows, though both played The Street, *Pins and Needles* in what had been the Princess Theatre and *The Cradle Will Rock*, after it was forced out of Maxine Elliott's Theatre, in the Venice, which, as the New Century, later hosted *Up in Central Park, High Button Shoes*, and *Kiss Me, Kate*.

Pianos and ditties, no. What we're looking for is something re-flecting the power that musical comedy enjoys in the theatre, that Life Is Wonderful Because the Songs Are So Good mentality. Decca's lively three-disc set of *The Boys From Syracuse* in 1938, with Rudy Vallee, Frances Langford, and Harry Sosnik's orches-tra, was closer than *Pins* and *Cradle* to what we mean by the term "cast album," though none of the participants had any connection with the show.

What if the participants did? What if Ethel Merman made a *Panama Hattie* album, Gertrude Lawrence a *Lady in the Dark*? They did, and all right; these were studio dos, more like short radio concerts than Broadway. But then came a breakthrough: Decca recorded the 1942 *Porgy and Bess* revival.

Of course, that low-budget production tolerated extremely cut-down orchestrations, and this was in fact the *second* volume of Decca's *Porgy and Bess*, the first having been taken down in 1940 with just Todd Duncan and Anne Brown, the show's original leads, singing various characters' solos, as Tibbett and Jepson had done in 1935. Still, the 1942 album brought in *Porgy*'s other play-ers; and a third volume, with Avon Long and Helen Dowdy (of the 1942 cast) backed by Leo Reisman's orchestra in amiable dance-band readings, filled out Decca's overview of the piece. It's a tangled history. But, a decade later, the bulk of these three 78 albums, transcribed together onto one LP, produced what, even today on CD, appears to be Broadway's first original-cast album, albeit of a revival (using, however, most of the original 1935 cast).

Well, *now* the history can be made, surely; but something hap-pened first. Six months after *Porgy and Bess* opened, the Petrillo Ban went into effect: no member of the Musician's Union could take part in any recordings, anywhere, at any time. James Caesar Petrillo, head of the union, deeply resented the use of recorded music on the radio and in the newly popular jukebox, for his constituency received no royalties for what was in effect their infinitely repeated performances. Petrillo demanded compensation, the recording industry refused, and, on August 1, 1942, all professional recording ceased.

The major labels—Victor, Columbia, and Decca—had plenty of recordings as yet unreleased, so they were prepared to ride out the strike. However, they could market only music that had been made before the ban went into effect. Any new popular song, even a potential gold-mine hit, was verboten. Of course, radio could present any music live, including the latest hit. But it could not be recorded: so no new Broadway show could get a cast album, not a single cut of any kind, no matter how popular its score. But how could a score *be* popular without recordings?

However, the Petrillo Ban contained one amusing loophole. It naturally excepted any recording made as part of the War Effort. Jack Kapp, now at Decca, took advantage of this exemption to record *This Is the Army*, with the profits assigned to Army Emergency Relief. This was even more strictly a cast album than Decca's *Porgy and Bess*es, for now every performer in the set was heard in his actual stage role; and the orchestra was of regulation Broadway pit size. Decca had a hit, and Kapp must have been chuckling at his coup, not least because the competition over at Victor and Columbia depended heavily on their classical backlist, unaffected by the ban, while Decca dealt strictly in pop music and thus needed to keep up with the hot new performers, titles, events.

This Is the Army was a chance stopgap, no more. What was Kapp to do when the *Oklahoma!* phenomenon hit in March of 1943? Here was the ontological successor to the insignificant *Pins and Needles* and *Cradle Will Rock*, the understaffed *Porgy and Bess*, the patriotically apropos but all the same ephemeral *This Is the Army*. Like the last title, Kapp's *Oklahoma!* could bear a full-cast cover shot, with photographs of the individual numbers on the inside left cover, and perhaps a leaflet of lyrics and synopsis, so the album would function not only as a souvenir for theatregoers but as a substitute for those across the country who didn't have access to the show. What an album that would be! Kapp must have been thinking—not some pop concert but the music of a *story*, a series of characterological transactions. It was what American culture loves: something new. And all for $5.85, the price of an *Oklahoma!* ticket.

Months passed; still Petrillo maintained his ban. Finally, in September 1943, Decca signed a separate peace with the union and rushed *Oklahoma!*'s cast and orchestra into the studio. As Kapp had foreseen, the album proved as phenomenal as the show itself, selling well over a million units at a time when very few *single* discs reached that level: and this was a set of six. As the banned Victor and Columbia looked helplessly on, Decca went on to *One Touch of Venus*, the *Connecticut Yankee* revival, *Winged Victory*,* *Carmen Jones*, *Mexican Hayride*, *Song of Norway*, *Bloomer Girl*, and *Sing Out, Sweet Land!*. By then, it was very late 1944, and Victor and Columbia at last capitulated to the union.

Note that Decca varied its recording aesthetic from show to show. *Oklahoma!* fiddled a bit with the orchestral arrangements, turned "Out of my Dreams" into Laurey's solo (in the show, chorus women introduce the refrain), and presented the first in the grand history of the Concocted Medley Finale that has convinced many a listener that musicals end with a table of contents. *One Touch of Venus* used only two of the leads; *Mexican Hayride* found Bobby Clark extraneous (in his own vehicle!) and gave his main song to Wilbur Evans; *Song of Norway* offered Kitty Carlisle in

---

* This now outstandingly forgotten and at the time extravagantly misleading recording was probably seen as the Air Force's answer to Decca's *This Is the Army*. However, *Winged Victory* (1943) was a play (by Moss Hart) with some incidental music and choral work. It had an eye-catching cast, taking in among others Private Red Buttons, Private Whitner Bissell (later the Whit Bissell who gave so much to the B-line horror film of the 1950s; who can forget, or even watch, *I Was a Teenage Frankenstein*?), Private Karl Malden, Private Lee J. Cobb, Sergeant Ray Middleton, and Sergeant George Reeves (later television's Superman). *Winged Victory* did make a bit of history in that it was the first Broadway cast album released on twelve-inch discs (two of them), a format hitherto reserved for classical matter such as opera and symphony. It paved the way for shows with "bigger" music, like *Carousel* and *Song of Norway*, which naturally needed the longer sides, but which also needed to be perceived as "larger" than pop music.

Irra Petina's role (as Petina, billed as "prima donna of original production," made her own *Song of Norway* album for Columbia, with Robert Weede and a stormload of authentic Grieg).

Decca gave *Bloomer Girl* its biggest album yet, eight ten-inch 78s, so expansive for the tenuous 78 album bindings of thin cloth that well-played sets fell apart before the show did. Yet Decca simultaneously scanted *On the Town*, reducing the score to six vocal numbers, all studio mock-ups with Nancy Walker and Comden and Green, with Gabey's two ballads assigned transexually to Mary Martin. (Victor, jumping into the cast-album business after its concord with Petrillo, also made an *On the Town* album, this one emphasizing the ballet music, with the songs performed by the Robert Shaw Chorale.)

Columbia and Capitol entered the lists in 1946, the one with the *Show Boat* revival and the other with *St. Louis Woman*, mainly because Johnny Mercer, *St. Louis Woman*'s lyricist, was a co-founder of Capitol. That same year, Decca demonstrated how loose the working concept of an "original-cast" reading could be with *Annie Get Your Gun*, using Ethel Merman and Ray Middleton but otherwise nothing but studio ringers except for the black porters' trio backing up "Moonshine Lullaby." Victor entered the competition, after its half-there *On the Town*, with a superb preservation of *Brigadoon* in 1947, the same year in which Columbia also challenged Decca's hegemony. *Finian's Rainbow* was a smart choice, a score in which every number seemed to have hit potential; but Columbia generously also recorded *Street Scene*, the first Absolutely Guaranteed Flop to get an album.*

This proliferation of "cast albums" of varying authenticity, all very suddenly in this decade without a single antecedent of quality in any earlier age, has had the same effect as the acculturation of the talking picture in 1929. It creates a Before and After, reclassifying all that came Before, at least in the popular perception, as

---

* *Sing Out, Sweet Land!* and *St. Louis Woman* had failed commercially, and, after *Street Scene*, *Allegro*, *Miss Liberty*, *Lost in the Stars*, and *Texas, Li'l Darlin'* would also post losses. But *Street Scene* was the first succès d'estime to be recorded more out of admiration than capitalist self-interest. It's an imposing precedent, the recording industry's admission that it's not merely presenting a buying public with ware but making historical declaration as well.

inadequate. How different our short list of classics might have been had Jack Kapp gotten the bug a decade earlier and caught full-out theatre readings of *The Cat and the Fiddle, Face the Music, Music in the Air, Revenge With Music, Jubilee, Babes in Arms, Knickerbocker Holiday,* and *DuBarry Was a Lady.* At that, while the 1940s is the first decade of musicals that we know intimately in terms of performing style, aren't we misled by the record labels' *selection* of titles? What's a forties show that didn't get recorded? Debris.

Let me expand this idea with two examples from the middle of the decade: *Are You With It?* (1945) and *Lute Song* (1946). Two more unlike shows there could not be in this time, the one a down-and-dirty musical comedy with a carnival background and the other based on a fourteenth-century title from the Chinese repertory, *Pi-Pa-Ki,* by Kao-Tong-Kia, though some say Tse-Ching. Yea, casting could be tricky for this tale of a man of the Middle Kingdom who deserts his family for the capital, and whose faithful wife knows that the lute is the symbol of their honorable love. At length, there is little to keep the wife at home, what with typhoons, famine, and her irritating in-laws. But see: they have just dropped dead of starvation in a highly stylized manner. The wife will journey long, to the capital to find her husband. Lo, they will sing the Lute Song.

This is a musical? Who on Broadway would play these roles, even given that the production, under John Houseman's direction, will revel in the piquant spectacle of the Eastern stage, Robert Edmond Jones' designs backing Yeichi Nimura's exotic choreography? Well, it could be done with the then-unknown Yul Brynner as the husband; he has the look and can even play the lute. Nancy Reagan (then Davis) will add that touch of je ne sais quoi in a small part. And of course the wife is a natural for . . . Mary Martin? Wearing her Valentina gowns even during the famine?

Are You With It? was much easier to put together. This was a genre show. The protagonist was the generic cute nerd (Johnny Downs), an accountant who fumbles a decimal point, loses his company a fortune, and runs away to join the circus. The comic was the generic finagler with throwaway delivery (Lew Parker), and the girl friends were generic, Downs' fond sweetheart (Joan

Roberts) and Parker's leathery broad (Dolores Gray). The Harry Revel–Arnold B. Horwitt score was generic, too, counting the main couple's up-tune ("Slightly Perfect") and ballad ("This Is My Beloved"), Gray's slam-bang spots ("Are You With It?," "You've Gotta Keep Saying 'No' "), the breezy ballad with the dancey release ("Just Beyond the Rainbow"), the minor character's comic lament ("Poor Little Me"), and, *bien sûr*, the dream ballet ("Vivian's Reverie," as Roberts envisions the cheap carnival as a Ringling Brothers rival).

There were novel bits—an opening called "Five More Minutes in Bed" in which the chorus girls were seen rising and dressing in naughty silhouette; a singing quartet like *Louisiana Purchase*'s Martins; the freaks of the Midway, not mere bric-a-brac but very integral in the action; and, as with *Lost in the Stars*, two title songs, that of the show and that bearing the title of the novel it was drawn from, George Malcolm Smith's *Slightly Perfect*. Anyone could write a show like this; in the 1930s and 1940s, it was the most prevalent kind of show. It didn't have to be wonderful to succeed: just fast, funny, and bright.

Anyone *did* write *Lute Song*, judging by its confused authorship. The 1946 version dates back to a collaboration between veteran playwright Sidney Howard and a besotted amateur of Chinese theatre named Will Irwin. Their *Lute Song*, a play without music, was first staged in summer stock in 1930 and made the rounds of academic and theatre-society circles before producer Michael Myerberg ordered it for Broadway with a great deal of incidental music and dances by Raymond Scott and seven songs by Scott and lyricist Bernard Hanighen.

Why Mary Martin thought *Lute Song* a sound followup to her flash success in *One Touch of Venus* is anybody's guess, though it certainly was a star vehicle . . . for the scenery. The miscast Martin came in second. Perhaps everyone was taken aback by the ceremonial nature of the production. Asian theatre is likely to begin with a stage manager sort of character coming up to the footlights to say things like:

It is a venerable tale of the time when the gods walked upon earth and wrought their magic in the eyes of men . . . But

> still through the ages the voice of an ancient lute sings on
> . . . sings of harshness, but of pity also; sings of love, which
> is stronger than the Voice of Jade from the Imperial Throne.
> And now, with your permission, our play begins.

As if we could stop them. Houseman incorporated many traditional usages of the Eastern stage—the Manager taking a role in
the story; the black-robed property and "effects" personnel we're
not supposed to notice; even the Lion Dance. Those who saw
Sondheim's *Pacific Overtures* will know the style.

Lute Song failed. It almost had to have done, given the crossed
signals it sent to Martin's following and the generally farouche
nature of Asian theatre. *Are You With It?* was a hit: but who got
the album: and who made the history? Granted, *Are You With It?*
would have made no more than pleasurable listening. On five ten-
inch discs, with an overture and nine numbers, little actual story
could have been inferred. It's love and fun, as vague as that. But
it would have caught standard-make mid-forties musical comedy
in all its populist energy, not to mention one of the greatest singers in Broadway history, Dolores Gray.

Lute Song's album is nice but incorrect, suggesting that this
was one of those sui generis Rodgers and Hammerstein things, a
revolutionary musical. No. It wasn't even a musical, but rather a
play that acted like a musical, with all those people in crazy costumes sauntering in and out and striking poses and turning
around real sudden as a gong strikes. The seven vocal numbers,
all for Martin and/or Brynner, are an odd collection, now reflecting the Eastern feeling ("Willow Tree," pentatonic to a fault), then
trying to give Martin a pop tune that would not be embarrassed
on the radio ("Where You Are"); now trying a theme song ("The
Lute Song," conventional yet soaring and quite lushly harmonized), then going off-the-wall on an irrelevant idea ("See the
Monkey"); now finding just the right mood of timeless beauty
("Mountain High, Valley Low," a rare title that is somehow utterly
forgotten yet a standard at the same time).

Decca's album featured Martin alone, in five numbers on four
sides, devoting the fifth and sixth sides to incidental music that
emphasizes the pageantry of the piece. Okay, that's reasonable,

and we're all glad to have it—but it only exists because Decca, Martin's home label, saw a commercial opportunity to reanoint the diva. Why was Brynner omitted? Why leave out "Willow Tree" and "The Lute Song," the best numbers after "Mountain High"? Did this recording lead to the 1959 City Center revival of *Lute Song*—complete with the Jones sets and Nimura movement—in its spring season usually devoted to real-life musicals such as *Carousel* and *Brigadoon*? Did *Are You With It?*'s lack of a cast album prompt Universal to give its film version, in 1948, an entirely new score (a new title song included), even while retaining Lew Parker from Broadway?

It was as if a musical without a cast album were a musical without a score. Recordings were controlling history: and the history went particularly astray in the fall of 1948, when Petrillo reimposed his Ban and no cast albums were made, not even of *Magdalena* (1948). Here was the latest floperetta from the west, as Edwin Lester flourishes yet another Wright and Forrest show drawn from the music of _____ and starring anodyne, dauntless Irra Petina. In this case, _____ was Heitor Villa-Lobos. "South America's foremost composer," the posters claimed; that was true. The prolific Villa-Lobos oeuvre had yet to be absorbed up north beyond his nine *Bachianas Brasileiras* (especially the fifth, for soprano and eight cellos, popularized on a two-sided Columbia 78 by Bidù Sayão), so, unlike *Song of Norway*, and, later, *Kismet*, *Magdalena* could not draw on foolproof tunes like "Strange Music" and "Stranger in Paradise." In fact, the score was written not from drams of Villa-Lobos but in fresh collaboration with him, carried on in fractured French and, somehow, bits of Portuguese. I'd like to say that this extraordinary music tells of a lost masterpiece, but the subject matter is so idiotic that *Magdalena* could never have been anything *but* a cast album; and, thanks to Petrillo, it wasn't one.

Maybe it couldn't have been one in any case. The gigantic score, composed for the opera-weight voices that Broadway could field almost routinely then, would have had to come out on two volumes of twelve-inch discs, two *Street Scenes*. For to omit any episode of this already incredible plot would render it stupefyingly incoherent. "The story is unintelligible," groused Brooks Atkinson. It isn't—that's the problem. One understands just how ridiculous it is, scene by scene.

In brief: Magdalena is a river in Colombia. The settings are jungle and Paris (yes, that Paris), the characters natives and French colonists. Petina is a restaurateuse, Hugo Haas a general and her gluttonous lover, John Raitt a freedom-fighting jungle bus driver and atheist, Dorothy Sarnoff his pious girl friend. The lady chef eventually lures the general into eating himself to death, and the bus driver sort of finds God.

Uh . . . *what?* Arthur Kay looked over everyone's shoulders to guarantee the musical side of the evening, and Jack Cole got up his usual wicked dances. But director Jules Dassin was no Rouben Mamoulian—and, as on *St. Louis Woman*, even Mamoulian could do nothing for a show without a good story. So the music was in effect lost: but only for fifty years. In 1988, *Magdalena* reappeared, in concert in New York with Judy Kaye, George Rose, Kevin Gray, and Faith Esham, and the legend held. This is a truly marvelous piece of music, wed to the stupidest libretto in the musical's history.

I'm not talking about spiffy tunes; Villa-Lobos is too rich for that. Those who know his ninth *Bachiana Brasileira* can reckon the style—lush and jungly yet sophisticated, Parisian, as well. Epic, intimate. Dapper, brutal. Broadway had heard nothing like it: operetta characters going beyond Romberg–Friml into . . . what? Villa-Lobos is indescribable, except to say that he is unlike the great symphonic *dramatists* such as Beethoven, Brahms, Bruckner, and Shostakovich, and more like the great symphonic *melodists* such as Schubert, Dvořák, and Vaughan Williams. Then add the jungle.

At times, Villa-Lobos seems absurdly precise in pinning down international operetta style and deciding how to redefine it: as in Petina's "Food For Thought," a comic gender-war piece, suave and cynical, literally whipped by the percussion section in what sounds like a musical rendering of the S & M Handbook. As Petina elaborates her theory of enslaving men by feeding them *au cordon bleu*, the chorus repeats her main strain underneath her new theme—but then, this is a highly contrapuntal score. Villa-

Lobos loves piling melodies upon each other. The title song at first seems simple—or relatively so, given its lavishly undulating accompaniment—till Villa-Lobos brings in a broken-down player piano in fits and starts as the stage fills with dancers and the orchestra takes on the riotous grandeur of the *Bachianas Brasileiras*.

That number does end peacefully; but this is the least peaceful of operettas. It isn't orderly or merry. There's no "Freddy and His Fiddle." It doesn't even sound like an operetta, not as Broadway knows the style. *Magdalena* is too rich, too smart, too South American. Too brilliant? Its song titles may suggest Romberg–Friml, giddy with bad jokes and useless glamor, sodden with sparkless exotica—"The Omen Bird," "Plan It By the Planets," "Bon Soir, Paris," "The Forbidden Orchid." But its *music* is unique, spectacular.

Wright and Forrest would write better lyrics, to *Kismet* and *Kean*, but, given the spot they were in—it can't be easy to create an operetta with a classical composer who doesn't speak your language—they did a fine job. One problem was the high tessitura of the roles, which consistently pulled mezzos Petina and Sarnoff and baritone Raitt into soprano and tenor ranges (in the 1988 concert, higher voices took these roles) and thus made it difficult for the public to hear the lyrics. The many choral scenes also were hard to absorb verbally; and the critics came down evenly mixed, from rave to pan.

Magdalena gave up after eleven weeks, so, even if it had had an album, it couldn't have come out in time to publicize its score. But then came *Love Life*, whose half-year run might easily have been prolonged if the public had had access to a take-home kit of its tunes. Five ten-inch discs would have done the trick:

My Name Is Samuel Cooper	Economics
Here I'll Stay	Love Song
Progress	Is It Him Or Is It Me?
I Remember It Well	Minstrel Parade
Green-Up Time	Mr. Right

It's enough of the plot to keep us up to speed, a balance between the character and vaudeville numbers, and, most interesting of all, it would have stopped Lerner from recycling "I Remember It Well" in *Gigi*.

Strangely, the following *Where's Charley?* (1948) also lacked an album, though it ran two-and-a-half years, while the musicians' strike lasted only a few months. Was it the bizarrely mixed reviews, some suggesting an inept piece of junk? Was it the feeling that Ray Bolger was carrying an otherwise inconsequential work, as he did *By Jupiter*? But that show, despite its shallow book, had a recordable score (given no more than a four-side Hildegarde studio set at the time), as did *Where's Charley?*.

This was the Broadway debut of producers Cy Feuer and Ernest Martin and composer–lyricist Frank Loesser, though some may have seen the work as another of those George Abbott shows. Abbott directed and also wrote the book, from Brandon Thomas' late-Victorian farce *Charley's Aunt*, David Ffolkes ("Bunty Kelley's got the wrong socks on again!") designed both sets and costumes for the Oxford University setting, and George Balanchine staged the numbers. It's a sound lineup, with the credentials that expectably create a prominent title: and isn't that where the cast album comes in?

Where's Charley? did get a cast *single*, Bolger's show-stopper, "Once in Love With Amy" (so big a hit that he was able to bring the audience in on a singalong in one of the number's encores), backed by "Make a Miracle," his duet with Allyn McLerie in the typical Loesser style of interknitted phrases, each singer's line answered by the other singer's line so closely that they touch at the ends. It created a mini-genre during the 1950s—"Small Talk," "Paris Loves Lovers," "I'm Past My Prime," "Flattery," not to mention Loesser's own "Marry the Man Today" and "Happy To Make Your Acquaintance."

This is not, however, a distinctive score in general. Not till *Guys and Dolls* in 1950 did Loesser discover—and then vary—his voice, shifting style from work to work to give each a unique *tinta*. In *Where's Charley?*, he constructed a conventional late-forties musical-comedy score, sharper than, say, *Billion Dollar Baby* but uninspired. The ballads "My Darling, My Darling" and "Lovelier Than Ever" have a hit-parade feeling, though there are satisfactory situation numbers in "Better Get Out of Here" (in which two students and their dates consider the danger of remaining behind closed doors together) and "The Gossips," and a really nifty chorus, "The New Ashmolean Marching Society and Student Conservatory Band." There's also one out-and-out dud, or perhaps simply an excrescence, a Latin American rhythm special called "Pernambuco" that had no purpose other than to provide Balanchine with a showpiece for the first-act finale. "Unbelievable town!" the lyric runs; "unbelievable song!" the wags countered.

So, yes, there were holes in the show. Overall, it had the George Abbott things—up-and-coming kids supporting Bolger (including Doretta Morrow, ready for her *Kismet*), a lot of fun without realism, and of course all that hideously vivacious drag comedy.

All right, drag wasn't an Abbott trademark. It hadn't been anybody's trademark since the first decades of the century, when the halcyon Julian Eltinge and the tempestuous Bert Savoy held sway. There was drag in *This Is the Army* (*Winged Victory*'s casting preferred biological women) and drag bits in shows like *Early To Bed* and *Follow the Girls*: transvestism as a sight gag. Audience whoops, guy exits.

But *Charley's Aunt* depends on one character's extended drag episode, fully exploited in *Where's Charley?*.* That can't be why the musical missed getting recorded, but it did surely put the show in an odd light during the extraordinarily homophobic 1950s. Literally *phobic*: feared. Gay is well-known today, and hated. But gay in *Where's Charley?*'s time was as unknown and feared as witchcraft. It was unpredictable. Scary. "Straight" drag acts like Bolger's here were all but unknown once the Cold War got going, with its infinitely hidden evil of "eggheads" (intellectuals) and spies and queers. Some were all at once, quite an achievement. At the very end of the decade, Billy Wilder's film *Some Like It Hot*, with Tony Curtis and Jack Lemmon spending most of the action in cop-baiting drag, seemed like a satiric scream of terror, perhaps an exorcism.

Obviously, in such a time, such a show must undergo devalu-

---

* In Thomas' play, a supporting player dons the dress; but why would Ray Bolger let an assistant upstage him?

ation. The lack of a cast album hid the score, and the faithful movie, filmed at Oxford in 1952, became elusive very early on. The show didn't vanish. London saw it, with Norman Wisdom, in 1958, and it was revived twice in New York: at the City Center (with Eleanor Steber as the aunt) in 1966 and at the uptown Circle-in-the-Square in 1974, with Raul Julia gamely trying the musical in an early case of cross-race casting. This doesn't sound like a classic-manqué, perhaps, but, while Wisdom had a hit in a culture that celebrates drag performers, both New York revivals sold badly. There is simply no interest in this work now that Ray Bolger has vacated it.

Meanwhile, strike or no strike, nobody thought that Sigmund Romberg's *My Romance*, based on Edward Sheldon's 1913 play *Romance*, deserved a recording. *Magdalena* had come in during September, *Love Life* and *Where's Charley?* in early October, and now here was this mad, sad, bad duet operetta, the kind in which the lovers have love or nothing and everyone else in the show has nothing, including the lovers. The original 1913 play was, basically, an anticipation of *Rain*, except set in New York and with Sadie Thompson as an Italian opera singer with a heavy accent. *Song of Norway*'s Lawrence Brooks and *Street Scene*'s Anne Jeffreys played the leads, in a debacle that managed to eke out three months of grueling houses.

As the Girls Go (1948), in November, was a Michael Todd–Bobby Clark show, so expensive that only *My Fair Lady*, *Candide*, and *Camelot* broke its record cost.* But they were spectacles. *As the Girls Go* was a nonsense about the first woman president.

So Clark, of course, is the First Man, Waldo Wellington, married to Madame Boss (Irene Rich) and father of the juvenile (Bill Callahan), who does the romance with Betty Jane Watson. There was virtually no plot, just a series of Clarkian sketches using the

---

* A big-sized musical was still running at around $200,000 by the late 1940s. Todd saw prestige in being the guy who produced the most expensive shows on The Street, and thus brought this one in at an unheard-of $340,000. No musical had yet approached that figure, except possibly *Jumbo* (1935), Billy Rose's circus piece, whose titanic logistical problems so protracted rehearsals that Rose may have ended up spending something like a third of a million dollars—in Depression money!

White House for coloring. Remember when "music and girls" were "the soul of musical comedy"? *As the Girls Go* was one of the very last of the type with that soul. Indeed, Todd was the last major showman who thought in those terms. George Jean Nathan rejoiced when, just before attending *As the Girls Go*'s opening, a man who had seen it in Boston said, "Thank God, it's like a 1920 show and not one of those 1948 affairs."

Except, while filling his show with girls, Todd forgot about the music. *As the Girls Go*'s score, by Jimmy McHugh and Harold Adamson, is the dullest of the decade, rock-bottom tuneless and lacking even the shred of an idea, an image. Unambitious flop musicals can have lively scores—*Miss Liberty*. They can have moderately pleasing scores—*Are You With It?*. They can even have one decent number—*Walk With Music*'s "The Rhumba Jumps!."

This hopelessly unambitious musical had such ballads as "I Got Lucky in the Rain," with its irritatingly repetitive A strain; "You Say the Nicest Things, Baby," dead on arrival; and the funereal "Nobody's Heart But Mine." The raffish beguine flirtation is "There's No Getting Away From You," the sarcastic comedy number "It Takes a Woman To Get a Man," the big waltz for Hermes Pan's dancers "It's More Fun Than a Picnic." It's a morgue of a score; *Nellie Bly*'s isn't worse.

Moreover, this hopelessly unambitious musical was a flop. That extravagant budget killed it despite a year's run, normally the term limit of a smash. And how could it have had an album, for, besides its bum score, it had no character beyond that of Clark, and it is in the nature of the cast album to locate a show's characters. The cast album changed our view of the musical's score, from sounds that are functional to sounds that are definitive. And note that this happened just when the shows were ready to define and not just function. That is, Americans started getting cast albums just when the scores were getting interesting.

Yes, there were plenty of wonderful scores in the 1920s and 1930s. Still, save an obvious exception such as *Show Boat* and *Of Thee I Sing*, the shows weren't strong in plot and character and thus could not field solid storytelling scores.

But now consider the converse: if a cast album *revealed* a good score, it also *exposed* a bad one. Perhaps this was on Cole Porter's mind when he wrote *Kiss Me, Kate* (1948), his greatest hit, his most celebrated score, and, its having opened in December, the first post-strike cast album. After all, Porter's only previous cast recording, *Mexican Hayride*, preserved a show that even he thought tawdry. From the large amount of songs that Porter wrote for this new show, and his constant attempts to better them with new pieces for the same spots, he was apparently trying to write his version of a Rodgers and Hammerstein show, with all their variety and ingenuity and character profile.

And, yes, *Kiss Me, Kate* made a dynamite album, in a very full reading on six twelve-inch discs. However, a recording, reducing a show to its score, can inadvertently misrepresent the show. It's easy to come up with great songs if you're Cole Porter and desperate for a hit. But it can be hard for a number of different people to come up with a great show, and it is arguable that *Kiss Me, Kate*—classic though it inarguably is—is not a great show. It may not even be a good one.

First, a little backstage: there are two explanations of how the piece came about. Its co-producer Saint Subber says that he got the idea from Alfred Lunt and Lynn Fontanne's 1935 staging of *The Taming of the Shrew*. This was a famously lavish and eccentric production, involving among other things two men in a horse suit, three acrobats, and four midgets. Working as production assistant on the Lunts' 1940 tour of the show (and others, to champion Finnish War Relief), Subber was enchanted by how the Lunts' turbulent relationship mirrored the war between wooing Petruchio and the ungovernable Kate, the at times sordid clash so at odds with the demented poetry of the staging. This would be *Kiss Me, Kate*: a musical based not on Shakespeare but on the Lunts' production.

Bella Spewack, who with her husband, Sam, wrote the show's book, recalls it differently. The original idea, she says, was simply to turn *The Taming of the Shrew* into a musical, as when *The Comedy of Errors* became *The Boys From Syracuse*. Apparently, no writer could figure out how to do it—update the action? Shift the setting? Use Shakespearean dialogue, modern dialogue, some compromise?—till Bella was brought on board. I'm going to guess that she alone realized that, as *The Boys From Syracuse* had already pulled off the stunt of borrowing the Shakespearean plot and characters and setting but phrasing it all in modern Broadway-musical English, no musical could adapt Shakespare in just that way again. However, why not contain the authentic Shakespearean text within a backstager format, not adapting the *Shrew* itself so much as showing the lives of a theatre company putting on someone else's adaptation of the *Shrew*: thus pulling off a different stunt altogether?

Whoever is right, the finished *Kiss Me, Kate* reconciles both versions, for it was indeed a look at a direly bickering man-and-wife team (divorced, here, but still enamored) who feud in both contemporary and Elizabethan English, all in Lemuel Ayers' sets and costumes, perhaps the most magnificent in all the decade, contrasting the bare stage, theatre alley, and dreary dressing rooms of the real life with the Renaissance riot going on "on-stage."

Smart Broadway went, "Oh, really?" while the show was pulling itself together. That washed-up Porter, that drunk of a director (John C. Wilson, who co-produced the 1940 *Shrew* revival), the strange idea. *Is* it the *Shrew* or isn't it? Like *Oklahoma!*, *Kate* had to hustle to get its backing; no less than seventy-two angels finally took the trick. Alfred Drake, as the hero, Fred Graham, may suggest plush casting, but he had been in nothing but flops since *Oklahoma!*. The Czech opera soprano Jarmila Novotna, who had played the lead in *Helen Goes To Troy* (1944), Max Reinhardt's Broadway version of Offenbach's *La Belle Hélène*, was to have been Kate's heroine, Lilli Vanessi. But Porter was especially taken with Patricia Morison, who had appeared in two minor Broadway musicals (including one opposite Alfred Drake, *The Two Bouquets*, in 1938) and had a great look for period (or any) costumes. She had as well soprano enough to handle Kate's odd tessitura, which stays low most of the time but climbs high now and again, even if not to truly operatic heights. Porter had a thing about legit sopranos: he found them useful, or perhaps just unavoidable, in certain minor duties (such as Corinna Mura's solos in *Mexican Hayride*), but he vastly preferred belters like Ethel Merman. At least they had good diction. Porter was obsessive about audiences hearing his lyrics, and, in rehearsal, would blow a whistle when they were fudged.

Kiss Me, Kate had a belter built into it, in the "Bianca" role, so to say, Kate's sweet younger sister but played by a kid who's Wise in Men's Ways—a much-decorated campaign veteran, in fact. Her "Lucentio" is *Kate*'s hoofer. With Lisa Kirk and Harold Lang in the parts, *Kiss Me, Kate* was cast, for all the rest is small parts except for the First Man and the Second Man (as they are billed in the program), and I'll get to them in a second. What I must emphasize right now is that the washed-up Cole Porter so succeeded in his determination to awe his detractors that he didn't write but rather incessantly *rewrote* this score. Fans of the show will be amused at the tunestack that Columbia's album might have drawn on had the show been recorded around the time that it went into rehearsal:

Act One: Another Op'nin', Another Show
Why Can't You Behave?
It Was Great Fun the First Time (replaced by Wunderbar)
We Shall Never Be Younger (replaced by So in Love)
We Open in Venice
If Ever Married I'm (replaced by Tom, Dick or Harry)
I Sing Of Love
I've Come To Wive It Wealthily in Padua
Were Thine That Special Face
Kiss Me, Kate

Act Two: What Does Your Servant Dream About? (replaced by Too Darn Hot)
Always True To You in my Fashion
Where Is the Life That Late I Led?
A Woman's Career (replaced by Fred's reprise of So in Love)
Brush Up Your Shakespeare
I Am Ashamed That Women Are So Simple
Finale: Kiss Me Kate

Of course, any musical drops and adds songs before its premiere. What's arresting here is that the five deleted titles, virtually unknown today (though they have been recorded), are good enough to have stayed with the work throughout its history. But Porter knew that the cast album made this an age of Great Scores or Else, and Porter wanted the Greatest.

And it is: but what of the *show*? Critic Ken Mandelbaum points out odd goofs among and between all those wonderful numbers, a true incoherence of material that, for Mandelbaum, throws *Kate* off the short list—even the long one—of truly inspired shows.

First, it is never made clear whether this company is putting on Shakespeare's *The Taming of the Shrew* or a musical version of it. Yes, the Shakespeare characters sing during the *Shrew* scenes. But, Mandelbaum asks, is that because they are in a musical or because they are in *Kiss Me, Kate*?

Second, if it *is* a musical version of the *Shrew*, where are the adaptors? Where's, say, Comden and Green, Harold Arlen? Where's, even, Saint Subber? Is this show simply happening by itself?

Third, Porter's lyrics during the *Shrew* scenes don't match the Shakespeare that we hear, with such typical Porter references as those to L. B. Mayer, Lassie, and so on.

Fourth, why is all that Shakespearean dialogue there in the first place? Is it fill? Snob-bait?

Fifth, the Kirk–Lang subplot *isn't* a subplot. They're just there to sing and dance. Her "Why Can't You Behave?" suggests an important union, but ultimately they seem just so much decoration, each getting an irrelevant solo, her "Always True To You in my Fashion" and his "Bianca."

Sixth, what is the emotional reality of this story, once "So in Love" has been sung? This is the decade of *Carmen Jones, On the Town, Carousel, Brigadoon, Street Scene*, a time when musical comedy sought more and more to move its public sentimentally. Yet isn't this show steeped in that old Porter marinade of sex and laughs?

Actually, it *is* clear that *Kiss Me, Kate* is about a company putting on a musical based on the *Shrew*: because in 1948, as the overture was about to end, the curtain unexpectedly rose on a bare stage filled with milling players. Alfred Drake came down the theatre aisle, listening to the music as if monitoring some solution to a problem. Cutting off the players on a startling, inconclusive note, *Kate*'s conductor, Pembroke Davenport, turned to Drake, now moving onto the stage, and asked, "Is that all right, Mr. Graham?," and Drake answered, "Yes, the cut's good, leave it in."

Straight plays of 1948 didn't have overtures, so this *is* a backstager about a musical. Unfortunately, since the last City Center revival, in 1965 (with Patricia Morison and Bob Wright), the original opening has been invariably modified, and the stopped-dead ending of the overture has never been recorded, not even on the archeological double-CD boxes that plume themselves on authenticity. So this one defining moment when *Kate* is seen to be a musical-within-a-musical is lost. Then, too, where *are* the writers? We infer that Drake is an actor–manager, his own producer, and he makes an offhand reference, seemingly in jest, to "the six other fellows who've been sitting up nights rewriting [Shakespeare]." But surely Drake isn't Cole Porter, too. Backstagers are supposed to include writers and staff. Where's the choreographer, for instance? True, he or she may have fainted in the wings, for *Kate* is the most relentlessly danced show since *On the Town*, with full-out spots after six numbers, plus a "Rose Dance" and a pavane, covering everything from ballet to jitterbug. Choreographer Hanya Holm may have held 51 percent of the production.

As for Porter's lyrics not matching the Shakespeare, the songs go astray also in other ways that we would never forgive in, say, *Annie Get Your Gun*. For one thing, does anyone know what "We Open in Venice" is about? It would appear to serve as the opening number of the *Shrew* musical. But why do Drake, Morison, Lang, and Kirk (i.e., Petruchio, Katherine, Lucentio, and Bianca) pass themselves off as "a troupe of strolling players" when we never hear of these players again once the number has ended? Is this Porter's "adaptation" of Shakespeare's *Shrew* prologue, often cut, built around Christopher Sly, a character who vanishes once the *Shrew* proper begins? Then, too, "Bianca" begins surrealistically, as messengers suddenly appear at the stage door during a performance—literally, feet away from the performing area—with presents for Kirk. Worse, the song that caps this grotesque charade is pure hit-parade wannabe, comparable to "Old Fashioned Garden" and "True Love," numbers Porter wrote (respectively, near the start and end of his four-decade career) to appeal to idiots. One cannot blame him; "Bianca" was created simply because Lang was dissatisfied with his part.

What part? Aside from some singing and a load of dancing, Lang has a few lines early in the show and nothing else save his Lucentio in the *Shrew*. But Lang's role hides a secret; he's why *Kiss, Me Kate* gets away with all its dramaturgical persiflage. Because he's the one who brings in the First and Second Men.

As I see it, a *Kiss Me, Kate* audience is just about to realize how flimsy its realism is and how little reason there is to hear all that unanchored Shakespeare, when these two characters walk in. Instantly, the show is transformed by their vaguely disturbing manner and Runyonesque argot:

> FIRST MAN: (*to Morison*) Miss Vanessi, you have been my ideal for years. I married my wife because, in a certain light, she might pass for your sister.
> LILLI: How sweet.
> FIRST MAN: Your glorious voice has been an inspiration to me in my work.
> SECOND MAN: What a trouper!
> FIRST MAN: What a personality!*

The men are gangsters, and it is they who give the show its plot power. Lang has dropped a small fortune while gambling. They want to collect the debt. Lang signed *Drake's* name to the IOU. Morison is about to walk out on the show in the middle of a performance in a jealous rage because Drake sent flowers—in fact, Morison's wedding bouquet—to Kirk. So, in a way, the show does come together, as Drake persuades the two gangsters to don costumes and physically "escort" Morison on and off stage . . . and now I hear Ken Mandelbaum saying, "If you buy that, you believe that Jessie Matthews really was being chased by spies while working on *The Lady Comes Across*."

But it's my contention that *Kiss Me, Kate* is a show we love not

---

* Producers Feuer and Martin had just landed *Where's Charley?* and were looking for their next project. Could they have seen *Kiss Me, Kate* and, from the Spewacks' clever stylization of punctilious gangster rap, got the idea for *Guys and Dolls*?

despite its sloppy realism and irrelevant hunks of Shakespeare but because the score is so good that the rest doesn't matter. "We Open in Venice," for instance: maybe it is an out-of-story frame for the *Shrew* musical. (The 1958 television version, with Drake and Morison, explicitly presented it as such.) And maybe it isn't. Still, it doesn't matter, because it serves as the perfect transition from the black-and-white backstage world into a wildly picturesque Italy, and because the song itself is irresistible, as is its impish quotation of the "Miserere" from Verdi's *Il Trovatore* in its last four bars. (It's easy to miss, as the original is a curvy line heard over triplet phrases, while "Venice" is in 4/4.)

Or what about the devilish ingenuity with which Porter creates his Shakespearean sound, so "pipes and tabors" in "I've Come To Wive it Wealthily in Padua," so tarantella in "I Sing of Love," yet so jiving in "Tom, Dick or Harry"? No, this is not a backstage number. It comes up in the *Shrew*, yet it's pure Porter ribaldry. How does it relate to Shakespeare?

It doesn't. *Kiss Me, Kate* is the most inconsistent of classics in the decade that created the Consistent Classic, all of a tone in sordid *Pal Joey*, dreamy-real *Lady in the Dark*, funny-sad *On the Town*, funny-political *Finian's Rainbow*. Great shows are true to themselves. *Kiss Me, Kate* isn't true.

Yet it's magnificent. "So in Love"? "Wunderbar"? "Too Darn Hot," which sets forth the Cole Porterest line of all time while listing potential dates: "A Marine for his queen"? Or, now, what of the gently intimate "We Shall Never Be Younger," the title drawn from the final line of Shakespeare's Christopher Sly prologue? What of the unusual device of having Harold Lang not exit before Lisa Kirk's "Why Can't You Behave?," as any other show would have had him do? It's her solo, and a good cover-up for a scene change. No: Lang sits and listens, adding just one sung line to the song's coda—"Gee, I need you, kid"—which supplies his sole moment of emotional involvement in his love plot.

Ironically, the more *Kate* makes no sense, the more no sense it gets away with making. Its last two new numbers show us how unsettled the show is stylistically. First, we get the two gangsters, who, leaving the theatre, take a wrong turn, find themselves on stage, and bang into "Brush Up Your Shakespeare," a Porter list song in the form of a Bowery waltz with a tune accidentally bor-rowed from *Love Life*'s "Mother's Getting Nervous." Now, wait a minute: are these two buffoons actually *singing a number* onstage *during a performance* of the *Shrew* musical *with orchestral accom-paniment*? Who wrote the song? When did they learn it? When was it orchestrated?

You see the problem. But then comes Kate's "I Am Ashamed That Women Are So Simple," asserting a new tone in this show of warring tones: Porter's setting of Shakespeare, neat. And, I pro-pose, in this one number, all the mess of the show neatens up, even unites. This last piece is pure and true, even elegant, some-thing Porter seldom was if he could help it, and it excuses "Tom, Dick or Harry" and dismisses "Brush Up Your Shakespeare." It forgives them, being fantastical and contemporary at once: Eliz-abethan verse set by Broadway's most jazzy guy. It draws in all the show's parts, because the show, like this song, is a stunt. It's not *Carousel*: it's Cole Porter getting *as far from Carousel as he can get*. He says, "I won't have death and folklore, because if the Duke of Verdura doesn't enjoy it, it isn't a musical." But Porter did extend himself this much into the Rodgers and Hammerstein rev-olution: he wanted to show competitive work, earn his credentials as a *maestro di cartello* in the newfangled Broadway in which even an Ethel Merman vehicle could have some emotional reality.

Kiss Me, Kate made a stupendous album, not least because it leaves out all the book's quiddities. It also leaves out almost all the dance music, regrettable because Genevieve Pitot's arrange-ments are a marvel in the way they twist Porter into blues, pavane, juke box, gavotte, cape dance, hot trot, big-band brass parade, and *paso doble*. Too many forties musicals used the dance sections of the score simply to restate the potential hits over and over—*Annie Get Your Gun* almost destroys its melodies with these repetitions. Pitot enlarges Porter by essentializing him, in both his suave and sassy modes. Harold Lang's "Rose Dance," his solo during the *Shrew*, turns "Tom, Dick or Harry" into a kind of Renaissance hesitation waltz, with surging keyboard glissandi up to brass sfor-zando chords for Lang's leaps; yet the "Too Darn Hot" dance mu-sic is almost as freely derived as modern jazz.

The *Kiss Me, Kate* discs included some spoken lines, furthering the concept of the cast album as stay-at-home theatregoing. Decca's *Lost in the Stars* has so much dialogue that it was a miniature of the entire show. Recording a work on CD seems so easy compared with recording in the days of the 78-RPM format. With nearly eighty minutes to play with, one simply takes down the full score with connecting bits of underscoring and dialogue; and pop operas or Big Sing book shows such as *Follies* or *Ragtime* will need two discs.

Back in the 1940s, the ten-inch three-minute side or twelve-inch four-minute side imposed a process of selection on the recording's producer, a limitation in how he could depose his history. Before the cast album, shows could only be remembered, or, in rare cases, revived. Now shows stayed on, but only in the form in which they had been recorded. All else vanished. *Call Me Mister* was easy: save the ten best songs. *Carousel* was difficult: *all* of the music was best, and much of it came in sequences too developed even for the twelve-inch side.*

Columbia's *Kiss Me, Kate* worked so well that the music invented a classic that lives on without revivals. It is performed, certainly. By the time that Capitol rerecorded it in stereo in 1959, retaining the four original principals, conductor, and one minor player, retaining the same recording decisions made by Columbia (such as substituting the entr'acte for that unended overture), *Kiss Me, Kate* had been a London hit, a Hollywood hit (in 3-D, where available), on television, as we know, and was traveling the world, especially popular in Nordic countries. The City Center of course featured it, with its focus on famous forties titles, and it enjoyed a brilliant revival in London in 1987 at the Old Vic, with former rocker Paul Jones, Nichola McAuliffe, American Tim Flavin, and Fiona Hendley. Directed by Adrian Noble and choreographed by Ron Field, this *Kiss Me, Kate* showed once again why the show transcends its own flaws: a great score, a great look (costume

---

* The "Soliloquy" was given two sides, not only complete but with a short section that is never heard today, the "When I have a daughter" transition into the "My little girl" melody. The cut presumably encourages the Billy, who has a lot to sing and act over the course of the evening. However, such other sequences as the "Carousel Waltz" and the Bench Scene were knocked down to a single side, completely misguising these numbers.

designer Liz Da Costa quite went to town on this one), and wonderful opportunities for the four leads. Noble vulgarizeed the
gangsters, who turned up onstage in the *Shrew* in drag; isn't that
whole business unbelievable enough as it is? Field showed his
awareness of the work's chancey construction by trying to natu-
ralize "We Open in Venice" as an intimate quartet among actors
in dressing gowns, a backstage number. It still makes no sense.
But Jones, however overextended by the music, was just right, and
McAuliffe, a wonderful actress not known for musicals, displayed
an intensity in "So in Love" that, I have to say, overruled even
Patricia Morison.

The show *plays*, and the rest doesn't matter. That's what it is.
The 1940s is filled with smash hits that no one needs to see again.
*Something for the Boys. Follow the Girls. Up in Central Park.
Where's Charley?. This* smash hit must come around again and
again.

Yet it hasn't. To the date of this writing, *Kiss Me, Kate* has never
had an open-run New York revival—the one title on the chart of
classics not to have been seen in half a century.

Meanwhile, Columbia had introduced the long-playing disc in
mid-1948, so quickly habilitated that cast albums became culturally central. Playing them was how you knew you belonged to the
Informed Middle Class. Lighter than the 78 and virtually unbreakable, the LP had a particular advantage in the latitude that
it gave to the record producer in the timing of each cut. Where
the 78's short sides necessitated tailoring theatre scores to the fit,
the LP accommodated music more generously. Most important,
it was the format that an entire generation responded to. The LP
disc replaced the 78 album virtually overnight, and *Kiss Me, Kate*
was one reason why.

South Pacific (1949) was the other reason, though it was ideally
suited to the album made of ten-inch 78 sides: no major dance
music, no expansive musical scenes, and a score so characterful
(there are a couple of atmosphere numbers, but no situation numbers: all people, no plot) that one doesn't need a synopsis to know
what's happening.

What's happening is a lesson in racism. I don't mean "Carefully
Taught." That's but a moment of *South Pacific*. The *entire show*

is about racism—an arresting realization, as it deals with the war against the Japanese, not at all about the war against the Nazis, whose fight was explicitly one of racial overlordship and extermination. Yet it was the same war.

James Michener's war. His *Tales of the South Pacific*, particularly the stories "Fo' Dolla' " and "Our Heroine," gave Rodgers and Hammerstein (and co-librettist Joshua Logan) their principals: naive American ensign Nellie Forbush (Mary Martin) and worldly French planter Emile de Becque (Ezio Pinza); cynically Ivy League lieutenant Joe Cable (William Tabbert) and Tonkinese girl Liat (Betta St. John); the Rodgers and Hammerstein earthmother figure, Bloody Mary (Juanita Hall), who is Liat's mother; and the comic, Luther Billis (Myron McCormick). Noting that de Becque has two children by a deceased Polynesian wife, and that Nellie has conventional American ideas about race (of the southern kind), we see some interior contradictions already built into the narrative: Nellie loves but must surely reject de Becque, and Cable has a comparable problem with Liat, one involving class as much as race.

But there's a war on, so all this is subsumed by the *other* throughline in this deceptively complex show, that of the intelligence mission that Cable wants to interest the officially neutral de Becque in: monitoring the movement of Japanese convoys from an island that de Becque used to live on. It's a dangerous undertaking. As navy commander Harbison puts it, "Let's say that every time they send out a message they move to another hill . . . Realistically, they could last about a week."

There's another throughline, a most subtle one, more interesting, perhaps, to moderns than to audiences in 1949: the two male leads are respecters of women, and every other male is a raving slut. This is an unusually sensual show for its age—not lewd like *Star and Garter* and *Early To Bed* and *Follow the Girls*, but very, very appetitive. To the sheltered young Nellie, de Becque is clearly an erotic figure, as a European can seem to an American bourgeoise; but he is also an older man, almost fatherly, for all Ezio Pinza's reputation as a womanizer. Remember, he was the Don Giovanni of the age, trim and blatantly sensual, a very odd yet effective partner for the state-fairish Martin.

As for the other romantic pair, we meet up with Cable in what is unmistakably his first ecstatic sexual experience—at that, on Bali Ha'i, an island famed for the everything-goes Ceremonial of the Boar's Tooth. Bloody Mary literally gives Liat to Cable for sex, intending that Cable marry Liat and take her back to the States. Mary herself is smitten with Cable—another "romance" that crosses generation lines, as the Cable-Liat romance *and* the Nellie–de Becque romance (because of de Becque's children) cross racial ones.

The staging of Cable's union with Liat in 1948 was highly suggestive: alone with him, she was reaching up to him as he started to remove her blouse and the lights faded out. Music and strolling lovers covered the scene; but when the lights came up again he was shirtless and about to launch into the rhapsodic "Younger Than Springtime." Out of context on the album, it's just a song, a fine one. In the show, it's a bold touch of realism. The four previous Rodgers and Hammerstein titles treated murder, suicide, spousal abuse, and adultery, but they were shy about sex. *Carousel*'s Julie and Billy are obviously going to spend the night together after the Bench Scene; and a bedroom argument between *Allegro*'s hero and his wife is settled when she manipulates him into guilty self-doubt while she plays the martyred innocent and finally cues him into picking her up and carrying her to bed as the chorus men call out, "That's all, brother!"

However, *South Pacific*'s erotic moment is a lengthy one, and not pre-marital or conjugal sex but sex as pure bliss between two beautiful youngsters. It was shocking in its day, and it questions Hammerstein's assertion that he and his partner wrote "family shows." Yes, compared with what Cole Porter wrote. But it measures the salient quality of Rodgers and Hammerstein—their honesty—that *South Pacific* is above all a hot show, hungry, bedazzled.

Like all Rodgers and Hammerstein works, it is is unlike other works. Yet it embodies the forties style in musicals. It may be a summit, perhaps an index, full of the decade's entries: the war theme, of course, so of the time (whether in the heavily uniformed *Something for the Boys* or the period *Bloomer Girl*) that no major fifties musical dealt with even the peacetime military; the mixed-race casts of *Beggar's Holiday* and *Finian's Rainbow*; the mixing of legit and musical-comedy voices, as in *Up in Central Park* and *Street Scene*, that leads to a new sound comprising the vernacular and the exalted (in *Central Park*'s "When You Walk in the Room" and "April Snow" or *Street Scene*'s "Moon Faced, Starry Eyed" and "Somehow I Never Could Believe" or, here, "Honey Bun" and "Some Enchanted Evening"); or simply the teaming of a raga-muffin and a Big Opera Guy, as in *Mexican Hayride, Annie Get Your Gun*, and *Love Life*.

What *was* the 1940s? It was Rodgers and Hammerstein them-selves, proposing a new Essential: the story. That really was it. True, there are certain identifying practices, as in the complete lack of genre numbers, of "The Rhumba Jumps!," "Tschaikowsky," "Farming," "Ev'rything I've Got," "Where You Are." The Rodgers and Hammerstein revolution so exposed "type" songs that, a mere five years after *Oklahoma!, Love Life*'s score could collide char-acter songs with format songs, counting on our ability to distin-guish the one set from the other set in order to appreciate the show's encompassing irony.

Or there was the highly particularized use of choreography, so varied from show to show that to jump from *Oklahoma!*'s "Kansas City" two-step to *Carousel*'s opening pantomime (not danced: en-acted in motion) to *Allegro*'s surrealistic title-song ballet on mod-ern life suggests discontinuity, chaos. No; a liberation from cliché. True, there were a lot of dream ballets. But what better way to articulate the unutterable?

That's the forties musical's revolution in brief: staging the un-stageable. *South Pacific* is rich in it, so racial, erotic, poetic, and tragic; so busily plotted that it's almost Shakespearean in breadth, filled with such niceties as Nellie's being asked to spy on de Becque or Billis' implausibly antic snafu that inadvertently aids Cable's mission.

Yet there is a center: Bali Ha'i, a place we visit but cannot imagine, a dream come true but only for those *with* dreams. De Becque and Bloody Mary (and, by extension, Liat) have dreams. The unfocused but large-souled Nellie can share a dream. Cable cannot. Submitting to pressures of class and family background, he has renounced dreams for protocol: that's why he dies. He

wasn't deserving, wasn't even alive, but for that afternoon with
Liat. "Your own special dream," Bloody Mary warns Cable in "Bali
Ha'i," the romantic version of the theme. And "You got to have a
dream," she reminds him in "Happy Talk," the comic version. She
is, in effect, ambassador from this dream world to the mortal kingdom, the deity but also gatekeeper of Bali Ha'i. It is she who signs
Cable's death warrant: while renouncing Liat, he presents her
with a family heirloom, a lucky watch that saved his grandfather
from harm in World War I. Furious at Cable's resistance, Mary
grabs the watch and smashes it as if it were Cable. It is.

Those not familiar with *South Pacific* as a theatre experience
may be anticipating a dream ballet built around all this imagery
of the island Bali Ha'i. But *South Pacific* has no ballet. No choreography, even. Of all great Rodgers and Hammerstein shows,
South Pacific has the most book and the least music—one reason
why it won the Pulitzer Prize for drama. It almost seemed more
a drama than a musical. What else, in 1948, didn't have a dream
ballet? *Mister Roberts? Anne of the Thousand Days?* The dream
ballet, after all, had become one of the Essentials by then. But
the Essentials didn't hold any more; each new good musical created its Essentials from scratch.

Actually, *South Pacific* has a touch of dance here and there,
but informally—Nellie's joyful strutting about during "A Wonderful Guy," the seabees restlessly pacing during "There Is Nothing
Like a Dame," the "Honey Bun" drag act of Nellie and Billis at a
Thanksgiving variety show (she in a man's uniform, he in a grass
skirt and coconut halves). This lack of presentational choreography enhanced the show's realism, just as *On the Town*'s incessantly presentational choreography unveiled its shy romanticism.
This isn't a song-and-dance show. It's a song show.

The songs emphasize themselves, often dispensing with the in-
troductory verses to cut right to the melody, largely avoiding de-
velopmental sections, and using almost no chorus except in
"There Is Nothing Like a Dame." Those songs that do have verses
seem to feature them unduly—doubly ensonging them, so to say—
as in the waltz for plucked strings and harp cut by brass razzmatazz at the start of "A Wonderful Guy," or the grandiose beginning
of "Bali Ha'i," as if Bloody Mary were an oracle: as indeed she is.

These are songs *as* songs, a tour de force in which the musical play redevises the hit parade for its own uses. We get virtually none of *Carousel*'s detailed play of fragments and musical scenes to expand the musical dramatization—the way a now-sung, now-spoken conversation "turns into" "Mister Snow"; the choral bits that precede "June Is Bustin' Out All Over" (Carrie and the girls' "Get away, you no-account nothin's" answered by the boys' "Now, jest a minute, ladies"); the omnibus structure of the "Soliloquy"; and of course the Bench Scene.

South Pacific has a sort of Bench Scene, however, a sequence of three separate numbers that, like Julie and Billy's duet, serve to bring the main couple together, just after their entrance scene, on his estate. First, "A Cockeyed Optimist" gives us Nellie: gregarious, content, wishful, and a touch serious as well. Dialogue follows. To break the tension—for the two are clearly nervous—de Becque suggests brandy. This ushers in the "Twin Soliloquies," as each gives way in song to unspoken thoughts of romantic yearning and insecurity. The music builds, speeding up on a jagged vocal outline, till de Becque approaches with the brandy glasses and the two drink while the orchestra steals the climax from them. It's the opposite of operetta, where strangers think nothing of soaring into a rhapsody. These two daren't soar: so Rodgers soars for them, on a single undulating phrase of strings and woodwinds, repeated obsessively and growing in volume as the pit players join in desk by desk till the music's glowing red hot.

What can top that? Nothing less than "Some Enchanted Evening," the third number in the scene and the ideal wooing piece for a man in love at first sight. There's no reason in love—no class, no race. It overwhelms reason. And, of course, if Hammerstein's lyric doesn't persuade you, Rodgers' melody will.

Try to put aside all your knowledge of this show and imagine how it seemed to first-timers back in 1949. The exotic setting, the appearance of Mary Martin and Ezio Pinza pseudo–blithely chatting away, the incredible music when they drank their brandy, and now this. "Some enchanted evening," he begins: so appropriately, so poetically, so beautifully. It's inventive and unique and, mainly, it's absolutely correct, as story and character converge in such alarming clarity that you realize that you are in the hands of masters who are larger than the form they're working in. How could they not have reinvented Broadway?

So this is a showy score, yet even so an integrated one. It may be splitting hairs to say so, but, of the three Rodgers and Hammerstein shows preceding *South Pacific*, *Oklahoma!* never quite matches the Ado Annie–Will Parker share of the score to the rest; *Carousel* contains extraneous numbers in "Blow High, Blow Low" and "The Highest Judge of All" (the latter of which originally covered an elaborate scene change that today is executed in a whisk; it is almost invariably cut); and *Allegro*, so intricately divided between sung and spoken parts, is an unimportant score. *South Pacific* is perfect.

It made a perfect album, with every song on site. The sole vocal portion missing was a snatch of continuity between "Carefully Taught" and "This Nearly Was Mine," de Becque's furious arraignment of the evil men who love making war and destroying lives ("I was cheated before . . ."), and the sole "for the album" adjustment was the substitution of Nellie and de Becque's reprise of "Some Enchanted Evening" for the Act Two finale, which is in reality a taste of "Dites-moi" and a crashing orchestral peroration that would only have mystified the home listener. Omitted, of course, was all the show biz that lightened this weighty piece, the Broadway stuff expected more of *Panama Hattie* or *By Jupiter*: the star entrances, Martin and Pinza promenading into the first scene in mid-conversation; Bloody Mary's first appearance, a sudden revelation of some unholy religion as a line of sailors parted and grinning, wicked Juanita Hall appeared; Mary Martin's eight-times-a-week onstage shower for "I'm Gonna Wash That Man Right Outa My Hair"; Martin's clowning in "Honey Bun," so musical comedy in the middle of a musical play—that is, so outrageous yet so captivating—that photographs of her in her navy whites with the overhung black tie became a kind of signature for the show.

One other thing typifies the forties musical—the growing prominence of the director. In the 1920s, when the American musical asserted itself in *Dearest Enemy*, *Show Boat*, and *Strike Up the Band*, Broadway was producers and performers: Florenz Ziegfeld hires writers to showcase Marilyn Miller, the Astaires, some star comic; and that's a musical. Directors had no importance till the 1940s, when Hassard Short, Rouben Mamoulian, and George Abbott, by their success in shows without star personalities (think of *Carmen Jones, Oklahoma!, On the Town*) called attention to their post. Furthermore, we have seen, in these pages, George Balanchine, Agnes de Mille, Jerome Robbins, and Gower Champion move from choreographer to supervisor. This further defined the mysterious job of "director." Later on, we could speak of "Bob Fosse shows" or "Hal Prince shows," when the director had assumed total command as editor of composition and conceiver of production style. That's as near to auteur as one can be without actually writing book, lyrics, and music.

But in 1949, when Joshua Logan directed (and co-produced) *South Pacific*, no one spoke of a "Joshua Logan show." *South Pacific* was a Rodgers and Hammerstein show. A Mary Martin show, a war show, even the James Michener show. Logan got credit for his cinematic scene changes, in which characters strolled offstage as characters from the next scene rushed in. As I've said, this was novel but not original; Logan's long career as a director of musicals depended to some extent upon fooling everyone into thinking how inventive he was when he in fact was a solid journeyman of the George Abbott sort who could play a trick or two beyond the limited Abbott and was also not afraid—most were—to confront the erotic.

Rodgers liked him. Logan had done good work with Rodgers and Hart and staged the spectacularly successful *Annie Get Your Gun*, though it's hard to imagine that that Red Sea parting of Merman and Berlin needing anything more than capable direction. What really recommended Logan to *South Pacific* was his military experience, which helped Hammerstein get into the enlisted man's lingo and worldview. Had Rodgers and Hammerstein gone to any of the regular directors of the forties musical—Edgar McGregor, John Kennedy, Robert H. Gordon—they would have ended up with . . . not the same show. Not one as precisely enamored as when Nellie and de Becque lock eyes during "Twin Soliloquies"; or as ebullient during "A Wonderful Guy"; or as deftly ironic as when Tabbert delivered "Carefully Taught"; much less as nakedly passionate as when Cable holds Liat like a man who has come for the first time,

Hammerstein was a fine director himself—he not only wrote but staged *Show Boat*. If Hammerstein thought that, with all Broadway to choose from, they needed Logan for *South Pacific*, then Logan must have had something special. Nevertheless, this piece is so strongly and fully written, so complete as made, that all it really needs is the two stars; and it doesn't even need them.

No *stars*? Yet the show does keep succeeding without them. The original Broadway run saw Martha Wright take over for Mary Martin, Wright then spelled during a vacation by Cloris Leachman, with Ray Middleton, Paris Opéra bass Roger Rico, and George Britton replacing Pinza. Among the others, Myron McCormick and William Tabbert avoided leaving hit shows for potentially ephemeral work, and Bloody Mary, a star role of a kind, was passed from Juanita Hall to Diosa Costello (Desi Arnaz's opposite in Rodgers and Hart's *Too Many Girls*), operetta veteran Odette Myrtil, and one Musa Williams. A number of future Broadway principals came and went in the smaller roles, including Shirley Jones, Virginia Martin, Patricia Marand, and Biff McGuire.

But it doesn't matter who plays these parts. They're almost as performer-proof as the *On The Town* leads, even if Nellie needs charisma and de Becque *voce profunda*. London saw Martin with our own Wilbur Evans; the movie offered the astonishingly appropriate Mitzi Gaynor and Rossano Brazzi (even if he had to be dubbed by Giorgio Tozzi); and Rodgers' own revival, at Lincoln Center in 1967, put forth Florence Henderson with Tozzi. All gala bills. Yet New York has seen it also with nobodies, and a 1987 London revival with the superb Gemma Craven made do with the lackluster Emile Belcourt.

Casting of the other roles varies—there are dangerous Bloody Marys, comic Bloody Marys, sharp or lugubrious Billises, though Cable is invariably a cute young tenor—but, again, this is not a star show. It started as one, but unlike *Lady in the Dark*, *Annie Get Your Gun*, and *The King and I*, it isn't one as a rule. It's a bit like *Oklahoma!* or *Guys and Dolls*, shows that started without stars but *can* use them—or, at least, use particular talents smartly cast. Marlon Brando filmed a marvelous Sky Masterson; but *Guys and Dolls* goes over with Peter Gallagher's understudy.

Anyway, whether one saw Martin and Pinza or Leachman and Britton, *South Pacific* ran five years on Broadway and another five years on the simultaneous tour (with Janet Blair, Dickinson Eastham, and the four Migeneses, mother Jeanette as Bloody Mary's understudy and, as de Becque's kids, brother John and, alternating, sisters Maria and Julia: the future world-famed Lulu and Carmen). It's no accident that the age of very-long-running musicals exactly coincided with the age of the cast album. It was a case of elective affinities: when the music was ready, so was the technology.

What Has Happened So Far: in the First Age of the American Musical, the nineteenth century, the work was primitive. The Second Age, from 1900 to 1920, saw at once an absorption of European influences and a rejection of them, a time of the continental Victor Herbert and the homegrown George M. Cohan, but also of Irving Berlin and Jerome Kern, separately collaborating on the creation of American popular music. "Alexander's Ragtime Band" and "They Didn't Believe Me" are breakthroughs, as are the Gershwins, Vincent Youmans, Cole Porter, Rodgers and Hart, De Sylva, Brown, and Henderson: but now we are in the Third Age, the Golden One.

The American musical is finally invented in the 1920s, suffers an artistic setback in the financially oppressed and therefore conservative 1930s, and at last reflowers for good in the 1940s. Before, it was fit but primitive; it is now rich, sophisticated. It has status, a powerful economic base, and is becoming globally important, like Coca-Cola. It is culturally secure, and that makes it experimental, bold. Flops have nothing to lose but money; hits generate not only profits but an understanding of American civilization. The musical *is* America: democratic, fast-moving, innovative.

Of course, the Fourth Age brings us to decadence and ruin; but that's not for years and years yet.

Index

NOTE: Bold page numbers indicate primary discussions of topics.

Aarons, Alex, 4, 5–6, 13, 15, 17, 27, 29, 69, 71, 90–91, 92, 114, 133–34, 170, 207
Abbott, George, 8, 10, 11, 12, 25, 49, 51–52, 55, 56, 125, 127, 128*n*, 129, 130, 178, 189, 192, 198, 204, 205, 248, 249, 268
Adair, Yvonne, 178, 196
Adamson, Harold, 26, 197, 251
Albert, Eddie, 78, 198, 199, 200
Allegro, 62, 74, 84*n*, 87, 183, 196, 210, 211, **212–18**, 213*n*, 219, 220, 221, 223, 224–25, 226, 232, 234, 241*n*, 263, 264, 267
Allyson, June, 11, 12
Alton, Robert, 9, 49, 55, 57, 58, 211
Alvarez, Anita, 166–67, 197
Andersen, Hans Christian, 151
Anderson, Eddie "Rochester," 47
Anderson, John Murray, 145, 219
Anderson, Maxwell, 147, 164, 228–29, 230, 231, 233, 234, 235
Andrews, Nancy, 178
Angel in the Wings, 177–78
Angelus, Muriel, 9, 94–95
Annie Get Your Gun, 20, 66, 71, 89, **111–18**, 116*n*, 117*n*, 126, 165–

66, 174, 197, 198, 199, 217, 221, 241, 256, 259, 264, 268, 269
Arden, Eve, 15, 16–17, 16*n*, 197
Are You With It?, **242–45**, 251
Arlen, Harold, 4, 19, 47, 47*n*, 97, 99–100, 108, 110, 111, 255
Armstrong, Louis, 47
Aronson, Boris, 45, 59, 224, 227
Around the World, 62, **201–3**, 213*n*
Artists and Models, 177, 186
As the Girls Go, 250–51
Astaire, Adele, 4, 237, 267–68
Astaire, Fred, 4, 237, 267–68
Atkinson, Brooks, 46–47, 55, 57, 143, 150, 167, 168, 197, 214, 221, 246
Auden, W.H., 68
Ayers, Lemuel, 77, 98, 109, 254

Babes in Arms, 242
Bailey, Pearl, 109, 110
Baird, Bil and Cora, 177
Balanchine, George, 7, 18, 30, 47–48, 59, 138, 139, 151, 152, 153, 155, 158, 162–63, 170, 211, 248, 249, 268
Ballard, Kaye, 211
Ballet Ballads, 62, **218–20**, 218*n*, 221

271

Banjo Eyes, 26
Barefoot Boy With Cheek, **203–9**
Baronova, Irina, 187
Battles, John, 129, 215
Beat the Band, **8–9**, 10, 11, 18, 71, 129, 130
Beggar's Holiday, 189–90, 200, 264
The Beggar's Opera, 189
Behrman, S.N., 233
Bel Geddes, Norman, 180
Bell, Marion, 174
La Belle Hélène, 253
Bells Are Ringing, 126
Belmore, Bertha, 33
Bennett, Robert Russell, 81, 82, 98, 152*n*, 180*n*
Benson, Sally, 108
Berle, Milton, 177
Berlin, Irving, 7, 17, 18, 19–20, 35, 37, 41, 96, 97, 100, 111, 114–15, 116, 117, 198, 199–200, 236, 268, 270
Berliner, Emile, 236*n*
Bernstein, Leonard, 121, 122, 125*n*, 126, 127–28, 129, 130, 131, 134, 134*n*
Best Foot Forward, **10–13**, 116, 129
Billion Dollar Baby, **134–37**, 185, 196, 248
Bissell, Whit, 240*n*
Bizet, Georges, 79, 80, 81, 82
Blackbirds of 1928, 47, 237
Blair, Janet, 165, 270
Blane, Ralph, 10, 12–13
Blitzstein, Marc, 87*n*, 101, 143, 144
Bloomer Girl, 47*n*, **97–100**, 98*n*, 103, 112, 130*n*, 136, 166, 197, 221, 240, 241, 263
Blossom Time, 23, 57, 138, 153
Bogardus, Stephen, 218
Bohn, "Peanuts," 24
Boland, Mary, 15*n*
Boles, John, 159
Bolger, Ray, 24, 32, 33, 34–35, 36, 48, 183, 197, 248, 249, 249*n*, 250
Bolton, Guy, 5, 27, 139, 186, 218*n*
Bond, Sheila, 148, 183, 184
Bontemps, Arna, 108–9
Booth, Shirley, 25, 108
Bordoni, Irene, 17, 18, 20, 22, 59, 170
Bosler, Virginia, 174
Bowers, Kenny, 11, 12, 116
The Boy Friend, 179
The Boys From Syracuse, 94–95, 198, 238, 252, 253
Brecht, Bertolt, 124, 163, 165, 189, 190, 228
Brice, Fanny, 6, 57–58*n*, 205
Brigadoon, 5, 62, 133–34, **165–66**, 169–

75, 169*n*, 172–73*n*, 175*n*, 196, 213, 221, 225, 241, 245, 255
Britten, Benjamin, 68, 143
Britton, George, 269, 270
Britton, Pamela, 78, 174
Brooks, David, 98, 174
Brooks, Lawrence, 250
Brotherson, Eric, 197
Brown, Anne, 238
Brown, Lew (with B.G. De Sylva and Ray Henderson), 41, 185, 270
Bruce, Betty, 104
Bruce, Carol, 17, 18, 58, 59, 92, 198
Bryant, Glenn, 82
Brynner, Yul, 242, 244, 245
Bubbles, John W., 47
Buloff, Joseph, 74, 78
Burns, David, 78, 136, 183
Buttons, Red, 204, 240*n*
By Jupiter, **32–35**, 35*n*, 56, 71, 112, 121, 179, 197, 248, 267

Cabaret, 54, 116, 133*n*, 150, 226, 226*n*
Cabin in the Sky, 30*n*, **43–48**, 59, 60, 62, 65*n*, 69, 75, 157, 211, 231
Caesar, Sid, 183
Cahn, Sammy, 205, 206–7, 208
Call Me Mister, **181–83**, 182*n*, 260
Calloway, Cab, 44
Candide, 125*n*, 134*n*, 250
Cannon, Maureen, 11, 104
Cantor, Eddie, 4, **25–27**, 28, 35, 36, 223
Carlisle, Kitty, 5, 143, 240–41
Carmen, 23, 79, 80
Carmen Jones, **79–82**, 92, 130*n*, 177, 180, 189, 211, 240, 255, 268
Carmichael, Hoagy, 4, 5, 197
Carousel, 10, 13*n*, 82, **83–89**, 90, 91, 92, 93, 95, 103, 104, 106–7, 109, 111, 112, 116, 118, 125, 127, 133–34, 148, 150, 154, 156, 157–58, 162, 168, 175, 175*n*, 196, 207, 213, 216, 217, 218, 231, 240*n*, 245, 255, 259, 260, 260*n*, 263, 264, 266, 267
Champion, Gower, 30, 31, 33, 178, 210, 268
Channing, Carol, 29, 178, 195, 196, 197, 203
Chapman, John, 136, 146, 158
Charley's Aunt, 248, 249
Chicago, 133*n*, 233
The Chocolate Soldier, 139, 140, 141
Chopin, Frédéric, 141, 158
Clark, Bobby, 120, 139, 140, 200–201, 205, 240, 250–51
Clark, Harry, 161
Clayton, Jan, 85, 92

Cohan, George M., 7–8, 39, 95, 111, 142, 270
Cole, Jack, 177, 246
Coleman, Herbert, 234
Coleman, Robert, 214
Coleman, Warren, 234
Comden, Betty, 121, 122, 123, 127, 129, 132, 134, 204, 241, 255
Company, 212
Concert Varieties, 181
A Connecticut Yankee, 71, 79, 240
Connelly, Marc, 43
Conte, John, 215
Cook, Joe, 205
Cooper, Melville, 145, 146
Cordon, Norman, 147, 148
Cornell, Katharine, 61, 229
Costello, Diosa, 269
The Cradle Will Rock, 101, 144, 237–38, 239
Crawford, Cheryl, 68–69, 107, 143, 160
Cullen, Countee, 108–9
Curran, Homer, 151

da Silva, Howard, 73
Dance Me a Song, 137n
Dancing in the Streets, 159
Daniels, Danny, 11, 136, 148, 183, 184
Darling, Jean, 85
Dawson, Mark, 33, 206, 208
The Day Before Spring, 170, 171
de Laria, Lea, 132
De Marcos, The, 26, 45, 112
de Mille, Agnes, 75, 79, 83, 85, 98, 99, 100, 112, 159, 161–62, 163, 165, 171, 172, 173n, 175, 175n, 195–96, 209, 210–11, 215, 268
De Sylva, B.G., 17–18, 37, 41, 185, 270
The Desert Song, 102, 237
Dickey, Annamary, 215
Diener, Joan, 152
Dietrich, Marlene, 159, 160
Dietz, Howard, 113, 184
Dodson's Monkeys, 24
Dolan, Robert Emmet, 193, 194
Dowdy, Helen, 92, 238
Down in the Valley, 147
Downs, Johnny, 242
Drake, Alfred, 73, 101–2, 145, 190, 197, 254, 255–56, 257, 258
Dream With Music, 158
DuBarry Was a Lady, 33n, 37, 185, 193, 242
Duke, Vernon, 26, 29, 29n, 30, 43, 45, 46, 47n, 59, 65n, 113, 164
Duncan, Todd, 43, 81, 234, 238
Dunham, Katherine, 43, 48, 181
Durante, Jimmy, 24, 205

Eager, Edward, 101, 158
Early to Bed, **9–10**, 179, 185, 249, 262
Ebb, Fred, 136, 226
Ebersole, Christine, 218
Ebsen, Buddy, 92, 92n
Eggerth, Marta, 7, 138
Ellington, Duke, 108, 189, 190, 200
Elliott, Maxine, 218, 218n, 238
Ernst, Leila, 55
Errico, Melissa, 165
Esham, Faith, 246
Evans, Wilbur, 104, 145, 201, 240, 269
Eythe, William, 178–79

Fabray, Nanette, 15, 100–101, 205, 206, 206n, 207, 209, 220, 221
Face the Music, 126, 242
Fain, Sammy, 182
Fancy Free, 121, 121n, 122, 124–25, 131
Feigay, Paul, 121, 129, 134
Feuer, Cy, 248, 257n
Ffolkes, David, 171, 172n, 173n, 248
Fields, Dorothy, 13, 15, 37, 103, 107, 114, 200
Fields, Herbert, 13, 15, 37, 61, 103, 107, 114, 200
Fine and Dandy, 185
Finian's Rainbow, 18–19n, **165–69**, 172, 173–74, 175, 197, 221, 227, 241, 258, 264
The Firebrand of Florence, **144–46**, 147, 156, 163, 164
Die Fledermaus, 138
Florodora, 179, 236, 236n
Follies, 14n, 76n, 130, 134, 150, 176–77, 180, 221, 226, 227, 233, 260
Follow the Girls, 102, 121, 130n, **185–88**, 249, 261, 262
Forrest, George, 151, 153, 153n, 154, 155, 158, 245, 247
The Fortune Teller, 236n
Fosse, Bob, 58, 137n, 210, 268
Foy, Eddie, Jr., 140, 141
Freedley, Vinton, 4, 5–6, 13, 15, 17, 27, 29, 46, 47, 69, 71, 84, 90–91, 92, 114, 133–34, 170, 207
Friml, Rudolf, 103, 155, 237, 246, 247
Froman, Jane, 24, 177

Gallagher, Helen, 57, 131n, 206, 219
Garde, Betty, 74
Garrett, Betty, 39, 182
Gateson, Marjorie, 140
Gaxton, William, 17, 18, 20, 21, 22, 59, 108, 203n
The Gay Life, 184
Gaynor, Charles, 178

Gentlemen Prefer Blondes, 195–97, 196n
Gershwin, George, 4, 19, 37, 41, 43, 63, 68–69, 107, 125, 270
Gershwin, Ira, 19, 37, 41, 61, 144, 164, 190, 191, 270
Gibbs, Wolcott, 34, 229
Gilbert, Billy, 139, 140
Gilbert, W.S., and Sullivan, Arthur, 19, 108
Gillette, Priscilla, 143
Glad To See You!, 207
Gleason, Jackie, 24, 177, 185–86, 188
Godkin, Paul, 206, 211, 219
Goldsby, Helen, 111, 111n
Goodman, Benny, 180, 181
Gordon, Bert, 27, 28
Gordon, Max, 145, 164, 190
Gould, Morton, 134–35, 136, 181
Grable, Betty, 5n, 33n
Gray, Dolores, 118, 180, 181, 243, 244
Great Lady, 170
The Great Waltz, 164
Green, Adolph, 121, 122, 123, 124, 127, 129, 132, 134, 204, 241, 255
Green, Mitzi, 5, 6, 136
Green Grow the Lilacs, 70–71, 83, 148, 177n
Grieg, Edvard. See *Song of Norway*
Griffies, Ethel, 198
Guys and Dolls, 116, 248, 257n, 269, 270
Gypsy, 28, 63

Hale, George, 27, 29, 33
Haley, Jack, 7, 184–85
Hall, Juanita, 102, 262, 267, 269
Hambleton, T. Edward, 218, 218n
Hamilton, Nancy, 183
Hammerstein, Oscar II, 41, 71, 72–73, 76, 79–80, 81, 82–83, 84, 84n, 88, 89, 90, 94, 95, 104, 215, 218, 222n, 228, 266, 268, 269. See also Rodgers and Hammerstein
Hanighen, Bernard, 139, 243
Hanley, Ellen, 204
Harburg, E.Y., 4, 27, 47, 47n, 97, 99–100, 166, 167, 168, 169, 182
Harris, Sam H., 61, 111
Harrison, Ray, 131n
Hart, Lorenz, 4, 11, 34–35, 49, 56, 57, 58n, 71, 73, 80
Hart, Moss, **60–62**, 63, 64n, 65, 66n, 180, 184, 198, 222n, 240n
Havoc, June, 55, 113, 200, 201
Hayden, Michael, 85
Heckart, Eileen, 58
Helen Goes to Troy, 253

Hello Again, 87n
Hello, Dolly!, 29, 224
Hellzapoppin, 25, 118, 176
Henderson, Florence, 156, 269
Henie, Sonja, 91
Hepburn, Katharine, 6, 32, 33
Herbert, Victor, 39, 62n, 139, 141, 236n, 270
High Button Shoes, **205–10**, 206n, 211, 219, 221, 238
Higher and Higher, 7–8, 10, 49
Hill, Ruby, 109
H.M.S. Pinafore, 107, 108
Hodges, Joy, 203n
Hold On to Your Hats, **26–28**, 112
Holiday, Billie, 81, 121n
Hollywood Pinafore, 108
Holm, Celeste, 74, 98, 100, 221
Holm, Hanya, 219, 256
Horne, Lena, 47, 47n, 58, 189–90
Horwitt, Arnold B., 181, 183–84, 243
Hughes, Langston, 148, 149
Husmann, Ron, 131
Huston, Walter, 229
Hutton, Betty, 39, 40, 41

If the Shoe Fits, 158
Ingram, Rex, 43, 44, 47, 109, 111
Inside U.S.A., 184–85, 188
Irene, 126, 270
Irving, George S., 197
Ives, Burl, 96, 102

Jeffreys, Anne, 147, 148, 250
Jenkins, Allen, 39, 40
Jerome Robbins' Broadway, 133, 210
Johnny Johnson, 67, 148, 163, 222
Johnson, Bill, 39, 118
Johnson, Chic, 176
Jolson, Al, **26–28**, 35, 36, 223
Jonay, Roberta, 215
Jones, Robert Edmond, 242, 245
Jones, Shirley, 269
Jumbo, 80, 80n, 250n

Kálmán, Emmerich, 141–42
Kander, John, 136, 226
Kapp, Jack, 237, 239–40, 242
Kaufman, George S., 60, 61, 62, 108, 180, 190, 193
Kay, Arthur, 151–52, 152n, 153, 155, 246
Kaye, Danny, 15–16, 22, 64–65, 77–78, 151
Kaye, Judy, 246
Kazan, Elia, 159, 178, 220

Kean, Jane, 9–10
Keep Off the Grass, 24, 25
Kelly, Gene, 11, 54–55, 57
Kern, Jerome, 4, 19, 41, 71, 89, 90, 103n, 218n, 228, 236, 270
Kidd, Michael, 165, 169, 210, 220, 221
Kiepura, Jan, 138
The King and I, 84n, 139, 218, 269
Kirk, Lisa, 215, 218, 254, 255, 256, 257, 258
Kismet, 139, 152n, 245, 247, 249
Kiss Me, Kate, 89, 102, 118, 156, 197, 238, **252–61**, 257n
Knickerbocker Holiday, 67, 148, 163, 228, 229, 231, 242
Knight, June, 139–40
Kollmar, Richard, 9, 33, 34, 35n

LaChiusa, Michael John, 87n
The Lady Comes Across, 29–32, 33, 35, 43, 257
Lady in the Dark, 15, **59–68**, 62n, 66n, 69, 75, 76n, 77–78, 82, 88, 144, 157, 163, 164, 174, 228, 230, 238, 258, 269
Laffing Room Only, 130n, 176, 182
Lahr, Bert, 33n, 179–80, 181, 183, 193, 202
Lane, Burton, 27, 166, 225
Lang, Harold, 57, 58, 131, 131n, 183, 192, 192n, 193, 254, 255, 256, 257, 258, 259
Lapine, James, 228
Latouche, John, 26, 29, 30, 43, 45, 46, 47n, 59, 121, 189, 190, 218, 219
Laugh, Town, Laugh!, 25
Laurence, Larry (aka Enzo Stuarti), 202
Laurence, Paula, 39, 40, 41n, 159, 161, 165
Lawrence, Gertrude, 60, 61, 63–64, 65, 66, 67, 159, 238
Le Gallienne, Eva, 84
Leave It to Me!, 54, 55, 159
Lee, Gypsy Rose, 120
Lend an Ear, 178–79, 188, 196, 197
Lenya, Lotte, 144–46, 226
Lerner, Alan Jay, 169n, 170, 174, 220, 221, 222, 223, 224, 225, 227, 228, 248
Lester, Edwin, 151–52, 152n, 245
Let's Face It, **13–17**, 22, 39, 112, 121, 191, 197, 200
Levene, Sam, 25
Levey, Ethel, 95, 142
Lewis, Brenda, 143, 152
Lewis, Robert, 143, 171, 172–73n
Lieberson, Goddard, 56, 57, 58, 192n
Liliom, 83, 84, 86, 95, 148

Lillie, Beatrice, 180, 181, 184, 185, 188
A Little Night Music, 116
Littlefield, Catherine, 27, 187
Loesser, Frank, 151, 248
Loewe, Frederick, 170–71, 172, 225, 225n
Logan, Ella, 166
Logan, Joshua, 200, 213n, 262, 268, 269
Long, Avon, 107, 108, 190, 238
Long, Huey. See Louisiana Purchase
Longstreet, Stephen, 205
Look, Ma, I'm Dancin'!, 190, **191–93**, 195, 205
Loos, Anita, 195, 196, 197
Lorelei, 197
Loring, Eugene, 82
Lost in the Stars, 163, **229–35**, 241n, 243, 260
Louisiana Purchase, 7, **17–22**, 59, 92, 112, 114, 126, 154, 164, 198, 243
Love Life, 163, **220–28**, 222n, 247–48, 250, 259, 264
Lunt, Alfred, 229, 252
LuPone, Patti, 58
Lute Song, 62, 242, **243–45**

McCarty, Mary, 198, 199
McCauley, Jack, 102, 197, 206, 206n, 207, 209
McCormick, Myron, 262, 269
McCracken, Joan, 98, 100, 135, 136–37, 137n
MacDonald, Jeanette, 4, 7
McDonald, Ray, 190, 191
McGregor, Edgar, 27, 268
McGuire, Biff, 169, 269
McHugh, Jimmy, 251
McKechnie, Donna, 131
McKneely, Joey, 133
McLerie, Allyn, 198, 199, 200, 248
McQueen, Butterfly, 47
Magdalena, **245–47**, 250
Make Mine Manhattan, 183–84
Mamoulian, Rouben, 75, 83, 109–10, 113, 233, 234, 246, 268
Mandelbaum, Ken, 255, 257
Marand, Patricia, 269
Marinka, 141–42
Marion, George, Jr., 8, 9, 142
Markova, Alicia, 180
Martin, Ernest, 248, 257n
Martin, Hugh, 6, 10, 12–13, 18, 22, 30, 191, 192, 196
Martin, Mary, 55, 84n, 101, 113, 159, 160–61, 197, 221, 241, 242, 243, 244–45, 262, 266–67, 268, 269, 270

Martin, Virginia, 269
Mathis, Stanley Wayne, 110
Matthews, Inez, 234
Matthews, Jessie, 29, 30, 31, 35, 257
Mayer, Edwin Justus, 144–46, 228
Me and Juliet, 84n, 137n
The Medium, 143
Memphis Bound!, 107–8
Menotti, Gian Carlo, 142–43
Mercer, Johnny, 4, 5, 108, 110, 193, 194, 241
Merman, Ethel, 10, 28, 29, 33n, **35–39**, 40, 41, 41n, 48, 60, 63, 100, 101, 112, 113–14, 115, 116, 146, 186, 193, 198, 200, 202, 221, 238, 241, 254, 259, 268
Merrily We Roll Along, 212
The Merry Widow, 102, 138
Mexican Hayride, 130n, **200–201**, 240, 252, 254, 264
Michener, James, 200, 262, 268
Middleton, Ray, 115, 220, 240n, 241, 269
Mielziner, Jo, 117, 139, 145, 214, 224
Migenes, Julia, 270
Miller, Ann, 193
Miller, Marilyn, 36, 60, 101, 221, 237, 267–68
Miss Liberty, 20, **198–200**, 232, 241n, 251
Mitchell, James, 136, 137n, 174
Molnár, Ferenc, 83, 95
Moore, Constance, 33, 34, 35n
Moore, Victor, 10, 17, 18, 21, 22, 59, 108, 203n, 205
Morgan, Helen, 92, 237
Morison, Patricia, 254, 256, 257, 258, 261
Moross, Jerome, 218, 219
Morrow, Doretta, 249
Mostel, Zero, 181, 190
Mr. Strauss Goes to Boston, 141
Mura, Corinna, 201, 254
Murphy, George, 55
Music in the Air, 185, 242
Music in My Heart, 141
My Fair Lady, 10, 30, 250
My Romance, 250
Myerberg, Michael, 243
Myrtil, Odette, 77, 140, 141, 269

Nash, Ogden, 159, 164–65
Nathan, George Jean, 9, 81, 82, 100, 169n, 177, 195, 206, 251
Naughty Marietta, 23, 62n
Nellie Bly, 203n, 251
Nelson, Gene, 178

Neuwirth, Bebe, 58
The New Moon, 94, 102, 237
Nicholas, Fayard, 109, 110
Nicholas, Harold, 109, 110
Niesen, Gertrude, 186–87
Novotna, Jarmila, 253
Nymph Errant, 136
Nype, Russell, 143, 165

O'Brien, Virginia, 24
Of Thee I Sing, 52–53, 185, 251
Offenbach, Jacques, 210, 254
O'Hara, John, **48–54**, 50n, 52n, 56, 58
O'Hara, Paige, 165
Ojeda, Perry Laylon, 133
Oklahoma!, 21, 62, 69, **70–79**, 72n, 76n, 80, 83, 84n, 85, 86, 89, 91, 92, 93, 94, 95, 96, 98, 100, 101, 104, 106, 109, 111, 112, 113, 116, 117, 117n, 118, 125, 126, 127, 129, 130, 130n, 134, 136, 142, 148, 150, 159, 161, 162, 164, 172, 175n, 177n, 179, 185, 187, 194, 196, 198, 200, 209, 211, 213, 216, 217, 218, 227, 231, 236, 239–40, 254, 264, 267, 268, 269, 270
Olsen, Ole, 176
On the Town, 62, 103, **121–34**, 121n, 123n, 125n, 128n, 130n, 131n, 132n, 134n, 135, 136, 172, 203–4, 209, 211, 219, 227, 231, 241, 255, 256, 258, 265, 268, 269
Once Over Lightly, 80
One For the Money, 55, 183
One Touch of Venus, 125, 126, 129, 130n, **159–62**, 163, 164–65, 196, 197, 219, 227, 230, 240, 243
110 in the Shade, 166
Osato, Sono, 129, 137n, 160, 160n, 162, 219
Osterwald, Bibi, 102, 183

Pacific Overtures, 226, 244
Pal Joey, **48–59**, 50n, 54n, 60, 62, 66, 69, 75, 126, 131n, 154, 174, 192n, 231, 258
Panama Hattie, **37–40**, 41, 42, 59, 115, 121, 200, 238, 267
Park Avenue, 190–91, 195
Paton, Alan, 229–30, 234–35
Paul Bunyan, 68
Pearce, Alice, 129, 197
Perelman, S.J., 159
Peters, Bernadette, 131
Petina, Irra, 152, 153, 241, 245, 246, 247
Petrillo, James Caesar, 238–39, 240, 241, 245

Pickens, Jane, 25, 143
Pins and Needles, 182, 237–38, 239
Pinza, Ezio, 262, 266–67, 269, 270
Pipe Dream, 74, 84*n*
Pitot, Genevieve, 210, 259
Polonaise, 141
Porgy and Bess, 23, 43, 68–69, 72, 92, 107, 110, 143, 234, 237, 238, 239
Porter, Cole, 12, 13, 14, 15, 16, 17, 22, 29, 30, 35, 37, **39–41**, 48, 58*n*, 61, 103, 113, 115, 136, 159, 164, 180, 180*n*, 181, 187, 190, 191, 200–201, 202–3, **251–59**, 263, 270
Premice, Josephine, 58
Price, Leontyne, 92
Prince, Harold, 23, 90, 133*n*, 212, 228, 268

Ragland, Rags, 39
Rain, 113, 218*n*, 250
Raitt, John, 85, 246, 247
The Rape of Lucretia, 143
Raye, Martha, 27, 28
Reagan, Nancy Davis, 242
Reams, Lee Roy, 165
The Red Mill, 140–41, 140*n*
Redfield, William, 204–5
Regina, 62, 143–44, 144*n*
Reinhardt, Max, 138, 224, 254
Reinking, Ann, 133*n*
Rent, 116, 227
Revel, Harry, 243
Rhapsody, 130*n*, 141
Rice, Elmer, 146, 146*n*, 148–49, 228, 233
Richards, Donald, 166
Riggs, Lynn, 70, 76, 78
Robbins, Jerome, 121, 122, 127, 129, 131*n*, 133, 134, 135, 181, 191, 192, 193, 198, 199, 200, 205, 208–9, 210–11, 268
Roberts, Joan, 73, 95, 142, 242–43
Robeson, Paul, 233, 234, 237
Robin, Leo, 195
Robinson, Bill, 107, 108
Rodgers and Hammerstein, 3, 11, 18–19*n*, 23, **71–92**, 96, 97, 98, 99, 104, 106, 111–12, 114, 115, 117, 127, 137*n*, 143, 150, 156, 157, 163, 166, 170, 172, 174, 176, 178, 179, 183, 192, 198, 203, 207, 210, 212–14, 215, 217, 218, 235, 244, 252, 259, 262, 263, 264, 265, 267, 268
Rodgers and Hart, 7, 8, 11, 12, 29, 32, 33, 35, 41, 50, 50*n*, 53–54, 56, 79, 80*n*, 157, 268, 269, 270

Rodgers, Richard, 4, 11, 19, 32, 35, 35*n*, 49, 53, 54, 55, 71, 73, 77, 82, 111, 125–26, 177*n*, 215, 225, 266, 268, 269. *See also* Rodgers and Hammerstein; Rodgers and Hart
Romberg, Sigmund, 71, 85, 94, 102–3, 104, 105, 106, 107, 155, 236–37, 246, 247, 250
Rome, Harold, 4, 182, 211
Roosevelt, Franklin Delano, 17, 22, 25, 98*n*, 130, 183, 198–99
Rosalinda, 138–39, 140*n*, 151
Rose, Billy, 80, 80*n*, 81, 82, 179, 180, 180*n*, 181, 250*n*
Rose-Marie, 60, 78, 155, 237
Russell, Lillian, 221
Russell, Rosalind, 66
Ryskind, Morrie, 17, 18, 22, 30

Sadie Thompson, 113, 130*n*
Saidy, Fred, 98, 166
St. John, Betta, 262
St. Louis Woman, **108–11**, 111*n*, 231, 241, 241*n*, 246
Sarnoff, Dorothy, 139, 246, 247
Saxon, Luther, 82
Scholl, Danny, 194
Schwartz, Arthur, 37, 184, 190, 191
Scott, Raymond, 243
Segal, Vivienne, 54–55, 56, 57
The Seven Lively Arts, 130*n*, 179–81, 180*n*, 201
Shakespeare, William, 169*n*, 229, 252–53, 254, 255, 256, 257, 258–59, 264
Sharkey (trained seal), 7
Sherwood, Robert E., 198–99, 233
Short, Hassard, 41, 61, 82, 142, 180, 268
Show Boat, 10, 13*n*, 23, 42, 52–53, 57, 59, 61, 62, 72, 77, 82, **89–92**, 92*n*, 113, 133*n*, 170, 215, 215–16*n*, 221, 227, 237, 241, 251, 267–68, 269
Shubert Brothers, 25, 26, 28, 31, 102, 138, 176–77, 201, 205, 209–10
Side Show, 226
Sillman, Leonard, 158, 158*n*
Silvers, Phil, 193, 205–6
Sing Out, Sweet Land!, 101–2, 130*n*, 240, 241*n*
Smith, Mildred, 190
Smith, Muriel, 82
Smith, Oliver, 121–22, 129, 130, 134, 171, 172, 195, 198, 205
Something For the Boys, 37, **38–41**, 59, 72*n*, 121, 200, 261, 263
Sondheim, Stephen, 22, 58*n*, 87, 136, 212, 228, 244

278 INDEX

Song of Norway, 62, 103, 130*n*, **150–56**, 152*n*, 153*n*, 158, 211, 240–41, 240*n*, 241, 245, 250
Sons O'Fun, 176
South Pacific, 62, 66, 84*n*, 87, 89, 113, 136, 197, 213*n*, 218, **261–67**, 268, 269, 270
Spewack, Bella, 159, 252–53, 257*n*
Spewack, Sam, 252, 257*n*
Spialek, Hans, 54*n*, 57, 58, 142, 152*n*
Star and Garter, 120, 262
Star Time, 130*n*
Stewart, Johnny, 206*n*, 209
Stolz, Robert, 141
Stone, Dorothy, 140, 141
Stone, Paula, 140
Stoska, Polyna, 147, 148
Street Scene, 126, **146–50**, 146*n*, 147*n*, 163, 183, 226, 230, 233, 241, 241*n*, 245, 250, 255, 264
Stritch, Elaine, 58, 178
The Student Prince, 23, 57, 102, 138, 155, 173
Styne, Jule, 57, 58, 195, 205, 206–7, 208
Subber, Saint, 252, 255
Sullivan, Brian, 147, 148
Sullivan, Lee, 5, 174
Sunny River, **94–96**, 103
Sweet Adeline, 94, 103*n*
Sweet Charity, 129
Sweethearts, 139–40

Tabbert, William, 136, 180, 181, 262, 268, 269
Tamiris, Helen, 90, 105, 106, 178
The Telephone, 143
Texas, Li'l Darlin', 190, **193–95**, 241*n*
Thank You, Just Looking, 178
That's the Ticket!, 211
This Is the Army, 96–97, 102, 120–21, 181, 239, 240*n*, 249
Three Men on a Horse, 25–26
Three to Make Ready, 183
Titanic, 116
Todd, Michael, 72, 72*n*, 103, 105, 107, 111, 120, 200, 250, 250*n*
Too Many Girls, 8, 203, 269
Toplitzsky of Notre Dame, 158
Touch and Go, 178
Tudor, Anthony, 108, 110, 170
Tune, Tommy, 217
Tunick, Jonathan, 152*n*
The Two Bouquets, 254
Two For the Show, 183
Tynes, Bill, 165

Up in Central Park, 90, 102, **103–7**, 112, 151, 156, 238, 261, 264

The Vagabond King, 138, 155
Valentina, 180, 181, 242
Vera-Ellen, 33
Verdon, Gwen, 60, 101, 131*n*
Verne, Jules, 201–2
Villa-Lobos, Heitor, 245, 246–47
Vye, Murvyn, 85

Walk with Music, **4–7**, 10, 71, 179, 251
Walker, Don, 58, 108, 125*n*, 152*n*
Walker, Nancy, 11, 12, 129, 133, 191–92, 193, 204–5, 209, 241
Waller, Fats, 9
Warnick, Clay, 108, 158
Waters, Ethel, 43, 46, 47, 65
Watson, Betty Jane, 250
Wayne, David, 166
Weede, Robert, 241
Weill, Kurt, 4, 61, 63, 65, 67, 68, 125, 126, **144–50**, 147*n*, 159, **162–65**, 170, 189, 190, 220, 222, **225–30**, 232, 233, 235
Welles, Orson, 201–2, 203, 213*n*
West Side Story, 13*n*, 131, 131*n*, 134*n*, 210
What's Up, 170, 171, 211
Where's Charley?, **248–50**, 249*n*, 257*n*, 261
White, Miles, 77, 98, 195, 205
Whiting, Jack, 5, 8, 27
Wilson, Dooley, 43, 44, 98
Wiman, Dwight Deere, 32, 35*n*
Winged Victory, 240, 240*n*, 249
Wodehouse, P.G., 218*n*
Wolfe, George, 132, 133
Wonderful Town, 134*n*
Wright, Martha, 269
Wright, Robert, 151, 153, 153*n*, 154, 155, 158, 245, 247, 256
Wrightson, Earl, 144, 145, 146
Wyckoff, Evelyn, 31–32, 64, 78
Wynn, Ed, 25, 205

Youmans, Vincent, 4, 27, 37, 41, 111, 270
Young, Stark, 72

Zenda, 29*n*
Ziegfeld, Florenz, 23, 26, 53, 77, 90, 103, 176–77, 180, 181, 237, 267–68
Zorina, Vera, 7, 17, 18, 20, 21, 22, 59, 158, 159